Feeling Extended

Feeling Extended

Sociality as Extended Body-Becoming-Mind

Douglas Robinson

The MIT Press
Cambridge, Massachusetts
London, England

© 2013 Massachusetts Institute of Technology

All rights reserved. No part of this book may be reproduced in any form by any electronic or mechanical means (including photocopying, recording, or information storage and retrieval) without permission in writing from the publisher.

MIT Press books may be purchased at special quantity discounts for business or sales promotional use. For information, please email special_sales@mitpress.mit.edu or write to Special Sales Department, The MIT Press, 55 Hayward Street, Cambridge, MA 02142.

Set in Stone Sans and Stone Serif by Toppan Best-set Premedia Limited. Printed and bound in the United States of America.

Library of Congress Cataloging-in-Publication Data

Robinson, Douglas, 1954–.
Feeling extended : sociality as extended body-becoming-mind / Douglas Robinson.
    pages cm
Includes bibliographical references and index.
ISBN 978-0-262-01947-7 (alk. paper)
1. Externalism (Philosophy of mind). 2. Philosophy of mind. 3. Cognition—Philosophy. I. Title.
BD418.3.R75 2013
128'.2—dc23
                          2012051751

10 9 8 7 6 5 4 3 2 1

Contents

Acknowledgments   vii

Introduction   1

1   Inside Out   31

2   Language as Cognitive Labels   67

3   Language as Conative Force   85

4   Qualia as Interpretants   119

5   Empathy, Face, and Ritual   147

Appendix: Liar-Paradox Monism   177
Notes   207
References   225
Index   249

Acknowledgments

This book began life as a manuscript of an article consisting of early drafts of what eventually became §2.1, §2.3, §3.0, and §5.1. Paisley Livingston, my colleague in the Philosophy Department at Lingnan University, read the manuscript and made helpful comments. I then submitted the manuscript to *Inquiry*, where an anonymous reader read it and recommended intelligent and sensible revisions. The article kept generating new ideas, and expanding, till it turned into a book. Paisley read an expanded version and continued to engage me in a challenging dialogue about the liar paradox and shared qualia. Another Lingnan colleague, Ding Ersu, a noted Peirce scholar and semiotic theorist, read my chapter on Peirce and made several significant contributions to that chapter's current form. Stephen Thornton published my article "Liar Paradox Monism" in *Minerva*; it sparked some very interesting and helpful comments, notably from Jeremy Barris. Christopher Hutton at the University of Hong Kong not only responded at some length to my queries about his reading of Peirce on the tone-token-type triad, but also invited me to give a condensed version of chapter 3 to the School of English at his venerable institution; thanks to Chris and his colleagues for their invitation and for the spirited discussion that followed the talk. Steve Palmquist, my colleague in the Religion and Philosophy Department at Hong Kong Baptist University, also read the entire manuscript and gave me a long list of queries and suggestions. Philip Laughlin at the MIT Press, a devoted supporter of the manuscript from the start, found three excellent reviewers quickly and managed to cajole three extraordinarily helpful reports out of them in record time. Thanks to Phil and the three anonymous reviewers.

Introduction

0.1 Border war

The extended-mind thesis (EMT), generally attributed to Andy Clark and David Chalmers (1998), is the notion that in specific kinds of mind-body-world interaction there emerges an extended mind or extended cognitive system that doesn't just use but *incorporates* the pencils, paper, computers, and other extracranial objects and environments we use to help overcome or work around our brains' klugey design flaws (see Marcus 2008). The tradition coming out of Clark and Chalmers holds that, because in some cases we could not function cognitively at all without such extracranial support, and in many more cases could not function as effectively without that support, it makes sense to think of those extracranial support systems as *part* of our cognitive or mental systems.

Of course, in one sense the idea wasn't new with Clark and Chalmers. As they themselves noted (1998: 10), AI and robotics researchers had been saying similar things for several decades, beginning with Manfred Clynes and Nathan Kline (1960/1995),[1] and Chris Hables Gray's important collection of major statements in those fields, *The Cyborg Handbook*, appeared in 1995, three years before Clark and Chalmers' article. Clark and Chalmers also discussed the Terminator cyborg of the movies in passing (1998: 16), and a few years later Clark (2003) reflected on the EMT in the explicit terms of cyborg theory. The significant difference between the EMT and cyborg theory is that, whereas cognitive externalists define the human-nonhuman coupling as an extended *cognitive* system, cyborg theorists define the human-nonhuman coupling as an extended *homeostatic* system: the crucial thing about a cyborg system is that it regulate its functioning unconsciously, so as to free the mind to make conscious cognitive decisions without distraction. Still, Clark and Chalmers (1998) describe their immemorious Otto's now-famous reliance on his notebook in terms that are strikingly reminiscent of many of the pieces in *The Cyborg Handbook*, such as David Hess' chapter "On low-tech cyborgs." Hess writes:

> I think about how almost everyone in urban societies could be seen as a low-tech cyborg, because they spend large parts of the day connected to machines such as cars, telephones, computers, and, of course, televisions. I ask the cyborg anthropologist if a system of a person watching a TV might constitute a cyborg. (When I watch TV, I feel like a homeostatic system functioning unconsciously.) I also think sometimes there is a fusion of identities between myself and the black box. (1995: 373)

The backlash against cyborg theory, famously characterized by Donna Haraway (1986/1991: 150) as a border war between the human and the nonhuman, also strikingly parallels the backlash against the EMT. Among the philosophers who reject the Clark-Chalmers EMT are Rupert (1999, 2004, 2008, 2009), Block (2005), and Prinz (2006, 2009). The philosophical critique of the EMT to which I mostly respond in this book is that offered by Adams and Aizawa (2001, 2008, 2009, 2010; see also Aizawa and Adams, 2005). The Adams-Aizawa critique has been challenged from several points of view. Menary (2006) insists that Adams and Aizawa oversimplify cognition, missing its hybrid nature and misconstruing manipulation. Wilson and Clark (2009: 69) argue that "even if we grant that every cognitive system needs to trade in intrinsic contents, it does not follow that each part of every such system needs do so." (See also Clark 2008, 2010.) Chemero (2009) argues that the insistence that cognition consist of mental representations constitutes a speciesist prejudice in favor of the human. Rupert (2010b), while agreeing with Adams and Aizawa on most points, argues that cognition does extend beyond the skull into the mind's own body.

I propose to take a rather different tack in this book. While fundamentally siding with the pro-EMT side of the debate, I argue that the tendency on both sides to ground the EMT in *materialist claims about extension*—that mind *actually* or *literally* does extend in some material sense, and that therefore the EMT should be susceptible to empirical proof or disproof—is debilitating and should be renounced.

In conversations with other philosophers of mind I have met with considerable resistance to this chain of assumptions—that truth claims about "literal" or "actual" extension imply materialism and therefore the specter of empirical proof or disproof—so, for the record, let me state unequivocally that I am entirely open to the notion that it may be beneficial to debate the viability of an ontological truth claim *as* an ontological truth claim without necessarily putting it to the test of empirical proof. I also recognize in this particular case that both the proponents and the critics of the EMT have stipulated that empirical evidence either for or against the EMT will be set to one side, and the case argued on its *philosophical* merits.

Let me also state for the record that I have no axe to grind with materialism, and that my arguments here should emphatically not be read as a denial or rejection of materialism. As I will have multiple occasions to show, the "liar-paradox monism" that I outline in the appendix recognizes that [a] there is a material world outside our minds, [b] our senses keep trying to represent that world to mind as accurately as possible, and [c] it requires a radically quixotic brand of extreme philosophical idealism to reject (a) or (b). (My use of parentheses and brackets is explained below.) All that I reject in general—and obviously I am far from being the first to do this—is the naive materialist claim that we can *know* material reality in any reliable or transparent way.

More specifically, however, I also reject the notion that mind is material. As we'll see, the Hard Problem of Consciousness of which Chalmers (1995/1997) writes is precisely that mind appears to us *in* the material world, and therefore theoretically must have *some* sort of material reality, but that it is utterly unlike anything we can understand as matter. This makes materialist claims about extended mind extremely problematic— and my brief is that EMT proponents have not paid enough attention to the problems. Instead, they tend to set up functionalist analogies that effectively function like idealist/qualitative/phenomenalist *models* of material reality, which suggests that anything that *seems to function* like mind *is* mind—and, most problematically of all, insisting that the qualitative *seeming* in that functionalist equation somehow shows that mind extends *materially*.

Some of my colleagues have even gone so far as to say that the EMT is not a materialist truth claim at all; that it is a *hypothesis*, a thought experiment that doesn't have to have real-world applications. And perhaps it is that for some of its proponents; and perhaps that's a viable project. That isn't how Andy Clark sees the EMT, though, and many later EMT proponents would agree: if the EMT is valid, it does have significant real-world ramifications. Such ramifications proliferate in, say, Clark 2008 and Chemero 2009, and to the authors' minds constitute strong support for the viability of the EMT. If the EMT can do all this useful work in the material world, they suggest, then it is specifically a materialist hypothesis that may some day be empirically confirmed. Indeed, Clark (2008: xxvi) writes, "Such body- and world-involving cycles are best understood, or so I shall argue, as quite literally extending the machinery of mind out into the world—as building extended cognitive circuits that are themselves the minimal material bases for important aspects of human thought and reason."

On a superficial reading, this claim seems to justify my insistence on taking materialism (and so also empirical verifiability) to be definitive for the EMT, at least as it is propounded by Clark: mind *literally extends*, and in so doing cycles through the body and the world in ways that build "extended cognitive circuits that are themselves the minimal *material* bases for important aspects of human thought and reason." Certainly "minimal material bases" seems to imply that this is a specifically *materialist* thesis about mind.

A closer reading of the quotation from Clark, however, throws wrenches into the works. What exactly is "the machinery of the mind" (is it neural and thus material, or phenomenal and thus ideal, or some combination of the two?), and what does it mean for that machinery to extend "literally" into the world? Obviously "machinery of the mind" is specifically a *metaphor*, which makes the claim about its *literal* extension into the world problematic; but even if we overlook "quite literally extending the machinery of mind" as careless writing, and thus not really what Clark meant, the difficulty remains: is the machinery of the mind purely material? If so, are we talking specifically about the (metaphorical) machinery of the *brain*, the biological substratum of thought—neurons and dendrites and myelin sheathing and synapses and neurotransmitters and so on—out of which, by some process whose nature is contested, emerges the phenomenology that we call "the mind"? If so, in what sense does that neurological substratum "literally" extend out into the world? That, of course, is a *reductio ad absurdum*. No one would seriously claim that Andy Clark or anyone else is seriously claiming that the material substratum of mind literally extends into the material world. What the *reductio* is intended to highlight is the vagueness of the "machinery of the mind" that Clark says literally extends. Obviously he doesn't mean *just* the neurological substratum of the mind; but what else would (could) the metaphorical "machinery of the mind" entail? Would we want to include in the "machinery of the mind" that "literally" extends out into the world various cognitive processes that we associate with mind (and not directly with brain)—inference, generalization, instantiation, comparison, and so on? This seems a more defensible position than that neural pathways "literally" extend to the tools we use; but it achieves enhanced defensibility specifically by jettisoning the demonstrably material "machinery" of the brain (as it becomes mind). Clearly, if neural pathways in the brain are the machinery, they don't "literally" extend to the tools we use; the pathways through which the EMT postulates the "literal" extension of the "machinery of the mind" from the cranial mind to the extracranial mind are just as metaphorical as the "machinery" of thought inside the skull. The mind-body-world cycles through which thought passes, according to the EMT, are *like* neural pathways (this is precisely the functionalist argument)—and in fact it is precisely because they are only *like* neutral pathways without actually *being* neural pathways that many critics of the EMT reject it. The more explicitly materialist the claims made about extended mind are, the harder they become to defend; the more explicitly EMT proponents jettison their materialist claims, the more their critics are willing to go along with them.

The problem, of course, is that the claim that using tools is *like* thinking inside the brain is not a newsworthy philosophical position. It's something everyone can agree with, and therefore a nonissue. The EMT becomes philosophical news only if it is aggressively materialist—if the claim is that "the machinery of mind" *literally* (viz., materially, and therefore also, one might want to insist, empirically verifiably) extends into and through the tools we use.

The precarious position I propose to take here is a hybrid one. I accept the idea that mind extends—most enthusiastically in the context of the embodied mind, or the enactive mind, in which the mind's interactions with the body and the surrounding world are constitutive of thought and so inseparable from thought. And I accept the claim that these interactions are material events that can be studied empirically. To the extent that we want to understand those interactions as *mind*, however, they are, or so I shall argue, phenomenologies, felt by human subjects—*not* material events susceptible to empirical study. Mind may participate in material events; however, for that participation to be mind, it must be *experienced* as mind, which is to say, experienced phenomenologically.

Calling mind a phenomenology means understanding it as *qualitative* in origin and nature—as consisting of qualia—and while this is the "trap" that Andy Clark and others have long sought to avoid, I argue here that it is a trap into which we must be willing to step. (Given the nature of qualia, though, at least we can never step into the same qualia trap twice.)

This, then, is the new tack I take: I begin with mind-as-qualia. This will seem to materialist EMT proponents to be surrendering before the race even begins; but I suggest that there are (highly complex) *social* ways of framing qualia that will significantly transform the EMT debate, which to my mind has too long been mired in analytical oversimplifications. Indeed, I suggest that the crippling difficulty Clark and his followers have in arguing that mind has a literal machinery that extends literally into material circuits in the extracranial world points to a *materialist trap* in which the EMT has been lodged for some time now. Rescuing it from that trap will be my project here. (Note that that rescue emphatically does not mean a rejection of materialism. It means only rescue from the materialist *trap*.)

Specifically, I start from the following interlinked assumptions:

[1] Qualia are primary (extended mind *feels* extended) and shared (reticulated through the group) (§0.2 and §1.0, chapter 4, appendix).
[2] Cognition is internalized conversation: intracraniality is mostly transcranial (§0.3 and §2.3).
[3] Even verbal labels emerge out of preconative affect (§0.4 and §2.3).
[4] Language is not all cognitive labels: speech acts are conative *force* (§0.5, §3.1.2, §3.2, §3.3).
[5] Indirect speech acts can be preverbal (§0.6 and §3.4).
[6] Empathy, face, and ritual are managed through affective-becoming-conative communication (§0.7, chapter 5).
[7] The extended mind is actually an extended body-becoming-mind (§0.8).

Note 1. I use brackets for numbered items in lists, and parentheses to refer back or forward to those items and others in the lists and in the discussions that follow. Thus, (1) and (7) frame the argument, (2)–(5) offer a rethinking of the philosophy of language as it applies to the EMT, and (6) quickly considers a series of additional social phenomena that can usefully be studied as forms of extended mind. Proposition (4) in that list above could have been written "Language is not all (3) cognitive labels," to indicate that (3) refers back to the previous item in the list. Numbers preceded by § refer exclusively to the numbered sections of the book; for example, §3.4 refers to section 4 of chapter 3, and §A.1 to section 1 of the appendix.

Note 2. My use of hyphenated terms like "affective-becoming-conative" in (6) and "body-becoming-mind" in (7) and in the book's subtitle may annoy some; I hope you'll allow me the habit, as it reflects my concern throughout with entelechial becoming (the emergence of higher-level phenomena out of lower-level phenomena). I borrow the approach from Aristotle, Hegel, and Peirce, and the use of hyphenated terms partly from Hegel but also from Continental philosophers like Heidegger and Deleuze. I prefer this hyphenated style because my emphasis in each case is on the *becoming*, and thus on the emergent continuity between the hyphenated terms: it's not that affect exists, separately, and then undergoes some kind of transformation, at the end of which there is cognition, but that affect is always becoming cognition, cognition is always emerging out of affect.

This focus on becoming is also featured in the *sorites* series that I develop in §2.3, §3.0, §3.4, and §5.4, which has been criticized on the grounds that, despite all that stuff in the middle, there *is* a significant difference between the two extremes, the beginning in nonderivation and the ending in derivation. This inclination to binarize, and to protect binaries methodologically and rhetorically by excluding middles, is precisely the reason for my use of the *sorites* series, and for the becoming-terms.

Note 3. An eighth item, which I've left off the preceding list because it isn't reflected in the structure of this book, might have been something like "The EMT debate has been unnecessarily impoverished by the habit cognitive philosophers of mind have developed of not reading certain kinds of philosophers—notably, in the context of my argument here, Hegel, Peirce, Bakhtin, Austin, and Derrida—and needs to be enriched by broader reading habits." Crisafi and Gallagher (2010) have noted this impoverishment in regard to Hegel, who wrote extensively and usefully on the topic over two centuries ago, but whose usefulness to contemporary cognitive philosophy of mind seems to many to be minimized by his idealism and his tendency to use jargon that has fallen into philosophical disuse. The same might be said of Charles Sanders Peirce, the American polymath philosopher whose jargon-laden writing (along with the lamentable state of its publication) also tends to daunt many contemporary philosophers. The Continental tradition, from roughly Nietzsche to Derrida, appears here only in brief discussions of Derrida's deconstruction of Austin in §3.1; that work, along with the philosophy of language offered by Mikhail Bakhtin in §3.2, is generally thought to be of more interest to literary and cultural scholars than to cognitive philosophers of mind, but I suggest that there is much in those thinkers that can nudge the EMT debate forward. Sociological and psychological studies of situated affect (§0.6, §0.7, §5.0), ritualization (§1.3.1, §5.3), mood-dependent cognition (§1.3.2), habitualized social practices (§3.3), empathy (§5.1), and face (§5.2) also add important perspectives to the debate. My focus in the appendix on Oscar Wilde—not only a writer, but a writer who seems to flaunt his lack of seriousness and his unconcern for the truth—may seem especially frivolous; but I hope to convince you that the liar-paradox monism that I derive from his "Decay of Lying" dialogue points past apparent inconsistency to a strongly integrative understanding of the complexity of human epistemology.

0.2 Qualia are primary and shared (§1.0, chapter 4, appendix)

Qualia—our "experiences" of things, our "feelings" that things are a certain way—are not Andy Clark's favorite explanatory model for the extended mind. In fact, Clark praises Alva Noë's enactive theory of mind for "avoid[ing] the qualia trap" (2008: 180)—using non-qualia-related skills and interactivities to explain cognitive events—and works hard to avoid that trap himself. His suspicions about qualia as explanations of cognitive events and systems have a good deal to do with the fact that he is a materialist, and qualia, as they are traditionally conceived, are fleeting, private, and rather mysterious home movies shown in and by the mind—not a solid foundation for a philosophy of extended mind, if you are Andy Clark.[2]

It is rather unfortunate, then—again, unfortunate if you are Andy Clark—that one of the most commonly lodged criticisms of the EMT is that mind only *seems* to extend, since this would effectively make extended mind a quale (a collection of qualia).

It is even more unfortunate that, because of the way Clark and Chalmers (1998) originally set up the EMT and the way Clark has defended it since, it is hard to avoid the conclusion that their critics are largely right.

Clark is not adamantly opposed to qualia. He writes, for example, that when "fluently using a stick" we "*feel* as if we are touching the world at the end of the stick, not (once we are indeed fluent in our use) as if we are touching the stick with our hand" (2008: 31, emphasis added). That feeling of bodily extension into the stick is, obviously, a quale. And, given that the stick in this passage is in fact a sensorimotor anticipation of Otto's notebook a few pages later, we do only minuscule violence to Clark's argument by paraphrasing that line as "automatically using his notebook, Otto *feels* as if he is remembering the location of the Museum of Modern Art with the notebook, not (once he has indeed automatized the notebook's use) as if the notebook is a mere memory aid." That paraphrase would obviously make extended mind a quale.

Clark goes on: "The stick, it has sometimes been suggested, is in some way incorporated, and the overall effect *seems* more like bringing a temporary whole new agent-world circuit into being rather than simply exploiting the stick as a helpful prop or tool" (ibid., emphasis added). Substitute "notebook" for "stick" there and you have the EMT about Otto's notebook without even a hint of distortion—unless the emphasis I added to Clark's qualitative 'seems' seems to make cognitive extension sound too much like "mere qualia," which is to say, in the negative sense with which Clark typically injects his mentions of qualia, mere fantasies.

But in case you suspect that this is an isolated case that applies only to sensorimotor qualia, not to extended cognitive qualia, here is a later passage:

For example, imagine you are struggling to use a new piece of software to solve a problem. Phenomenologically, our experience in such cases is not at all suggestive of anything like tool-based cognitive extension. Instead, you are likely to *feel* quite alienated from the tool in question. The software package dominates as the local problem space that you confront rather than as a piece of transparent equipment through which you confront a wider world. (ibid.: 74, emphasis added)

The implication in this passage is that extended mind is the *feeling* that the external "epistemic artifact" (Sterelny 2004) on which you rely for a cognitive task of the specified sort is "a piece of transparent equipment through which you confront a wider world"—which is to say, yet again, that extended mind is a quale.

But I may still seem to be characterizing the EMT analogically rather than addressing Clark and Chalmers' (1998) or Clark's (2008) direct account of it. Note, then, that the EMT as Clark and Chalmers (1998) formulate it rests heavily and somewhat uneasily on two principles that pull it in different directions. The first is the functionalist Parity Principle, according to which anything outside the head that functions as a process that would be unquestionably accepted as cognitive were it to occur inside the head must be considered part of a cognitive process (ibid.: 8). The second is the principle of "endorsement," which in fact is never explicitly stated as a principle but which does form an essential plank of the thesis. Here are the four criteria by virtue of which Otto's reliance on his notebook may, according to Clark and Chalmers (ibid., 17), be taken as part of his cognitive process:

First, the notebook is a constant in Otto's life—in cases where the information in the notebook would be relevant, he will rarely take action without consulting it. Second, the information in the notebook is directly available without difficulty. Third, upon retrieving information from the notebook he automatically endorses it. Fourth, the information in the notebook has been consciously endorsed at some point in the past, and indeed is there as a consequence of this endorsement.

Clark and Chalmers clearly think of all four of these points as functionalist, intended to invoke the Parity Principle: because Otto's access to, use of, and endorsement of the contents in the notebook are all functionally highly similar to his friend Inga's access to, use of, and endorsement of her own biomemory, the notebook should be considered part of an extended cognitive system. In order to make the case that Otto's use of his notebook is a part of his actual cognitive processing, and not simply an external memory crutch, Clark and Chalmers want to show that Otto uses it "automatically"—that is, without thinking to himself some version of "I'd better check my notebook" or "I am now verifying the location of the Museum of Modern Art in my notebook"—and endorsement is the criterion they have set up to ensure that.

Now, I see nothing whatever wrong with a functionalist approach to mind. I employ one myself, at various points in my argument, whenever I argue that to the extent that the *feeling* the mind extends changes how the mind functions, or seems to function, that feeling is itself a form of extended mind. The problem arises when one attempts to adduce the *function* of mind while radically excluding the *qualitative experience* of mind—when one wants to make the function of mind an observable material event that a researcher or some other observer might notice and study and describe objectively, empirically, scientifically—and *a fortiori* when one wants to make functionalist (analogical) arguments stand in, exclusively, for both empirical proof (which is unavailable) and qualia (which are unattractive).

In the passage quoted just above, Otto's access to and use of the notebook (criteria 1 and 2) are *observable* functionalities, things we might notice, as Clark and Chalmers specifically say, by following him around for a while. His endorsement of the notebook's contents (criteria 3 and 4), on the other hand, is not observable in the same way—indeed one might argue that it is not observable at all. To know whether and to what extent Otto endorses the contents of his notebook, one would have to be Otto himself—one would have to have access to his endorsement-thoughts, which is to say, his qualia.

This is not just a matter of sequencing, or phrasing, or even of the whole example of Otto's notebook. Certainly it is not about any kind of problematic rift between the observable functionalities of *using* the notebook in criteria one and two and the non-observable functionalities of *endorsing* the notebook in criteria three and four: Clark and Chalmers' point is that all four functions have to be present for Otto's use of his notebook to count as extended mind. There's no question here that criteria one and two are observable and therefore susceptible to empirical proof or disproof and criteria three and four are non-observable and therefore "purely subjective." This is a hypothesis, a thought experiment, in which both Otto's consciousness and the consciousness of any potential outside observer are equally available to us. That simultaneous awareness of the thoughts of two different people is potentially problematic for actual empirical testing, but in the idealized Total Epistemology world of the hypothetical we can as easily watch Otto endorsing his notebook as we can watch him taking it out of his shoulder bag and flipping through it.

No, the real problem in Clark and Chalmers' formulation of the four functionalist criteria of extended mind is that the binary gate between extending and not-extending is hinged on the *automatic* nature of Otto's use of the notebook after he has endorsed it once. If he endorses it that one time, his use of it thereafter is automatic, and cognition extends; if he doesn't, certainly if he never endorses it, his use of it never becomes automatic, and cognition doesn't extend.

This rather unforgiving binary gate is reinforced in Clark's (2008: 102–105) response to Sterelny's (2004) argument that the very public nature of Otto's notebook problematizes the interface by introducing the possibility of deception: someone might doctor the notebook so that its contents are no longer reliable. As a result, Sterelny argues, the use of external memory aids like notebooks actually *increases* the load on the brain: new adaptive strategies must be developed to guard against the likelihood of malicious manipulation. I find Clark's response convincing: "[O]n a day-to-day basis, the chances of these kinds of espionage are sufficiently low that they may be traded against the efficiency gains of (for some cognitive purposes) leaving some information 'out in the world' and relying on just-in-time access" (ibid.: 103). And indeed the requirement that Otto *endorse* the contents of his notebook for his cognition to extend to incorporate it does specifically rule out possible situations in which, for whatever reason, Otto becomes suspicious that his notebook has been tampered with.

This seems eminently reasonable. But again the binary gate is in place: as long as Otto is using his notebook automatically, transparently, unthinkingly, but *feelingly*, his cognition extends to incorporate it; as soon as Otto's qualitative incorporation of the notebook into his cognitive system becomes problematic enough to sound alarm bells (that is, to move him from preconscious qualitative reliance on the notebook to conscious suspicion of its reliability), the notebook drops out of the cognitive system. In other words, regardless of how we construct that Ottonian mental state that Clark and Chalmers call "endorsement"—whether it is an objective recognition of some state of affairs or a mere phantasmatic seeming—it is clear that cognitive extension depends upon, and thus is constituted by, or even (the most radical possibility of all) arguably *is*, that mental state.

Given Clark's (2008) opposition to qualia as traditionally conceived, a generous reading of Otto's endorsement would make it not a quale but a judgment, and would invoke Clark's (2000a) two-step attempt to distinguish judgments from qualia: [1] distinguish judgments about qualia from the qualia themselves, and [2] show how grounding in the neurophysiological substrate can make such judgments *true*. This would obviously allow Otto to endorse the reliability of his notebook's contents veridically, to *recognize* or *register* its *objective* reliability rather than simply entertaining a fleeting and possibly phantasmatic mental image of that reliability. By imagining a metaquale that somehow magically leaps the epistemological chasm from the phenomenal to the material and thus the veridical, Clark would also seem to have solved Chalmers' (1995/1997) Hard Problem of Consciousness from a strictly materialist point of view—assuming, of course, we are willing to make the epistemological leap with Clark.

Even if we are willing to make that leap, however, Clark's solution doesn't address the mental state in which Otto uses the notebook. Presumably in Clark's terms the judgment that the notebook is or isn't reliable (endorsement/non-endorsement) is Otto's own binary gate, into either the "automatic" or "transparent" YES state in which the notebook becomes part of his extended mind or else a highly aroused NO state of cognitive suspicion. He doesn't keep making the judgment that the notebook is reliable while he is using it; if he did, his use of it wouldn't be automatic, and cognition wouldn't extend. He makes the judgment and then *sinks* into that automatized state in which, I'm claiming, it preconsciously *feels* to him as if his mind is extending to incorporate the notebook. Or even, as Clark (2008: 103) seems to suggest, that automatized qualitative YES state becomes his default choice: having judged the notebook reliable at some point in the past, he need not make that judgment every day, or on a use-specific basis, in order to slip back into the YES state.

Nor does Clark's solution address the issue of an outside observer's access to Otto's judgment that his notebook is reliable. Otto's cognitive extension still seems to depend on that judgment, and we have no empirical way to determine whether or how he makes that judgment. We can posit it, as Clark and Chalmers want to do, as part of a philosophical thought experiment, but that effectively traps the EMT in the world of the hypothetical. We can rely on Otto's verbal report, and claim with Clark (2000a: 33) that "there is a further fact of the matter that makes such reports typically true," but, given the potential for deception that Sterelny reminds us all public communication entails, that strategy would mire us in an infinite regress that could be halted only by consensus. Clark is essentially saying "I report that I believe that my judgments about our reports of our beliefs/judgments about qualia are typically true," which constitutes a convincing argument only if I (Doug Robinson) report that I believe that my judgments about Clark's report (etc.) are typically true, and if you do the same about my report, and nowhere along the line does a substantial body of nay-sayers rise up in vociferous protest.

The problem is that there are two competing constructions of Otto's reliance on his notebook, with no principled basis for adjudicating between them: [1] his cognitive processes remain purely intracranial and merely

rely on the notebook as a memory aid; and [2] his cognitive processes extend out beyond what Clark calls the skinbag to incorporate the notebook. Given that Clark further agrees with his detractors that the notebook is incapable of "thinking" or "cognizing" on its own, he is forced to fall back on functionalist (analogical) parallels between Otto's reliance on his notebook and the brain's reliance on its own part-systems, which are similarly incapable of "thinking" or "cognizing" on their own—well, on those parallels along with the fact that it often *feels* to us as if mind extends. Absent empirical proof that mind *does actually* extend (and Clark tends to defer the possibility of such proof indefinitely), Clark's exclusive reliance on functionalist analogues makes the EMT sound like pure philosophical speculation—and specifically like speculation resting heavily on the qualitative impression we sometimes have that mind extends, which is to say, as Clark constructs qualia, on fantasies.

To my knowledge Clark never addresses this particular problem; he mostly tries to sidestep it rhetorically, as if somewhere deep down he knows that it is a problem that he can't solve. To avoid the potential accusation that he is dealing in imaginaries, in fact, Clark typically escalates his functionalist rhetoric: "To decide, in any given case, whether the channel is acting more like one of perception or more like one of internal information flow, we must look to the larger functional economy of conscious vigilance and active defenses against deception. The lower the vigilance and defenses, the closer we approximate to the functionality of a typical internal flow" (2008: 104). The "decision" there regarding the functionality of "the channel" depends on qualitative experiences to which arguably only Otto has access; yet as Clark constructs the decision-making process, the "we" who make the decision are not Otto but Clark or Clark's readers, reflecting on Otto's cognition from outside Otto's head. Describing those qualia as a "functional economy of conscious vigilance and active defenses against deception" may make them *sound* like objects observable from the outside; but as qualia have been traditionally understood, they are purely subjective experiences available only to the subject, through introspection.

I propose to solve the problem in a way that Clark won't like, but that seems to me the only principled solution:

[1] to affirm that mind only *seems* to us to extend to our epistemic artifacts, but also
[2] to insist that that seeming or feeling or qualitative experience does actually enhance cognitive function, and further
[3] to reframe qualia as interactive channels of social communication and regulation, and finally

[4] to situate the phenomenalism of (1)–(3) in a complex monism predicated on the necessary recursive failure of both standard materialism and standard idealism.

The effect of (1) is to accept the qualitative nature of extended mind; the effect of (2) is to reappropriate the functionalist argument of Clark and Chalmers (1998) toward the end of ensuring that (1) remains externalist in Clark's terms; the effect of (3) is to reconstruct the EMT in new phenomenalist terms; the effect of (4) is to ensure that my phenomenalist claims remain defensible on materialist grounds.

A tall order.

The primacy that (1) would give qualia for the EMT, obviously, is precisely the "qualia trap" that Clark has worked so hard to escape: rather than invoking the functionalist argument *as opposed to* the phenomenalist, and *in lieu of* the materialist, as Clark does, in (2) I subordinate it to the reframed fractured-phenomenalist EMT in (3) and (4). (For an introduction to (4), see the appendix.) Rather than treating the primacy of qualia as a problem, therefore, or as a limitation on the kinds of claims one can reasonably make about cognitive extension, or as an embarrassment, the less said about which the better, I embrace it as the starting point for any realistic discussion of mind.

What I suggest in (3)—and in chapter 4—is specifically that qualia are not the mysterious, mystical, evanescent, private will-o'-the-wisps as which they have traditionally been portrayed. Rather, qualia are often shared, reticulated through groups. Qualia, in other words, are often transcranial—and to the extent that intracranial mind consists of qualia, it too is often transcranial (§0.3), and thus in some generalized sense "extended" even inside the skull. The reticulatory sharing of qualia also means that we do often have more or less reliable access to the qualia in other people's heads, with or without verbal reports. Recall that I noted above, in connection with Clark's (2000a) argument that we can (usually) trust verbal reports, that this view institutes an infinite logical regress that can be halted only by consensus. What I meant by that regress-halting consensus was a *group quale* that seems true because we all accept it as true. Such group qualia, I will argue, are the primary channel of the social construction of reality; see Searle (1990, 1995, 1999) and Tomasello (2008) for discussions of "shared intentionality" that don't quite coincide with, but strongly anticipate, my claims about shared qualia. It is by reference to this socially constructed reality, not some "real" reality beyond the social (Kant's *Ding an sich*), that we mostly seek empirical confirmation or disconfirmation of claims like "mind extends beyond the skull to the tools we use."

What I suggest in (4)—and in the appendix—is that from time to time our socially constructed realities crack and fissure, and the *really* Real breaks through, and we tend to use such moments as (traumatic) tests for our "automatized" assumptions about reality; but we don't have systematic or continuous access to the Real. (What Kuhn (1962/1970) calls "paradigms" are the scientist's version of those socially constructed realities; what he calls the "anomalies" that undermine and ultimately destroy a paradigm would be the "really Real" against which normal scientists are constantly seeking to shore up the paradigms they normatively take to constitute the reality whose nature they are exploring.)

Once again, then, into the storm. The fact that I strongly critique materialist accounts of extended mind doesn't make me an anti-materialist, any more than my recognition that idealism inevitably fails (is everywhere undermined by material reality) makes me an anti-idealist. Nearly every pre-publication reader of this book tried to squeeze my argument into a single binary pole: I'm some kind of radical idealist who denies materialism. Understanding the full complexity of the case I make here requires more complex thinking than that. I'm a materialist who recognizes that everything we know about material reality is a quale, and an idealist who recognizes that qualia are human groups' ultimately inadequate attempts to represent and control material reality. Any attempt to reduce the complexity of that tension to a pure singularity will make hash of my argument.

Obviously, my failed-idealist/quasi-materialist fractured-phenomenalism will not satisfy a hard-nosed materialist like Clark; but I submit that it is an explanatory model to which his own rebellious instincts keep leading him, and a model that he resists to the detriment of the EMT. And I think I have built enough safeguards into the model (especially (3) and (4)) to ward off the disgruntled complaint that extended mind is pure fantasy.

0.3 Cognition is internalized conversation: Intracraniality is mostly transcranial (§2.3)

What I find most problematic in Adams and Aizawa's (2001, 2008) critique of the EMT is not so much the notion that mental representations in extracranial objects are derived as it is the notion that mental representations in *trans*cranial communication are entirely derived and in *intra*cranial cognition mostly nonderived. This is a point on which Clark (2008: 91) provisionally ("for the sake of argument") agrees: noting that Adams and

Aizawa's "real worry is that the inscriptions in Otto's notebook . . . are out-and-out conventional" and that "they are passive representations that are parasitic, for their meaning, on public practices of coordinated use," he argues only that for a cognitive system to extend it is only necessary for *some part of it* to be nonconventional and nonderived. In other words, Clark believes that it is enough for cognitive extension to occur if extracranial objects, bodies, or environments that don't generate original content are coupled in the automatic or "transparent" ways Clark and Chalmers (1998) specify with a nervous system that does. I will argue that, on the contrary, intracranial thought is itself in large part collectively derived and conventionalized, "parasitic . . . on public practices of coordinated use," and thus not exclusively or even predominantly intracranial—that in fact intracraniality is itself mostly transcranial, and thus that Adams and Aizawa have even less of a case against Clark than Clark recognizes. What we take to be an individual's thoughts are always to a high degree conditioned by the thoughts and feelings of the other members of the groups to which s/he belongs.

This is not a new idea. According to George Herbert Mead, for example, mind emerges out of language; mind is an "internalized or implicit conversation of the individual with himself" (1934: 47); or, as he puts it later in the book, "the conversation which constitutes the process or activity of thinking is carried on by the individual from the standpoint of the 'generalized other'" (ibid.: 155); or, more pithily, 12 years earlier (Mead 1922/1964: 246), "thought is the conversation of the generalized other with the self." Mead's "generalized other" is the internalized composite voice of "society," or "the group"; in a sense it is the voice of transcraniality itself.

Of course there are obvious philosophical differences between Mead's symbolic-interactionist sociology of mind and the reductive-representationalist (Fodorian) philosophy of mind on which Adams and Aizawa rely; we will be taking a closer look at Fodor's (1975) language-of-thought hypothesis (LOTH) in §2.2. I am in any case less interested in the border war between the human and the nonhuman, which I cover briefly in chapter 1, than I am in *sociality* as extended body-becoming-mind. My main focus in chapters 2–5 is therefore in a sense peripheral to the key issue in Adams and Aizawa's quarrel with Clark and Chalmers and their followers, namely the extended cognitive system purportedly created when a single individual relies cognitively on tools, his or her own body, a workspace, or the like. As Gallagher (2009: 38) notes, the various combatants in the border war over extended mind have not been especially interested in sociality as an instance of extended mind. Indeed, while Clark and Chalmers (1998: 17–18) mention it in passing toward the end of their article, Clark (2008: 80) says specifically that "other people would typically not count [as parts of an extended cognitive system] (but could in rare cases)"—presumably because he thinks we don't rely on other people "automatically," the way we do on our own brains. In §0.7 and §5.1, I will show that we do.

0.4 Even verbal labels emerge out of preconative affect (§2.3)

Affect research has seen a resurgence in recent decades, after a longish hiatus roughly coterminous with the heyday of behaviorism. The early work done on affect by James (1890), Dewey (1894, 1895), McDougall (1908), and Durkheim (1912/1954), as well as the empirical research on affect in the early decades of the twentieth century reviewed by Scheff (1984a), fell into disrepute in the 1940s as behaviorism encouraged psychologists to suppress theoretical and empirical orientations to both cognitive and affective subjectivity and focus on observable behavior, and encouraged sociologists to champion functionalist and structuralist theories of role, status, and exchange. As psychologists, sociologists, and philosophers began to chafe at the exclusion of subjectivity from theory and research in the mid-to late 1960s, *cognition* was first elevated to pride of place, leading to the explosive growth of the cognitive sciences, with far-reaching consequences for cybernetics and robotics as well as the philosophy of the human sciences—but affect was still pushed aside. This is understandable, perhaps, given the assumptions we have inherited from Platonism, Christianity, and the Enlightenment to the effect that cognition or "thought" is what is truly and supremely human about us and affect is what we share with the lower mammals. But by the late 1970s persuasive new paradigms for the study of affect began to appear, and Silvan Tomkins (1981: 314) predicted that "the next decade or so belongs to affect."

The new sociological and social-psychological approaches to the study of affect were varied. Kemper (1978) developed a social-interactionist model that challenged individualized (what we might want to call "intracranialized") theories of emotion by exploring the ways in which emotions are "situated"—produced in and for social interaction (for reviews of more recent research in this area, see Parkinson et al. 2005 and Griffiths and Scarantino 2009). Shott (1979) applied Mead's (1934) symbolic-interactionist theory of cognitive role-taking to "empathetic role-taking" in order to explore the emotional channels of socialization and social control. Collins (1975, 1981) returned to Durkheim to explore the role of mundane shared affect in the creation and maintenance of social cohesion and solidarity. Hochschild (1975, 1979, 1983) developed a model of "feeling rules," cultural norms regulating the production and expression of emotions. Denzin (1980, 1984, 1985) channeled Mead's symbolic interactionism through Merleau-Ponty's phenomenology of "lived experience" in order to situate social actors and their interactive selves in the group. Jackson (1988) summarized the new "integrative orientation" that gradually took hold in social psychology over the course of the 1980s, noting that it involved the following:

[1] a shift of analytical focus from the individual to the social act
[2] a conception of the individual as a reflexive social actor
[3] an integrative focus on subjectivity as cognition, affect, conation, and behavior
[4] a conception of the self as a loose conglomeration of situated identities (and of identities as consisting of the situational presentation of self and management of others' impressions)
[5] an understanding of meaning as neither extracranial nor intracranial but interactive, reflexive, and situated (constantly being negotiated reciprocally with others, in what are called "reference processes")
[6] a conception of social action as coordinated around group norms (in deciding on a behavioral strategy, each group member takes other members' reference processes into consideration)
[7] a scene-based understanding of social behavior (each "scene" or interaction begins with the construction and mutual negotiation of situated identities and ends with a discontinuity of the social process that may involve a scene-change—a change in physical location or in the group of "actors" "on stage")

In general, as this summary indicates, the new integrative orientation to social psychology was interactive and situated in focus, conceiving the individual as an active and reflexive conduit for group concerns.

One of the most influential new approaches to the sociological or social-psychological study of affect was affect control theory (ACT), first sketchily outlined by Heise (1969, 1970) and developed into a full research paradigm by Heise (1977, 1978, 1979, 1985, 1987, 1999, 2002, 2007) and his colleagues (Smith-Lovin and Heise 1988; Smith-Lovin 1990; Averett and Heise 1988; MacKinnon 1985, 1988, 1994; MacKinnon and Heise 1993; Heise and Lerner 2006). As MacKinnon (1994: 4) summarizes it, ACT "proposes that people construct social events to confirm the affective meaning of their situated identities and those of other actors; and when events occur that strain those sentiments, people initiate restorative actions and cognitive revisions to bring affectively disturbing events back into line with established sentiments." One strong core of ACT is borrowed from situated identity theory (Alexander and Wiley 1981), which draws on Mead (1934), Heider (1958), Goffman (1959), Stone (1962), and McCall and Simmons (1966) to explore the ways in which situational role-taking encourages social actors to see themselves through others' eyes (by inferring others' "dispositional imputations"), and indeed to *adopt* those other-imputed dispositions strategically and purposefully in order to facilitate social interaction. Situated identity theorists follow McCall and Simmons in distinguishing among [a] human behavior, in which actors are unaware of others' subjective orientation to a situation, [b] human conduct, in which actors consciously or unconsciously orient themselves to the *potential* psychological presence of others in a situation, and [c] situated activity, in which actors consciously monitor real others' perspectives on a situation and align their conduct accordingly. Situated identities are fluctuating by-products of situated activity; as MacKinnon (ibid.: 94) puts it, "situated identities are properties of the social field of interaction and define the relation between an actor and his or her environment at any point in the flow of situated activity."

Of the 24 propositions MacKinnon (ibid.: 15–40) offers that together define his emerging synthesis of symbolic interactionism and ACT, four (1–4) modify Mead's symbolic interactionism by adding affective associations to the verbalized social cognitions of interactants; ten (5, 6, and 10–17) define "event production" in terms of situational identities and the interactive guidance they provide to social actors, especially in cases where affective disturbances must be resolved through event (re)interpretations; three (7–9) cover affective *reactions* to social events, affective *control* of events by aligning them wherever possible with "fundamental sentiments" (established affective orientations or traits), and affective *reconstructions* of events when fundamental sentiments fail adequately to explain them; three (18–20) deal with emotions as arising from the discrepancy between "the transient impression of the interactant that was created by the event" and "the fundamental sentiment associated with the interactant's situated identity" (ibid.: 39); and the last four (21–24) deal with actors' cognitive revisions of their situated identities in response to affective disturbances.

The propositions that are the most relevant to my assumption about verbal labels arising out of affect are the first four:

[1] Social interaction is conducted in terms of the social cognition of interactants.
[2] Language is the primary symbolic system through which cognitions are represented, accessed, processed, and communicated.
[3] All social cognitions evoke affective associations.
[4] Affective associations can be indexed to a large degree on universal dimensions of response. (ibid.: 38)

MacKinnon (ibid.: 16) clarifies (2) by noting that "Affect control theory assumes that social cognitions are *embodied* in language" (emphasis added), perhaps not quite deliberately anticipating my claim that language is body-becoming-mind. The quantitative research agenda of ACT is to collect and analyze data on people's attitudes toward "*words* designating the constitutents [*sic*] of social events—such as social identities, personality traits and status characteristics, and interpersonal acts" (ibid.: 16–18, emphasis added)—though ACT researchers also move past words to study attitudinal and affective responses to the semantics of simple sentences as well. While ACT researchers seem to echo Fodorian LOT theorists like Adams and Aizawa in modeling cognitive processes on the idealized semantics of simple grammatical structures, therefore, in fact they add two key elements to the LOT equation: [a] a focus on social acts or events ("*events* are structured in terms in terms of case grammar, and additional grammars are invoked to explain the cognitive constraints that occur within and between events" (ibid.: 17, emphasis added)), and [b] a focus on affective associations ("all cognitions evoke quantitatively measurable affective associations which vary in intensity and direction along several qualitatively distinct dimensions") (ibid.). Those dimensions, which proposition (4) posits as universals, are the so-called EPA dimensions of the semantic differentials developed by Osgood and colleagues (Osgood, Suci, and Tannenbaum 1957; Osgood 1969; Snider and Osgood 1969; Osgood, May, and Miron 1975): evaluation, potency, and activity.

The claim that language consists of syntax plus semantics (no situated pragmatics) and merely *evokes* affective associations would seem to dualize cognition and affect in fairly traditional (i.e., nonsituated) ways. But in fact MacKinnon (1994: 43–50) argues for a continuum from cognition to affect that might be taken to undermine this apparent dualism: if Peirce's emotional interpretant is affect, his energetic interpretant is conation, and his logical interpretant is cognition (see §4.2), then *every interpretive act* is affect-becoming-conation-becoming-cognition, and affect is merely a more intense form of cognition, cognition a calmer form of affect. MacKinnon (ibid.: 50) quotes Mook (1987: 449) to the effect that it is ultimately irrelevant which comes first and conditions the other: "A process is set in motion that may bounce information back and forth between 'cold' thought and 'hot' emotion in a dazzlingly complex trajectory. There is no reason to think that the process has only one starting point, or follows only one sequence each time." Or, as MacKinnon (ibid.) paraphrases that, the affective reaction, affect control, and reconstruction outlined in propositions 7–9 "describe a cybernetic process of lower- and higher-order feedback wherein past cognitions evoke affective reaction and current affective states influence subsequent cognitions." The EPA semantics of evaluation, potency, and activity that form ACT's primary analytical line of attack, then, are not purely cognitive structures that "evoke" affective associations: they are *saturated* in affect. To the extent that they are cognitive, they are affective-becoming-cognitive definitions (and redefinitions) of situations *and* cognitive-becoming-affective channels of control.

0.5 Language is not all cognitive labels: Speech acts are conative *force* (§3.1.2, §3.2, §3.3)

To the extent that affect for ACT researchers is a channel of *control*, of course, it is also definitively conative: it mobilizes or energizes the organism to act (in certain regulated ways). As MacKinnon's use of Peirce suggests, affect is part of a complex cybernetic affective-becoming-conative-becoming-cognitive feedback system. What ACT specifically misses, however, are the ways in which *language* is also an affective-becoming-conative-becoming-cognitive channel of control: for ACT researchers, language consists entirely of verbal labels that evoke affective associations and so signify attitudes and sentimentalized identities, but themselves have no conative force.

The fact that speech-act theory beginning with Austin (1962/1975) does specifically theorize language in terms of its illocutionary *force* and perlocutionary *effects*—as conation—helps move us past the impasse created by what Felman (1980/2003: 13[3]) and Robinson (2003, 2006) would call ACT's "constative" (label-based) philosophy of language. It is surely significant, for example, that the E in Osgood's EPA is itself a speech act, namely *evaluating*. It is not, in other words, simply that language uses evaluative verbs and modifiers that *signify* evaluative conations, as ACT would have it: it also *performs* those conations. As Austin's title tells us, he is interested in "how to do things with words." We *encourage* and *discourage* each other. We *approve* and *disapprove* of people and the things they do. We *warn, intimidate, threaten, browbeat, guilt-trip,* and *undermine* people; we *urge, push, remind, nudge, nag,* and *support* people.

And it's not, as Austin is careful to make clear, that we *state* (represent) our warnings or urgings or other speech acts and our listeners then process them cognitively, in order to decide rationally whether to act on them; we yell "Stop!" and the other person stops. We irritate someone and that person feels irritated. We have an actual bodily impact (perlocutionary effect) on our interlocutors. Speech acts are in effect *transcranial conations*. To the extent that communication in the speech-act sense is affective-becoming-conative-becoming-cognitive, a speech act is often *my* affect becoming *your* conation—as we'll see in chapter 1, when a teammate's speech act of encouragement reticulates supportive affect in her body as conative motivation in a competitive swimmer's body—*and* becoming labeled cognitively (by me or you or both) as the speech act of encouraging, or supporting, or motivating.

0.6   Indirect speech acts can be preverbal (§3.4)

As long as we have a verbalized speech act to refer to, of course, it is always going to be possible for "constative" philosophers of language to argue that the effective agent in this reticulatory event is the verbal label—"I'm warning you," we say, thus naming the speech act a "warning"—and that its perlocutionary effect is therefore activated purely cognitively, rationally, and only secondarily (and intracranially) "evokes" affect or "produces" conation in the listener's body. But of course not all speech acts name themselves. "Stop!" is only implicitly or indirectly a warning, and speech-act theorists recognize that indirect speech acts (Searle 1975) can be performed wordlessly as well, as when a parent warns a child with a significant look. In those latter cases speech acts are transcranially affective-becoming-conative without becoming overtly cognitive, making it far more difficult to reduce them to purely or even primarily cognitive events. In many cases it does seem undeniable that some sort of affective-becoming-conative *force* is being transferred from body to body—that in fact preverbal speech acts constitute a powerful form of extended body-becoming-mind.

0.7   Empathy, face, and ritual are managed through affective-becoming-conative communication (chapter 5)

It is ironic, given their situated conception of social identities and acts—their belief that the "individual" is a conduit of social forces in specific interactive events—that ACT researchers insist [a] that individuals use affect-becoming-conation to *read* other people's body language but to *control* only their own behavior, and [b] that the only form of transcranial communication that can mobilize the organism to act is verbal. §0.6 suggests (contra a) that the speech act is designed to control other people's behavior, and that it does so through situated and extended affect-becoming-conation; now let us consider the possibility (contra b) that there are other channels of transcranial conation besides language.

MacKinnon (1994: 52) specifically argues that "it is only through the symbolic representation made possible by language that human organisms are able to relate to incentives as objects of reflective consciousness, to assess alternative means for realizing goal objects, and to anticipate outcomes of actions in terms of their instrumental value"—and that is certainly true. But this claim appears only a few pages after his passionate defense of the notion that affect and cognition are not polar opposites so much as they are overlapping tendencies on a scale—that affect *knows* things and cognition *feels* things, or that cognition is simply a higher-order version of the same kind of feedback provided by affect. One corollary of what MacKinnon (ibid.: 45) calls the "principle of inextricability"—the inseparability of cognition from affect—must surely be that the ability "to relate to incentives as objects of reflective consciousness, to assess alternative means for realizing goal objects, and to anticipate outcomes of actions in terms of their instrumental value" that MacKinnon rightly attributes exclusively to "the symbolic representation made possible by language" cannot be separated from the ability to relate to incentives as objects of affective and thus preverbal consciousness. If affect and cognition are different orders or intensities of conative feedback on the same scale, surely preverbal indirect speech acts and verbalized direct speech acts are as well? Surely, in other words, natural language is not the only channel of transcranial communication?

Ironically enough, in discussing Mead's (1934) dismissal of affect as purely private and thus "asymmetrical"—I feel an emotion and you don't, you feel an emotion and I don't—MacKinnon himself identifies several moments in Mead's work that theorize an affective channel of transcranial communication. On the one hand, "On the emotional side, which is a very large part of the vocal gesture, we do not call out in ourselves in any such degree the response we call out in others as we do in the case of significant speech" (Mead 1934: 149, quoted in MacKinnon 1994); typically "we do not deliberately feel the emotions which we arouse [in others]. We do not normally use language stimuli to call out in ourselves the emotional response which we are calling out in others . . . as we do in the case of significant speech" (Mead 1934: 148, quoted in MacKinnon 1994). On the other hand, however, even if we don't do this *normally*, it does happen: the artist will work hard "to find the sort of expression that will arouse in others which is going on [emotionally] in himself (Mead 1934: 147, quoted in MacKinnon 1994); a poet "is seeking for those words which will answer to his emotional attitude, and which will call out in others the attitude he himself has" (Mead 1934: 147–148, quoted in MacKinnon 1994). For Mead it is only the artist who does this—but apparently it *is* possible to communicate affectively, below the verbal radar, as it were. Affective communication *can* be symmetrical, so that you and I feel the same thing—so that emotion is not merely situated but (at least sometimes) extended.

In §5.1 I will cite dozens of empirical studies of the social neuroscience of empathy to show that this "symmetricality" of affective communication is in fact much more common than Mead claimed—a fact that ACT researchers really ought to be incorporating into their empirical and theoretical work. If Mead's symbolic interactionism is one powerful model for ACT, another is Goffman (1959, 1967, 1974) on the dramaturgical presentation of self, interaction rituals, and interactive frames; and in §5.2 I will also be looking closely at a curious convergence of Goffman (1967) on face-loss and Aristotle on shame to suggest that extended (transcranial) conation is in fact our primary channel of social control—control specifically of *others*, of the members of groups, and not simply (as ACT would have it) of our individual selves.

0.8 The extended mind is actually an extended body-becoming-mind

It is not a novel idea to reconceptualize the extended mind as the extended body-becoming-mind. In fact, EMT advocates' heavy reliance on studies of embodied cognition everywhere suggests that the mind that extends is definitively a body-becoming-mind. Clark (2008), after all, titles the first part of his book "From Embodiment to Cognitive Extension," and his first two chapters "The Active Body" and "The Negotiable Body," and continues to explore the embodiment of cognitive extension throughout. And when Rick Grush (2003) explains the emergence of mental representations as closed-loop (feedback-driven) mock-proprioceptive simulations of fast intentional motor activities and argues that such representations are [a] the "mark of the cognitive" and [b] strictly intracranial, Clark (2008: 149–156) invokes the widespread human reliance on "surrogate situations" (externalized mock-ups of the kinds of internal representations Grush means) to enable a form of cognitive processing that is *"disengaged but not disembodied"* (155). One of Clark's recurring arguments against the classical model of cognition as building and employing relatively stable composite representations of the world that make it possible for the mind to *withdraw* from the body/world draws on research demonstrating the importance for cognitive processing of just-in-time access to just barely enough information through a quick succession of visual saccades (glances).

For Clark, clearly, mind is always embodied. The problem I have with his understanding of that embodiment, however, is that in his formulations the leap from body to mind is always of the quantum sort: from sensorimotor activity to complex cognitive and metacognitive processing. There are almost never intermediate steps between the coarsest kind of embodiment and the embedded recursivity of the human mind. Hence, I think, his fascination with robotics—with the possibility that emergent indications of mental activity might appear in machines. His interest in language (Clark 1996, 1998, 2000b, 2004, and 2006, the last reprinted in slightly abridged form in Clark 2008: 44–60) is focused on the cognitive power of simple labels, which, he says, as if apologetically, do "depend on the presence of something akin to a system of interpretation." "But," he adds, more hopefully, "it is their ability to provide simple, affect-reduced perceptual targets that (I want to suggest) explains much of their cognitive potency" (2008: 45). That push to minimize the importance of interpretation and reduce affect I think characterizes Clark's approach to embodiment: he is not particularly interested in the middle ranges of affective and conative representations as *transitions* from kinesthetics to cognition.

Ironically, in view of his strong anti-Cartesian research agenda and his whimsical characterization of Grush as a "born-again Cartesian" (2008: 149), Clark's relative lack of interest in affect, conation, and language as embodied speech acts leaves a sizable enough gap between body-as-motion and mind-as-representation that his modeling of embodied cognition retains a kind of implicit structural Cartesian mind-body dualism. It is indicative, for example, that after his nearly 40 opening pages of detailed discussions of research showing convincingly that in many cases we don't simply *use* tools but incorporate them into our body schemas, Clark (2008: 39) asks "Could anything like this notion of incorporation (rather than mere use) and the consequent emergence of new systemic wholes get a grip in the more ethereal domain of mind and cognition? Could human *minds* be genuinely extended and augmented by cultural and technological tweaks . . . ?" It is relatively easy to demonstrate empirically that tool use quite often changes our neural architecture, he says; "it is harder to know just what to look for in the case of mental and cognitive routines" (ibid.: 40).

In other words, the body functions physically, allowing researchers to run experiments that establish causal bridges between that functionality and changing neural architecture; because the mind functions experientially, qualitatively, without an objective signature that might yield to the kind of experimental design that would satisfy a materialist, it is difficult to establish that *anything empirical happens* when mind extends—that, say, cognitive extension is not just a quale. The incorporation of tools into body schemas seems suited to empirical research, and thus to materialist explanation; the incorporation of tools into mind seems suited only to idealist speculation.

In addition to assuming that intracraniality is primarily a localized channel or circuit through which transcranial qualia are constantly passing, then, I propose to fill in some of the gaps left by Cartesian mind-body dualism by taking a close look at the middle ranges of the extended body-becoming-mind. My brief is that affect and conation are the realms of mental processing that are most obviously and demonstrably transcranial, and thus that by omitting them from a consideration of extended mind Clark leaves himself vulnerable to the claims of internalists like Adams and Aizawa, Rupert, and Grush.

My suggestion is specifically that body is not so much *different* from mind as it is continually *becoming* mind, through a series of closely connected evolutionary steps. My model for this becoming is adapted from the neo-Jamesian neuroscientist Antonio Damasio, who claims that the appetites "map" (represent) body states like hunger and thirst, the emotions map appetites and other body states, the feelings map emotions and other body states, and thoughts map feelings and other body states. At each level "maps" or representations of body states are generated for purposes of homeostatic control of the internal and external environment. The appetites "tell" us that we're hungry so as to motivate us to scavenge up some food and eat it in a timely fashion (appetite-becoming-conation-becoming-action). The emotions may then "tell" us that our inability to locate food is extremely annoying, though we may not immediately *feel* that particular emotion; one of William James' (1890) innovations was the notion that there is a difference between *having* an emotion and *feeling* it, the difference being that the feeling represents the emotion to consciousness (affect-becoming-conation-becoming-rudimentary-cognition). And our thoughts may then "tell" us that drastic measures need to be taken (call for take-out, make a midnight run to the grocery store), and possibly also that we need some sort of rational regime for stocking up food stores in advance, so that we don't discover that our cupboards are bare right at the very pinch of hunger (affect-becoming-conation-becoming-cognition-becoming-action).

While I will periodically recur to Damasio's neo-Jamesian approach—especially his somatic-marker hypothesis—in the course of the book, my main entelechial models for the emergence of mind out of body will come out of earlier stages of the Hegelian tradition: the triadic thought of Charles Sanders Peirce (who influenced James) and of Hegel himself (who influenced Peirce). In §1.1, for example, I draw heavily on the "Philosophy of Mind" section of Hegel's *Encyclopaedia of the Philosophical Sciences* to explore the emergence of mind out of what Hegel calls "soul" (something akin to what James calls "feeling"), and his *System of Ethical Life* to explore the circulatory (internalization/externalization/internalization) ensoulment of tool use. In §2.3, §3.0, §3.4, and §5.4 I trace a soritic neo-Jamesian becoming-structure by which emotion becomes feeling and feeling is voiced first inwardly, then outwardly, then gets increasingly tangled up with another person's feeling through affective-becoming-conative-becoming-cognitive communication.

0.9 Structure of the book

I begin chapter 1, titled "Inside Out," with the core of the EMT, namely Clark and Chalmers' (1998) claim that mind extends to our tools, bodies, and environments—but specifically in order to shift the philosophical ground on which that claim has mostly been made, from the quasi-materialist/functionalist foundations on which Clark has worked so hard to base it to a quasi-idealist/phenomenalist foundation. In chapter 1 I draw heavily on Hegel's philosophy of mind, specifically his theory of tools as externalized mind and of mind as internalized tools from *The System of Ethical Life* and his theory of habitualized thought from the *Encyclopaedia of the Philosophical Sciences*, in order to explore the *qualitative* nature of the relationship between mind and tools—extended mind as quale. I approach that relationship from two directions, both "outside in" (the sense we sometimes have when we think that we are internalizing external tools) and "inside out" (the sense we sometimes have that our proprioceptive system is expanding into the world to incorporate the tools and workspaces we use—the EMT—as well as the ways in which cognition is mood-dependent and mood-congruent).

In chapter 2, "Language as Cognitive Labels," I branch off from the main trunk of the EMT by interrogating Adams and Aizawa's attempt to protect the intracraniality of "true cognition" by excluding the transcraniality of natural language from cognitive processing. I first trace this attempt back to Fodor's (1975) language-of-thought hypothesis (LOTH), first briefly rehearsing the history of the Computational Theory of Mind (CTM) in general and the LOTH as perhaps the most influential instantiation of the CTM, then offering a countermodel by tracing the actual emergence of thought out of embodied (affective-becoming-cognitive) communication with others. Throughout this chapter I stick to the verbal-labels model of language that Andy Clark shares with his internalist critics in order to show that a careful enough examination of even this extremely narrow conception of language uncovers far more transcranial connectivity than Clark argues for.

Chapter 3, "Language as Conative Force," is devoted to a series of readings of Austin's (1962/1975) speech-act theory—Derrida (1972/1988) on iterability and the displacement of force, Bakhtin (1934-1935/1982) on internal dialogism, and Bourdieu (1982/1991) on *habitus*—in order to explore the nonsemantic connections a language maintains among its users. The focal claim of this book, in fact, is that *something* connects us nonsemantically (nonpropositionally)—that sociality really is a form of extended body-becoming-mind—but what? My tentative suggestion in chapter 3 is that it is some sort of transcranial conative *force*, the force Derrida theorizes as the core of the speech act; but what is that force, exactly, and how is it transferred from body to body? Force is transferred in a car crash through collisions; bodies don't collide in speech acts. What is passed from person to person, and how?

In chapter 4, "Qualia as Interpretants," I suggest that those forces passed from person to person are in fact qualia, feelings, experiences—that qualia are not the private, ineffable, quasi-mystical things they are often made out to be, but rather the communicable reality-organizing forces by which social regulation is managed. To make this case I compare and consolidate Charles Sanders Peirce's theorizations of qualia from 1898, the tone-token-type triad from 1906, and the emotional-energetic-logical interpretant triad from 1907.

Chapter 5, "Empathy, Face, and Ritual," defines the type of qualia that circulate through groups as affective orientations, inclinations, pressures, and intensities. The chapter begins with a discussion of the socioneurological research on empathy, and continues with a close look at Aristotle's use of the noun *doxa* as it intersects with Erving Goffman's (1967) discussion of face—an important model for ACT—by way of setting up a reticulatory model of affective communication. It closes with a look at Connerton's (1989) sociological theory of ritual as collective memory, returning us to the discussions of iterativity (Derrida) and the unification of language (Bakhtin) in chapter 3 to suggest that the human body-becoming-mind is neither perfectly collectivized (which would deprive us of individuality) nor perfectly individualized (which would refute the EMT).

The appendix, "Liar-Paradox Monism," offers a background discussion of idealism/phenomenalism and qualia on which my argument in the main chapters more or less implicitly relies, and to which it occasionally refers. There, taking Oscar Wilde's "The Decay of Lying" as my exemplary text, I offer a tentative (though rather baroque) solution to what Chalmers (1995/1997) calls the Hard Problem of Consciousness, based on the famous attempt to have contradictory things both ways that has come to be enshrined in the liar paradox. Specifically, I argue that qualia are our primary contact with what we take to be the world, and we want to trust them, but our encounters with things and other people prove our qualia wrong often enough to render that trust problematic. To improve the fit between our qualia and the world, we try to master our environments—to control *things* affectively-becoming-kinesthetically (chapter 1) and *people* affectively-becoming-conatively (chapters 3–5)—but also to test our qualia by triangulating our qualitative experiences of the world. This latter project generates empirical science, which for many scientists has tended to mean the elimination of all human bias, which is to say the exclusion of qualia-based explanations—avoiding what Clark (2008: 180) calls "the qualia trap." But qualia cannot be excluded: they are our primary interface with the world. Empirical science has in fact never truly been about the *exclusion* of qualia; rather it deals in the *testing* of qualia, the maintenance of a fruitful *tension* between qualitative experiences and quantitative testing of those experiences. That tension, the conflicting pushes and pulls of our idealist/phenomenalist desire to trust our qualia and our materialist/empiricist desire to test and manage our qualia, lies at the core of liar-paradox monism.

1 Inside Out

We begin with the primary claim of the extended-mind thesis (EMT): that mind extends to incorporate what Sterelny (2004) calls the "epistemic artifacts" that we use—things like computers and workspaces. This extension of mind to incorporate inanimate things is not the core of the extended-body-becoming-mind thesis that I seek to flesh out in this book, and I don't propose to return to it after this first chapter; but we shall start with what we have been given.

As I began to suggest in the introduction, the reservations I have about the EMT as it is advanced by Andy Clark are that it seems grounded in [a] endless and possibly baseless speculations about future empirical verification, [b] functionalist analogues (versions of what Clark and Chalmers (1998) call the Parity Principle), and [c] the rhetorical suppression of the pressing question of qualia. Could cognitive extension into tools and workspaces turn out in the end to be (c) a "mere" quale—a feeling, a seeming—that (a) will never yield to empirical proof and so (b) must rely exclusively on analogical support? Presumably Clark would want to say no; but, no matter how strongly his own criteria, evidence, and analogies suggest that it is, he never even addresses the issue. His reliance on the functional analogues of the Parity Principle is unrelenting, almost certainly because it is his strongest argument for cognitive extension; the fact that the argument from analogy is not quite strong enough to count as empirical support makes his approach a kind of argumentative alchemy, in which leaden analogies are painted yellow and marketed as the next best thing to gold. (Not that Clark's analogies are actually leaden; "alchemy" is just an analogy, and perhaps a leaden one.)

Still, whether Clark and his followers ever establish that mind extends to inanimate epistemic artifacts in some objectively verifiable way, the fact that it does often feel as if it does can serve as a useful starting point for a phenomenalist cognitive science. Certainly a phenomenalist approach to cognitive extension can explain why so many cognitivists *want* to believe that cognition extends beyond the brain: if it feels true, it may well *be* true.

From a materialist standpoint, I'm sure, this all sounds dismissively, even sarcastically, anti-externalist, as if I were saying that cognitive extension isn't "real"—it just feels real. (It's not a doctor; it just plays one on EMTV.) From the fractured-idealist perspective that I bring to the EMT, however—for discussion, see the appendix—recognizing the unlikelihood that cognitive extension will ever be verified empirically is merely the first (negative) step in a positive research program aimed at exploring how (body-becoming-)mind *actually* extends.

The first positive step in that program, I suggest, is to recognize that we tend to invest our epistemic artifacts with (the feeling of) sentience. When we interact with them fluently or "transparently," we not only enhance our cognitive processing by relying complexly (often recursively) on our bodies, our tools, and our environments, as Clark and other proponents of embodied, embedded, and extended cognition have shown so brilliantly; we also project our "qualitative selves" or "affective selves" out onto or into those things, so that they feel like part of "us," part of an extended body-becoming-mind/self. Our affective selves are capable of expanding to encompass whatever we incorporate into them: specific tools or workspaces, living spaces (what we mean by "home" is typically something like "the living space that I/we have incorporated into my/our affective self"[1]), streets or neighborhoods, whole geographical regions, nations, the planet, and so on. In that expanded mode, an insult to my nation, or to my religion, or to some other social or geographical grouping with which I fervently identify, is an insult to me. Those selves are also capable of shrinking to exclude our own recalcitrant bodies, or affective or cognitive events that happen inside our skulls but seem to have a mind of their own (a tendency to cry at inopportune moments or lust after inappropriate people), or dreams and other productions of what Freud called "the unconscious," or capacities that don't function as we would like them to function (e.g., failing memory as we age). ("My memory's going," we say, as if memory were an autonomous division in our heads.) My explorations in this chapter of the affective-becoming-conative-becoming-cognitive interface between the intracranial and the extracranial are predicated on the hypothesis that this *felt experience* of extended cognitive systems not only fuels theorization of the extended mind to a great extent but also contributes to fluent functioning.

David Bohm (1992) theorizes this extended affective self in terms of proprioception, in two steps. The first step is to suggest that, just as the bodily proprioceptive system tells us ("from within," without visual confirmation) where our legs are, so too is there a *proprioception of the mind*, which enables us to track our cognitive processes. To apply Strawson's (1994/2010) notion of cognitive experience recursively, the experience of experiencing our cognitive processes is strikingly similar to the experience of experiencing our bodies from the inside. Just as there is a qualitative difference between the feeling that our legs are in a position that will allow us to stand easily and the feeling that we will have to adjust their position before we will be able to stand, so too is there a qualitative difference between the feeling that we have formulated a rebuttal well enough to jump into a debate and the feeling that we're still a little confused, and would be taking our chances opening our mouths to argue against a position.

This first step in Bohm's argument is in the same ballpark as Grush's (2004) explanation of mental representations as closed-loop (feedback-driven) mock-proprioceptive simulations of fast intentional motor activities. Bohm's second step, however, is to suggest that proprioception of the mind is not bounded by the skull. Whether our feelings to this effect are accurate are not, we do often believe that we know what other people are thinking and feeling (the topic of §5.1), or even—and this is my main topic in this chapter—what the objects and spaces around us are thinking and feeling. That latter belief, of course, is what Ruskin (1856/1891) called the pathetic fallacy: the feeling that the soughing pines are mournful, for example, or that the burbling brook is cheerful. Ruskin specifically derogates this emotional projection as a *fallacy*, as a logical and scientific error; and while in one sense I am as much of a naturalizer as Ruskin, utterly uninclined to offer a mystical reconstruction of the pathetic fallacy as somehow Romantically veridical, I do think that the realist/materialist dismissal of the experiences that would make it *seem* veridical is hasty.

For one thing, given that any empirical evidence against those experiences must be filtered through the experiences in our own heads, that dismissal is itself epistemologically suspect. When we finish a lecture in a state of elation caused by the belief not only that "it went well" structurally or aesthetically but that the students loved it, we have no way of verifying that we're right—but then, neither does anyone else that we're wrong.

For another, as we will see in greater detail in chapter 4, our experiences—our qualia—are deeply involved in our collective constructions of reality. Our inclination to enter into the *poetic* power of a literary scene, especially when augmented visually and aurally in drama and cinema, tells us something about "reality" as a social construct. Our susceptibility to shared or collectivized experiences through art, rhetoric, or advertising is really just a specialized instance of our larger susceptibility to the shared experiences that we take to be "the world."

In response to the hard-nosed materialists who would dismiss this affective experience as "only" phenomenal, only felt, and therefore not empirical,[2] we may adduce the impressive body of research documenting the affective substrates of memory and learning. (See §1.4.2 below.) As Eich and Macaulay (2000: 244) note, "Much of this interest has centered on two phenomena of memory: *mood-congruent memory* (MCM)—the observation that a given mood tends to enhance the encoding or retrieval of target events that share the same affective tone or valence—and *mood-dependent memory* (MDM)—the observation that events encoded in a certain mood are most retrievable in that mood, irrespective of the events' valence." These research findings are still several argumentative steps away from the claim that we *invest* our epistemic artifacts with affect, and that such affective investments facilitate computational cognition—making that case is one of the burdens of this chapter—but even before we have explored that possibility, the empirical evidence that affect informs and even enables cognition is suggestive here. At the very least it should make us willing to consider the possibility that the *feeling* of extended cognition actually facilitates nonextended cognition, and that the rigid inside-outside opposition of the intracranialists is therefore oversimplified.

The title of the present chapter, "Inside Out," is shorthand for this process; a fuller title might be "Inside Out and Outside In," since the qualitative interrelatedness of inside and outside in extended (body-becoming-)mind is actually a circulation: the feeling that our epistemic artifacts are moving in and transforming the way we think is actually an internalized image of those artifacts. Inside out: we project our affective selves onto our epistemic artifacts. Outside in: it feels as if those external artifacts are thinking/feeling agents that break into our embodied minds and become part of the inner workings of those minds. I will deal with these two directionalities in the opposite order, however—the felt order rather than the reconstructed chronological order: first outside in (what we are initially conscious of is our sense that our computers and cars and so on are external living creatures that we feel at work internally), then inside out (since computers and cars are not actually living creatures, they are inanimate objects, we eventually remember that the feeling that they are alive must be coming from inside).

I take the notion of mind-tool interaction as a *circulation*—tools as externalized mind and cognition as internalized tools—from Hegel's *System of Ethical Life* (1802–1803/1979). Let's take a look first at what Hegel has to say about extended mind.

(A reminder: It may seem, again, as if this approach trivializes the EMT by reducing cognitive extension to figments of our overactive imaginations. While I do believe that cognitive extension to inanimate objects is a qualitative experience, however, my intent is not at all to trivialize the EMT. It is, rather, to show how embodied minds actually do extend. I believe that cognitive extension is severely limited in the realm of mind-tool or mind-environment interaction, and so after this single chapter will move on to the realm that I argue is the true locus of affective-becoming-cognitive extension, namely sociality; but even in mind-tool and mind-environment interaction, the focus of this chapter, a phenomenalist approach doesn't trivialize the possibility of extension. It only seems to do so to those who would trivialize qualia.)

1.1 Hegel

1.1.1 Crisafi and Gallagher on Hegelian mind as social institutions

"Hegel is rarely mentioned in contemporary discussions of the philosophy and science of mind," Crisafi and Gallagher (2010: 123) note, but should be: his notion of objective spirit, and especially "his idea that the mind is expressed in social institutions" (ibid.), seem directly relevant to the discussion of extended mind. More than that, Hegel has a clearly elaborated understanding of the situated embodiment of mind, of mind arising out of the body's interactions with its environment, that seems like a largely wasted resource in recent discussions of the EMT.

To be sure, Crisafi and Gallagher emphasize the *rational* character of Mind or Spirit (*Geist*) for Hegel; this is potentially misleading. It doesn't imply Cartesian mind-body dualism—the view that "mind" is the rational or logical or computational part of each human's being, over apart from "body" as the organic part. Hegel recognizes the existence of a rational or logical or computational part of human being but calls it not mind but "intellect" or "intellectual consciousness," and associates its dualistic conception of the body as radically alien and separate from itself as the product of a process akin to what Freud would later call "repression." As intellect arises out of what Hegel calls the "soul" or "psyche" (*der Seele*), its emergence involves the soul's "cut[ting] itself off from its immediate being, and plac[ing] this being over against itself as bodiliness, which can offer no resistance to the soul's incorporation into it" (1830/2007: paragraph 412). The soul for Hegel is that "immediate" or habitualized part of mind that manages (and in some sense *is*) feeling and sensation, working almost entirely under the radar of conscious awareness; it saturates and is saturated by bodiliness (*Leiblichkeit*), in three stages:

Stage 1 (the "soul that just is" (ibid.: paragraph 411)): soul/psyche/*Geist* begins as unseparated from the body

Stage 2 (the "feeling soul" (ibid.)): soul/psyche/*Geist* only begins to emerge as an individual subjectivity as it trains the body out of which it arises, and begins to *feel* the body as external to it

Stage 3 (ensoulment, what Hegel calls the "actual soul" (ibid.)): soul/psyche/*Geist* transforms "identity with its body" into "an identity *posited* or mediated by the mind" (ibid.: paragraph 410)

Once the actual soul begins to think of itself as that separate "identity *posited* or mediated by the mind," which is to say as no longer embodied, no longer connected to the body in any significant way, it becomes intellect, and thus purely "cognitive" in the strict Cartesian sense of the *res cogitans*. This split, Hegel says, is possible (and thus in some sense inevitable) only because the soul is unable to "pervade" the body entirely:

The soul's pervasion of its bodiliness considered in the two previous Paragraphs is not *absolute*, does not completely sublate the difference of soul and body. On the contrary, the nature of the logical Idea, developing everything from itself, requires that this difference still be given its due. Something of bodiliness remains, therefore, purely organic and consequently withdrawn from the power of the soul, so that the soul's pervasion of its body is only one side of the body. The soul, when it comes to feel this limitation of its power, reflects itself into itself and expels bodiliness from itself as something *alien* to it. By this *reflection-into-self* the mind completes its liberation from the form of *being*, gives itself the form of *essence* and becomes the *I*. (ibid.: paragraph 412Z)

For Hegel, therefore, the rationality of mind consists not of purely disembodied logical computation but rather of the meaningful structure of the evolutionary phenomenology of Mind in all its forms, including many (in fact virtually all) of the forms and functionalities that Cartesian dualism would relegate to "body."

For example, Crisafi and Gallagher (ibid.: 125) note Hegel's insistence in the "Philosophy of Mind" section of his *Encyclopaedia of the Philosophical Sciences* on the "dialectical emergence of the mind out of nature," especially through the expressive power of body language: "Human expression includes, e.g., the upright figure in general, the formation especially of the hand, as the absolute tool, of the mouth, laughter, weeping, etc., and the spiritual tone diffused over the whole, which at once announces the physical body as the externality of a higher nature"[3] (ibid., paragraph 411; quoted in a different translation by Crisafi and Gallagher). Note, first of all, that Hegel doesn't mean the "the upright figure" and "the formation especially of the hand" in a purely organic sense; he means the ways in which our postures, bearings, gaits, gestures, and the styles with which we manipulate objects are *trained* forms of expressivity. Thus, "formation" as training[4]—see stage 2 just above, and §5.3 on ritual.

Note further that the diffusion of "the spiritual tone . . . over the whole" suggests specifically that mind is at this stage not reason but an emergent tonality[5] that is just beginning to "announce" the body as something more than sheer materiality. This tonality would include not only tone of voice (a tone of pride, say, or the happy self-awareness that rings in the laughter of a healthy young body on a sunny morning) but also a more physical tonality—for example, the way a body-builder displays his or her "ripped" "muscle tone" in a posture, a gait, or the casual scratching of a deltoid muscle. Mind early on takes the form, in other words, of bodily expressivity—and, obviously, continues to do so today, although it is now much more than that as well, including the rationality (or what Hegel calls the intellect) with which a narrow Cartesian dualism would want exclusively to associate it. Bodily expressivity communicates with unnamed others, signaling its rhetorical desire to be *recognized* (see Ikäheimo 2007[6]) as "a higher nature" by those others. Crisafi and Gallagher (ibid.) put this as follows: "Insofar as the mind (as self-conscious) recognizes itself as this body, it recognizes itself as exposed to others, and seeks fulfillment in recognition by others, from which comes 'the emergence of man's social life' (§433)."

Note finally that in Hegelian terms the phrase "recognizes itself *as this body*" doesn't mean that the mind remains itself, whole, separate, complete, and purely rational, and merely projects itself spectrally onto the body, or sees the body *as if* it were mind/self (all the while knowing that it is not). It means, rather, that mind is externalized as body and body is internalized as mind, and the "recognition" (*Anerkennung*) is both bidirectional and constitutive of self. In the social context others participate rhetorically in this bidirectional and constitutive recognition as well, on the model of (and as an extension of) the mind recognizing itself as the body.

In places, it must be admitted, Crisafi and Gallagher's formulations might be read as associating Hegelian Mind exclusively with computational cognition, mind as *logical reasoning*:

Extension and embodiment are of utmost importance to Hegel, because no idea or state of consciousness can be of any influence if it is not extended and embodied. Mind here must turn itself into a concrete form in order to accomplish anything. Moreover, this extension and embodiment is reflective of cognition as a rational act. The mind is motivated to identify itself with the Objective, and it does this by working on the physical, molding it and melding with it. It does this through work and actions that become manifest in cultural activities such as art, religion, and philosophy, and through social institutions, such as government and law. As Hegel writes in the *Philosophy of Right*, a person "must translate his freedom into an external sphere in order to exist as Idea" (40).

What is potentially problematic in that passage is the phrase "this extension and embodiment *is reflective of* cognition as a rational act": the dualizing fulcrum offered by the noncopulative predicate "is reflective of" seems to make "extension and embodiment" into a mere secondary index of "cognition as a rational act," and thus to separate the two in neat Cartesian fashion. I think Hegel's position would actually be that extension and embodiment *are* actions of Mind, and in that broad sense *are* "rational acts" or "cognitive acts" or "mental acts." It is only when we can imagine mind-becoming-body—mind melding with the physical, cognition melding with embodied habit and affect as will, motivation, desire, and emotion—as a rational act that we are ready to entertain the notion that for Hegel Mind is reason or rationality.

1.1.2 Hegel on mind and tools

Given that the debate over extended mind has tended to revolve around the issues laid out in Clark and Chalmers (1998), especially perhaps the use of tools—Otto's notebook—I would suggest that Crisafi and Gallagher's (2010) brief summary of Hegel's theory of mind as body, as affect, and as social institutions from the *Encyclopaedia of the Philosophical Sciences* (1830/2007) and *The Philosophy of Right* (1821/1991) should be supplemented with his discussion of the use of tools from *The System of Ethical Life* (1802–03/1979). There Hegel is concerned with the reciprocal development of need and enjoyment from the earliest stages of "natural ethical life," in which need is typically simple and primitive, like hunger or thirst, and enjoyment is eating a fruit or drinking from a stream, to the complexities of advanced (mass-production) capitalism, characterized by the alienation of surplus need to the collective as the abstract ideality of property, value, and law.

Hegel theorizes our relationship with a tool as part of the mediation of reason, which for him here is the synthesis of the antithetical relationship between the serial internalization of consumer objects as a desire to make them (*thesis: outside in*) and the externalization of desire as the desired object (*antithesis: inside out*). "Reason" thus becomes the mediatory *circulation* of images of objects that we internalize as desire and the somatics of desire that we project outward onto objects, transforming them into the attractive images that we then internalize as desire, and so on. If this circulation, which Hegel helped Marx understand as the engine of consumerism—commodity fetishism—doesn't seem particularly rational, that is only because, as we have seen, Hegel defines reason not as cold logical analysis but as the emergence of agency or control out of the mindless state of nature. In that natural state, we're hungry, so we pick a fruit and eat it, and that's that. The appetite arises, is noticed, is satisfied, and so (as Hegel says) "nullified." In this state "feeling . . . is something entirely singular and particular, but, as such, is separated, a difference not to be superseded by anything but its negation, the negation of the separation into subject and object; and this supersession is itself a perfect singularity and an identity without difference" (Hegel 1802–03/1979: 103–104). The apple I pick from the tree is an object, separated from my needy (hungry) subjectivity; by eating it I negate that separation and supersede (sublate, *hebe auf*) the difference between subject and object. The apple becomes me. "The feeling of separation is *need;* feeling as separation superseded is *enjoyment*" (ibid.: 104), pure and simple.

The thetic "outside-in" extended-mind moment arises when need is not entirely nullified or satisfied in eating—when, for example, I do something to the fruit before eating it (peel it, slice it, cook it, make a pie out of it, etc.), and discover not only that it is tastier that way, but that I really enjoy the process of preparing it. Because this displaced enjoyment of baking (or whatever) is not "nullified" when I eat the concoction, (the image of) each tasty dessert, affectively enhanced by my newfound pleasure in the *making* of fruity desserts, is serially internalized as desire. Through my dessert-making labor, I sublate each individual dessert, in series, by replacing it with another and investing my new dessert-making desire as deferred enjoyment in each new dessert:

> The nullification of the object or of the intuition, but, *qua* moment, in such a way that this annihilation is replaced by another intuition or object; or pure identity, the activity of nullifying, is fixed; in this activity there is abstraction from enjoyment, i.e., it is not achieved, for here every abstraction is a reality, something that *is*. The object is not nullified as object altogether but rather in such a way that another object is put in its place, for in this nullification, *qua* abstraction, there is no object or there is no enjoyment. But this nullification is labour whereby the

object determined by desire is superseded in so far as it is real on its own account, an object not determined by desire, and determination by desire *qua* intuition is posited objectively. (ibid.: 106)

In this process, "pure identity, the activity of nullifying, is fixed" as an addiction is fixed, one that begins in this case as a consumption addiction but, through sublation, becomes an addiction to producing *and* consuming *and* still possessing the object, which must thus somehow remain available for addictive enjoyment despite its consumption. Clearly, here, the failed or attenuated (but ideal and therefore perpetually renewed potential for) enjoyment lies not in consuming the object but in making-and-consuming-and-having the object, making your pie or cake or apple turnover and having it and eating it too, so that, in practical terms, as you finish one dessert you have to start making another. The subject thus becomes primarily addicted to the idealized (internalized) image of the object, secondarily to the (internal) desiring/laboring processes that provide for the satisfaction of desire.

That is the thetic outside-in movement. Hegel theorizes the antithetic inside-out movement, or what Andy Clark calls "quite literally extending the machinery of mind out into the world— . . . building extended cognitive circuits that are themselves the minimal material bases for important aspects of human thought and reason," in terms of a shift in focus in the subject-object relation from subject to object. As long as the focus on that relation is on the subject, objects tend to be idealized as the image-objects of desire, possessed inwardly by the subject; externalizing them means rethinking or refeeling them as external objects that partake of "the real," the world outside our desires, even though for Hegel they still are part of the inner idealized world of our desires. The difference is not an ontological one—whether the object *is* inner or outer, ideal or real—but a phenomenological or qualitative one, how we construct the object, how it seems to us. This is, obviously, the "qualia trap"—which in Hegel's idealist imagination is no steel jaw-trap that clamps around the unwary philosopher's ankle, but is capacious enough to encompass the entire world.

But the real external object in question is not yet the tool—not yet the stick that Andy Clark describes as feeling like part of us, so that, when we use it fluently, it feels not as if we are touching a stick but as if we are touching the world at the end of the stick. It is the object of desire, Hegel's primary example of which in this dialectic is food. It is only when Hegel gives us "the mediation of reason" as the synthesis of the thetic outside-in and the antithetic inside-out that he begins to unpack that mediation dialectically in terms of a new antithetical tension, between the child as thesis, the tool as antithesis, and speech as synthesis. The tool is a dead object where the child was a living being, but is equally invested with the maker's desire, and specifically involved in mediating between subject and object: the subject uses the tool to rework the world into object.

In a sense the child, the tool, and speech are all externalizations of desire, but in Hegel nothing is ever unidirectional; everything is enmeshed in reciprocity. Just as a heterosexual relationship produces a child as its living externalization, so too does the child transform the sexual relationship (in fact, renders the free expression of its sexuality problematic). Just as the individual's intelligence produces speech as its living externalization, so too does speech transform the individual's intelligence, channeling the group's "objective" reception of speech back into it as a collective regulatory effect. (This regulatory reciprocity between embodied speech as externalized feeling and embodied speech as internalized judgment is a subtheme of chapters 2 and 3, but we will see some applications of the parallels Hegel draws between tools and words in §1.2.)

And just as the subject produces a tool as an externalization of his or her desire to rework the object, so too does the tool transform the subject, making him or her more object-like, or, as Hegel says, "blunting" (*stumpf machen*) the subject. This blunting is first transformed inwardly into objectivity, then increasingly "severed," as Hegel says, split off from the subject, who, through this severing or splitting, enlists the object and the labor as means to the thinking of the subject's own intelligence. In the tool, feeling is subsumed under the concept, which grounds mediating rationality in dead matter; in addition, especially as we begin to move from the early capitalism of individuals making whole products (a cobbler making a pair of shoes, a seamstress making a whole dress, etc.) to the late capitalism of mass production, labor is increasingly divided up into subtasks that are given to different workers. This has the effect of sucking the feeling of "wholeness" (*die Ganzheit*) out of labor, reducing making to a mechanical repetitiveness that tends progressively to mechanize or deaden the laborer:

> The particular, into which the universal is transferred, therefore becomes ideal and the ideality is a partition of it. The entire object in its determinate character is not annihilated altogether, but this labour, applied to the object as an entirety, is partitioned in itself and becomes a single labouring; and this single labouring becomes for this very reason more mechanical, because variety is excluded from it and so it becomes itself something more universal, more foreign to whole. This sort of labouring, thus divided, presupposes at the same time that the remaining needs are provided for in another way, for this way too has to be laboured on, i.e., by the labour of other men. But this deadening [characteristic] of mechanical labour directly

implies the possibility of cutting oneself off from it altogether; for the labour here is wholly quantitative without variety, and since its subsumption in intelligence is self-cancelling, something absolutely external, a thing, can then be used owing to its self-sameness both in respect of its labour and its movement. It is only a question of finding for it an equally dead principle of movement, a self-differentiating power of nature like the movement of water, wind, steam, etc., and the tool passes over into the *machine*, since the restlessness of the subject, the concept, is itself posited outside the subject [in the energy source]. (ibid.: 117)

Here is objectivity gone viral: the object-quality of the tool, first internalized as a blunting, then as intelligence, and gradually as blunted or blunting intelligence, is increasingly externalized as the machine, which in turn is re-internalized as machine-like labor, purely quantitative, mechanical, repetitive, mindless labor, which tends to have the effect of self-canceling the subject's blunted or blunting intelligence, and so deadening the subject, leaving only the subject's restlessness and the machine's energy source. (*The self-canceling of the subject's intelligence*: the tool is "canceled"—sublated, *hebt auf*—once when it is transformed inwardly into the tool user's intelligence; that "cancellation" is itself "canceled" a second time when the intelligence so created is blunted out of existence by mindless repetition.)

This is obviously a far darker vision of mind extended to tool than anything we find in Andy Clark. Extending mind to tools for Hegel doesn't just help us think better—Clark's (2008) recurring refrain. It does that too, but it also blunts our thinking, makes it (and us) more tool-like, and ultimately turns us (to the extent that we work on an assembly line) into brain-fried zombies whose only trace of remaining humanity is our restlessness. Hegel was, of course, a German Idealist, highly attuned to the German Romantic assault on science and technology that would find its most brilliant bloom in Martin Heidegger; not for him the celebration of robotics, say.

More than 200 years have passed since Hegel wrote *The System of Ethical Life*, and we have now mainly outsourced assembly lines to the Third World, where we don't have to think about them. Cyborg theory and the EMT are far more current for the twenty-first century than Hegel and Marx on the alienation of labor. But perhaps it might be at least passingly realistic for EMT theorists to consider the bleaker effects of tool use, along with the exciting ones.

For example, consider what David Hess (1995: 373) calls "low-tech cyborgs": people watching television, or driving cars. Is there some sense in which the mild-mannered person who becomes a raging maniac behind the wheel is acting out a version of extended mind? Neil Postman (1985) claimed that watching TV makes us stupid and passive: could this too be a version of extended mind? Other explanatory models are available for those transformations, of course; and it may be that Andy Clark and other extended cognitivists have steered away from less rosy examples like this for a good reason. But I suggest that if the EMT cannot legitimately be applied to cases where epistemic artifacts make us dull or dangerous, there's something wrong with it.

1.2 Outside in

A Hegelian approach to the mind-tool interface that lies at the heart of Clark and Chalmers' (1998) EMT, and to the debate that ensued, requires us to consider that interface not as a statically spatialized *coupling*, as it is for Clark and Chalmers, but as *directionality*—and specifically as *bidirectionality*, both the internalization of tools as mind (outside in) and the externalization of mind as tools (inside out). The chapter is titled after the later directionality, largely because it seems closest to the central issues of the extended-mind debate; but let's begin with the former.

1.2.1 Mental math

How do we do math in our heads? According to Jerry Fodor's (1975) language-of-thought hypothesis (LOTH), we do it in Mentalese or the language of thought (LOT), a symbolic language that is somehow ideally sequestered from the body's interactions with the world, including natural language. That this model, offered in all seriousness as an "empirical" hypothesis, is pretty far from the mental reality of doing math (or for that matter thinking other kinds of thoughts) can be shown with a very few counterexamples; indeed as Clark (2008: 54–55) notes, Fodor (1998: 72) himself later had second thoughts about it:

> I don't think that there are decisive arguments for the theory that all thought is in Mentalese. In fact, I don't think it's even true, in any detail. . . . I wouldn't be in the least surprised, for example, if it turned out that some arithmetic thinking is carried out by executing previously memorized algorithms that are defined *over public language symbols for numbers* ("now carry the '2'" and so forth). It's quite likely that Mentalese co-opts bits of natural language in all sorts of ways; quite likely the story about how it does so will be very complicated indeed by the time that the psychologists get finished telling it.

Fodor immediately add the following: "For all our philosophical purposes (e.g., for purposes of understanding what thought content is, and what concept possession is, and so forth) *nothing essential is lost* if you assume that all thought is in Mentalese" (quoted in Clark ibid.: 55; emphasis added by Clark). The problem, of course, is that for Fodor Mentalese is purely internal, private, nonderived; natural language is external, "public," as Fodor says, and then "co-opted" in the sense of being internalized along the lines we have just seen Hegel theorizing. In Hegel's sense, mental math understood as "co-opt[ed] bits of natural language" would be public tools internalized as intelligence; more radically still, our ability to recognize those "bits of natural language" as internalizable tools would require that we first project our own need or desire for them out onto them, then convert them phenomenologically from disturbances of the sound waves or black marks on a page into tools that are available for our (internal) use. This would imply not merely what Clark (ibid.) calls "hybridity"—natural language mixed in with the LOT—but circulation, the inside-out and outside-in circulation of tools and reason that would make it impossible to distinguish inside from outside, private from public, and Mentalese from natural language (except of course by phenomenological fiat, *assigning* each a separate category).

Clark suggests that "the potential cognitive impact of a little hybridity and co-opting may be much greater than Fodor concedes." In order to explore just how much greater it may be, let us consider a case study of mental math—one from my own experience of counting laps while I swim.

As other lap swimmers will confirm, the tricky part of swimming distances is keeping track of how far you've swum. While you're swimming, presumably owing to the length of time you have to hold a lap or length number in your memory—too long (say 30–40 seconds in a 25-meter pool) for short-term memory but too short and too transient for long-term memory—it is somewhat difficult to do even the simple additive math involved in counting laps or lengths. As Clark (2008: 55) points out, the physical environment in which mental math is done, and specifically the interaction between the actor's body and that environment, has a significant impact on the actor's ability to count. For the shorter distances—50-, 100-, and 200-yard or meter events, the only ones I swam in as a child—counting is typically not a problem; but for 500-yard or meter events it is customary for one team member to position himself or herself at the end of each swimmer's lane with a plastic flipbook of numbers, and, as the swimmer approaches her or his station, to flip the book to the relevant lap number and jam it down into the water for the swimmer to see, so the swimmer doesn't have to count laps.

Obviously, if Clark and Chalmers' (1998) Otto were to get in the pool to swim a 500-meter freestyle, he would not be able to jot down the number of each length (down the pool) or lap (down and back) in a notebook. He would need some externalized form of memory—a friend showing him underwater numbers, or a mechanized counter or clicker that he could tap with his hand at the end of each lap. (For discussions of a roughly parallel version of the story, see Clark 2005 and Chalmers 2005.)

I have found, over several decades of mostly shirking experience, that the form of exercise I hate least is a daily 500-meter freestyle. For years I swam a kilometer three times a week, but over time I kept finding it harder and harder to force myself to go to the pool, so I changed my regime and began swimming 500 meters five times a week—half a kilometer less per week, but in the long run conatively more sustainable. And I do find that keeping track of how far I've swum is a cognitive problem for me, as it is for many other lap swimmers I've talked to. It is too easy for me to forget to voice a number at the beginning of a lap, and then, at the beginning of the next lap, to have no memory of how many laps have gone by since the last time I voiced a number; and then I've lost count, and must make the tricky ethical choice between assuming that I've done two laps (and perhaps getting out of the pool a lap early) and assuming that I've done only one (and perhaps doing a extra lap). But I find that if I concentrate, and use the right counting strategy, I can count laps fairly effectively.[7]

1.2.1.1 *Habitualization experienced as internalization*

For the purpose of counting laps, 500 meters can be segmented mentally in a number of different ways, the most obvious being five 100s, ten 50s (in a 25-meter pool, ten laps), or twenty 25s (twenty lengths). At first, when I was swimming a full 1,000 meters, I tended to count in 100s, marking each 25-meter length with a letter (1a, 1b, 1c, 1d, 2a, and so on); when I switched to 500 meters, that computational regime came to seem unnecessarily cumbersome and I switched to counting lengths (1, 2, 3, . . . , 19, 20).

Recently, though, for reasons I'll discuss below, I switched to counting laps *and* lengths—1/1, 1/2, 2/3, 2/4, 3/5, . . . , 9/18, 10/19, 10/20. At first, I found, somewhat to my surprise, that continuing the count as I made the turn into each new lap felt *cognitively* awkward. I'm not exactly a "math person," but I usually feel quite comfortable around numbers, and I have a good memory for them. I was somewhat surprised when I would come up the pool thinking "3/6, 3/6, 3/6," then make the turn, and not know what came next. Obviously the answer was 4/7, but it took me a few seconds to work that out: 3 + 1 = 4, 6 + 1 = 7. Or, even more ponderously, "the number after 3 is 4, 4 doubled is 8, but I'm on the first length of 4, so it's 4 and 8 − 1 = 7." 4/7 wasn't a familiar numerical collocation for me. It wasn't a category that my mind fell into easily after completing 3/6. To anticipate my argument somewhat, this particular counting regime was like an unfamiliar tool or workspace for me. My mind didn't feel at home in it, and therefore didn't perform the fairly simple addition task easily.

After a couple of weeks of this cognitive awkwardness or balkiness, however, I grew habitualized to the mathematical turn, and began to move easily from 3/6 to 4/7, from 6/12 to 7/13, and so on. Adding 1 to 3/6 and getting 4/7 began to feel easy. The numbers that initially gave me difficulty were words that were spoken inside my head, obviously, but at first they seemed not to belong there; the more I voiced them in my head, the more familiar I felt with them, and the more internal they felt to my cognitive process of counting laps. If numerical sequences like 3/6>4/7 and 6/12>7/13 felt phenomenologically alien at first—"outside," like tools I didn't yet know how to use—repeated use phenomenologically "internalized" them.

My initial question, then, is this: what is the difference between *feeling comfortable* when performing some mental math task and *feeling awkward, uneasy, and therefore somewhat stymied* when performing that task? And, by extension, could there be a phenomenological relationship of some sort between habit (the feeling of cognitive "comfort" or "familiarity" or "ease") and intracraniality, on the one hand, and the feeling of "discomfort" or "alienness" or "awkwardness" that precedes habit-formation and extracraniality, on the other?

1.2.1.2 Conation

I want to work through this problematic throughout this chapter in a series of steps. The first step, as Hegel's dialectic of objects and desire suggests, requires the introduction of *conation*, one of the mind's three irreducible faculties, along with cognition and affect. Conation—impulse, desire, volition, motivation—has often been neglected in the study of mind; Bagozzi (1992) argues that this neglect goes a long way toward explaining the predictive inadequacy of the behavioral models developed by researchers of cognition and affect.

The main reason I keep experimenting with different computational regimes (counting systems) for my daily swim, in fact, is that how I count laps has a direct and powerful effect on my motivation to keep returning to the pool day after day—my willingness to expend the energy required to walk there, change into my suit, get into the pool, and push myself to swim 500 meters. Conation is all about *energizing* the organism to perform certain actions. If the way I count off each segment of my swim makes the total distance seem too long, the fairly short time I spend in the pool—10 minutes or so—feels like an eternity, and the exercise like sheer drudgery, and the walk over to the pool like something that can be postponed indefinitely. Ten minutes spent reading, writing, eating, or chatting with family or friends seems like no time at all; the closer I can bring myself to that enjoyable sort of phenomenological sense of my swim time, the more likely it is that I will be able to sustain my exercise regime. The conative payoff for coming up with just the right counting system, therefore, is significant.

And indeed the reason I switched from counting lengths alone to counting laps and lengths together was that the end of my 1–20 length count began to seem interminable. This conative phenomenology is easily missed when one focuses exclusively on cognition, or even when one focuses on cognition and affect. Cognitively, after all, 20 is just the number that follows 19; in the conative phenomenology of my 20-length lap swim, it means "done!" By the same token, 16 is, cognitively, just the number between 15 and 17, but conatively it is 4 away from "done!" If I count laps, by contrast, 10 is "done!" and 8 (an alternative to 16 in counting off 400 meters) is only 2 away from it. Hence the usefulness of the lap count.

Why not count only laps, then? Why not, for that matter, count 250s, so that 1 is "half-done!" and 2 is "done!"? Because the conative phenomenology of "only a few numbers left till I'm done" conflicts with the conative phenomenology of "it's taking forever till I get to say my next number." Conatively speaking, the numbers that I voice inside my head to mark the distances I've swum are not mere computational units; they are little motivational speakers. Each one swims, as it were, in conation, and in the affective regimes that support conation, and in interactive attitudes and emotions like encouragement, congratulation, and satisfaction. And my motivation begins to flag if I have to swim too long without a new numerical motivator—that is, a new number to cry out cheerily "You're moving right along!" I need interim numbers, preferably one for each length, to cheer me on; but I also need to minimize the numerical values left to count before I'm finished, to make it seem like I'm almost done.

Hence the usefulness of counting both laps and lengths: the lap numbers climb in shorter increments and the length numbers go by faster, together giving me the composite impression that I'm closing in on my goal more rapidly.

In other words, I need my numerical method of keeping track of distance to give me two distinct kinds of support: cognitive and conative—that is, support both for [cog] my ability to *count* the full 500 meters and for [con] my continued willingness to *push myself* the full 500 meters, day after day. The "danger," after all, is not really that I will inadvertently climb out of the pool too early one day (who really cares whether I swim 450 meters or 500 or 550 or 1,000?), but that I will grow frustrated or disgusted with the regime and quit it altogether. The exercise regime has to be conatively as well as cognitively sustainable.

1.2.1.3 Extended affect-becoming-conation

How is this cognitive/conative manipulation of counting systems in my daily 500-meter swim different from swimming the same distance competitively and seeing a number plate thrust into the water at the end of each lap? The fact that the number plate is held in human fingers, and that the fingers belong to a teammate, does make a difference. Strictly speaking, this difference is "imaginary"—that is to say, it is imagined, and thus intracranial (inside my head), projecting imagined encouragement onto the slight waving back and forth of the number under the water, or imagining the teammate thinking encouraging thoughts. But affectively and conatively, imagining a teammate's encouragement does make a difference; and it is a difference that *feels* like an extended body-becoming-mind system. Imagining that I'm competing in a 500-meter event, and that as I approach the end of the pool a friend is waiting with the number plate, I begin to anticipate seeing that number; knowing that I will see it, and that its appearance will signal my completion of another significant chunk of the race, spurs me on. The combined facts that I am relieved of the need to count laps myself (freedom from an extra cognitive task), that the lap count comes from outside my head (like a birthday present), and that the person giving me the lap count is a friend (warm feelings of imagined encouragement) all conduce to motivation.

Note here the feedback system between socially situated emotion and motivation: supportive affect (an emotion or attitude like encouragement[8]) coming from a teammate increases my motivation; good strong motivation increases my inclination to project imagined encouragement onto that hand thrusting the number plate down into the water, where I am physically and emotionally isolated. If the teammate in charge of signaling the laps I have swum puts the same number down twice, or puts it down too early (so I can't see it) or too late (so I nearly crash into it), I can easily grow frustrated, which can in turn decrease both my motivation to push myself physically and my inclination to imagine (and thus vicariously feel) that my teammates are supporting and encouraging me. Because I feel "positive" or supportive emotion coming from outside my head inside my head, it qualitatively blurs into "my own" internal motivation; it is primarily with the breakdown of affective communication that individualistic constructs come to seem realistic, and "your" motivating emotions seem inaccessibly alien to me, something utterly other than "my" motivating emotions. Only in a radically individualized world where affective communication (see §5.1) didn't link them would conation and emotion be radically different and separate faculties of the mind.

1.2.1.4 Habit as extended body-becoming-mind

Hegel (1830/2007, paragraph 410) defines habitualization in terms of repetition: "This self-incorporation [*Sicheinbilden*] of the particularity or bodiliness of the determinations of feeling into the *being* of the soul appears as a *repetition* of them, and the production of habit appears as *practice*." If the phrase "the particularity or bodiliness of the determinations of feeling" is taken to refer to *my feeling* alone, and thus to the particular determinations of that feeling in my body alone, then habitualization-as-repetition is in a strict sense intracranial. If, on the other hand, feeling is determined in part collectively—if it is distributed through a group, as I have been hinting here, and as I will argue more fully in §5.2—it may be necessary to rethink habitualization-as-repetition as extended body-becoming-mind.

The interesting question for the interaction of mind and its extracranial environment (tools, body, workspace, etc.) is whether habitualization too is necessarily interactive. My reflections on counting laps in the pool suggest that it is—that the internalization implied in *Sicheinbilden* (self-incorporation or imagination[9]) puts habitualization into an ongoing interaction with the environment that fractalizes repetition—interrupts it, and necessitates a repeated starting-over, an endless and unpredictable repetition of repetition. It is, after all, not merely my unfamiliarity with the math of $3/6 + 1 = 4/7$ that makes it initially difficult for me to habitualize it; it is also the size of the pool and the viscosity of the water, and the fact that I am using my own body alone to move through it (and not, say, a Jet Ski). It is also the need I feel to accommodate my affective-becoming-conative-becoming-cognitive counting strategies to the use of my body in a specific environment.

This construction seems utterly congruent with Hegel's discussion of the internalization of tool use as mind and the externalization of mind as tools, but in discussing habit in the *Encyclopaedia* Hegel (ibid.) seems to miss the specifically interactive nature of habitualization:

> *Thinking*, too, though wholly free, and active in the pure element of itself, likewise requires habit and familiarity, this form of *immediacy*, by which it is the unimpeded, pervaded possession of my *individual self*. Only through this habit do I *exist* for myself as thinking. Even this immediacy of thinking togetherness-with-oneself involves bodiliness (deficient habituation and long continuation of thinking cause headaches); habit diminishes this sensation, by making the natural determination into an immediacy of the soul.

It is, of course, possible to individualize specific aspects of thinking-as-habitualized as "this immediacy of thinking togetherness-with-oneself," but the pressure Hegel seems to feel to undertake that individualization here may be a premature anticipation of his movement toward Absolute Mind. Habitualized thinking may be one way we exist for ourselves as thinking, but an equally powerful channel of the feeling that one is in fact thinking—indeed perhaps even more powerful, because more intensely felt—is the experience of dehabitualized *rethinking* (and thus constant reactive rehabitualization) necessitated by changes in our qualitative relationship with the extracranial world. And it seems to me that the kind of intellectual thinking that we most insistently dramatize in our own writing and teaching, most highly respect in our colleagues and best students, and most exasperatedly miss in our worst students is not this quality of being "wholly free, and active in the pure element of itself," but rather the power to rethink and rehabitualize large disruptive quantities of input from the extracranial world in coherent ways—ways whose coherence is rendered novel by the disruptive multiplicity of the input.

The empirical fact is that virtually everything we learn has its origins outside our heads. We attempt to control learning, and thus our relationship with our environment, by imposing an internal image on those external objects and events—and indeed what Hegel means by mind as internalization of world is specifically imagination, the conversion of external object or event, which is beyond our control, into an internal image, which we hope we can control—but external objects and events tend not to be exhausted by our imaging process. We are constantly reinternalizing external objects and people and events, reimagining them, adjusting our homeostatic images of them in order to maximize predictability and control—and they keep changing, or revealing new and surprising facets of their being. One day a familiar old shoe stabs us in the foot, or a comfortably domesticated spouse of 30 years announces a desire to do a two-year stint in Africa with the Peace Corps. Habitualization creates an autopilot that relieves us of the necessity of making minute decisions every moment of our lives; but to the extent that it is fully successful, it deadens our homeostatic response to our environment; and to the extent that we are capable of responding (i.e., we are not comatose), it can never be fully successful. (This partial failure of habitualization is close to the partial failure of idealism that I theorize in the appendix as liar-paradox monism: the world as mind, and thus as ideal, is a function of habit, because an image of the world can be thought of as reality, as the real world, only if it is thoroughly habitualized; when habit fails us, a reality from behind or beyond the veil of the habitualized ideal reminds us that habit, and mind, and thus the ideal, is not all.)

And in any case, habit is the product of the habitualization, not of specific intracranial thoughts, but of interactive relationships. And the numbers we have been considering here, and the words we'll be considering in §1.2.2, are themselves not purely intracranial thoughts but also habitualizations or internalizations of interactive relationships.

1.2.2 Foreign languages

1.2.2.1 Foreign math
Why is it that I would rather do any math, mentally or out loud, even the simplest additions or subtractions, in English, rather than in one of the foreign languages I speak well—even Finnish, in which otherwise I feel completely at home? In fact, I had been living in Finland for several years before I felt comfortable even counting out loud in Finnish (as when making change). I knew the numbers well, but I didn't feel comfortable with them—didn't feel at home with them. Even now that I can count out loud or perform other numerical tasks out loud easily, almost automatically, in Finnish, I can still feel the slight edge of discomfort that I am overcoming in doing so. Switching to English numbers feels like putting on that old favorite pair of shoes (and hoping they don't stab me). Many fluent speakers of foreign languages I have asked about this have confirmed that the same is true for them: foreign numbers are more alien to them too, more difficult to assimilate into an inner realm of familiarity or at-homeness, than foreign words.

Is there something about numbers that makes them retain an air or aura of alterity, of alienness? After all, we speak of words as *natural* language, and of numbers as *symbolic* (and therefore, perhaps, implicitly "unnatural") language. Perhaps not. Counting the laps of my daily swim in English feels as familiar as speaking sentences in words. But why do numbers continue to retain that alien feeling in a foreign language, long after the words have come to feel familiar?

1.2.2.2 Foreign Words

But then foreign numbers *are* foreign words, and *all* foreign words are difficult to assimilate into the realm of familiarity. (The same is true of the language or languages we learn in infancy, but we are more aware of the process when learning languages that we think of as foreign.)

There are many obstacles to acquiring fluency in a foreign language, but surely the persistent phenomenology of alienness is one of the most daunting—daunting in the complex multiple sense of decreasing the student's motivation to keep learning the language (when it seems like utter gibberish) and of hindering its effectiveness as a communicational and cognitive tool (speaking it doesn't feel like communicating, and thinking in it doesn't feel like thinking). Memorizing vocabulary and grammatical structures—learning the language computationally, as it were—can in fact make communication *functionally possible*, but doesn't make it *feel plausible*. If the words don't feel familiar, comfortable, self-incorporated, like the speaker's own, it is hard to believe that they are *language*—that anyone will understand them. Another way of putting that distinction would be that a computational or "strictly cognitive" knowledge of a foreign language makes *instrumental* communication possible—you can ask how much that trinket costs, and understand the price—but not *affective* communication, which is what we normally mean by a "human connection."

What makes a word feel familiar? And why does that feeling of familiarity seem to be so important in learning to *use* a foreign language effectively? Why does an instrumentally memorized foreign word or grammatical structure (or number) feel alien, as if it didn't really "belong" in our intracranial cognitive system but was a cuckoo's egg from the extracranial world? For Hegel speech is the synthetic mediation between the living child and the dead tool, but he doesn't theorize the process of *coming*-to-speak, or coming-to-be-able-to-speak, in terms of the internalizations and externalizations that he theorizes in connection with tool use.

I learned some Spanish in childhood—not much, it later turned out, but I grew up *thinking* I had learned a lot because, growing up in Los Angeles, I heard Spanish all around me, and it felt familiar. Of the four European languages in which I am reasonably competent, Spanish is my worst, but in many ways it still feels the most comfortable. I learned German in high school, using the now-despised Audio-Lingual Method and thus memorizing a lot of dialogues but also speaking only German in class and on field trips, and I spent a month in German-speaking countries on an Interrail pass the summer before I turned 18. As a result, German too feels very familiar to me. I spent the year before my Interrail trip in Finland, as an exchange student, and became fluent in Finnish before I left; later I spent another 13 years there. Finnish is now like a second native language to me. I took a semester of Russian that first year in Finland, but then did nothing with it until my early forties, when I was getting to know my Russian second wife—and despite my growing love for her, despite two semesters of Russian classes, despite our several extended stays in Russia, amounting to two years, her language felt alien inside my head for a long time. She almost never wanted to speak it to me; that was one factor. All her friends spoke good English; that was another. My age (and deteriorating memory) must have been another significant factor. For years I knew a lot more Russian than Spanish, and I had lived in Russia far longer than I had lived in Spanish-speaking countries as a child (which was not at all), and still I felt more at home in Spanish. It wasn't until our daughter was born, in fact, and we began to raise her bilingually, so that I heard my wife speaking loving Russian to her every day, that I began to feel at home in the language—that I began to incorporate it into an inner *feeling* of familiarity.

Tomasello (2008: 310–315), in the course of devastating the Chomskyan quest for a universal grammar, pauses to ask why languages differ from one another as much as they do. He confesses that he doesn't really know, but speculates that linguistic difference might serve as "a kind of cultural isolating mechanism" (ibid.: 314), arising out of each language group's need to maintain a sense of in-group coherence by policing the boundaries. If it were easier to learn a foreign language, it would be much harder to distinguish between in-groupers and out-groupers. Even within the same language, groups tend to use jargon and allusions and in-jokes and other linguistic differentiations to help maintain group boundaries. My speculation suggests that what helps language groups (and other groups) maintain their boundaries is not merely linguistic (say, syntactic and semantic) difference, but affective difference: how it *feels* to use each language natively, which is to say, using Clark and Chalmers' (1998) terminology, automatically. If it were easier to learn the tonalities through which in-group feelings are definitively expressed—easier to learn to feel those feelings, and to express them automatically in and through the kinds of tonalities that signal to other in-groupers that the speaker is one of them—it would be far too easy to move in and out of groups, and the all-important sense of belonging that we as mammals need would be diminished.

Krashen and Terrell's (1983: 26–27) influential model for the radical difference between first-language "acquisition" and second-language "learning"[10] posits that [a] we acquire our first language(s) unconsciously and pragmatically, intent to communicate meaning, and learn later languages consciously and analytically, taught by our instructors to value structural correctness; [b] we monitor our structural constructs in the acquired language self-consciously (non-automatically) in ways that we did not in learning our first language(s); and [c] we are often hindered in learning later languages by "affective filters," such as poor motivation, low self-confidence, and anxiety, that don't plague most first-language acquirers. My observations thus far in §1.2.2 would suggest that affect is far more significant a shaping factor in all language learning (and generally cognitive processing) than Krashen recognizes: that first-language learning is not so much (a) "unconscious" as it is affect-driven, focused more on tonalizations as channels of attitudes and emotions than on what Krashen calls "pragmatic meanings," and that what applied linguists call "second-language acquisition" (in the classroom) tends to be cognition-driven, focused more on computational structure than on a felt connection with other people; but that to speak a language well we must feel our way to that affective connection, through iterative immersion in the shared affect of native-speaker groups.

Could it be that the kind of familiarity with foreign (or otherwise new) numbers *and* words that enhances our ability to think and communicate with and through them is achieved through affectivization—that the learning of familiarity and comfort in a foreign language is in essence cognitive-becoming-affective? By contrast, first-language learning would be affective-becoming-cognitive: the infant understands tonalizations first, and only gradually grows into the ability to parse and produce language cognitively.

But note two things:

[1] Not all foreign-language learning is cognitive first. There's an old chestnut that says that the best way to learn a foreign language is to sleep with someone who speaks it natively; the idea behind that notion is surely that love and lust in a relationship both tend to foreground the body and its affects, and thus puts the conative focus in language learning where it was for us as infants, on affective communication first, abstract computational structure later.

[2] Second-language instruction in the classroom that moves from cognition (computational structure) in the vague general direction of affect (typically without ever coming within shouting distance of it) doesn't

necessarily promote even cognitive competence in the language. Working with pure structure purely cognitively, without affect, makes that structure extremely difficult to cognize. Like my turn from 3/6 to 4/7 in the pool, abstract linguistic rules that map out the structure with perfect computational accuracy and coverage are cognitively too complex for the beginner.[11] Those rules tend to be constructed by linguists for linguists; they are the equivalent for the second-language learner of flowcharts, algorithms, and programming code for the computer user. What gives words (and numbers) in a foreign language a feeling of familiarity, and thus gives the learner the feeling of being able to use them meaningfully, is, well, *feeling*—repeated exposure not just to the structures but to conative and emotional support in affect-rich use contexts.

But then exposure alone would obviously not be enough: we need to *internalize* what we are thus exposed to. If learning is largely an outside-in operation—the internalization of words, numbers, images, ideas to which we are exposed outside our heads—there must be a process by which things that are alien to us because they are outside us gradually become part of our affective-becoming-conative "tissue." Just what that process is, and how it works, are two of the main concerns of this book. A research-based explanatory model is offered in §5.1.

1.3 Inside out

In §1.2 I loosely followed Hegel in suggesting that we consider cases of cognition in which it feels as if the words and numbers with which we think are internalized tools—specifically, in Hegel's terms, instrumental objects internalized not only as cognition but as *desire*—as interactive affect-becoming-conation. Now let's flip that equation over, antithetically, and consider cases of cognition in which it feels as if the extracranial body parts and tools we use and the environments in which we use them are externalized forms of desire. This antithetic moment obviously brings us into the most hotly contested realm of the extended-mind thesis.

By coming at this issue through a Hegelian dialectic focused on the *phenomenology* of tool use, I have evaded the major sticking point: the question, as Adams and Aizawa put it, of whether "cognitive processing *literally* extends from the brain" into the environment. From the perspective of liar-paradox monism (see the appendix) the only principled answer to that question is "It *feels* as if it does, and so I want to assert that it does, but of course I could be lying (to myself)." At the same time, I hope I have also reframed the question in potentially useful ways. At the very least, a phenomenalist approach will allow even the staunchest intracranialists to admit that it may well *feel* as if cognition extends beyond the brain without having to violate their principles by admitting that it literally does. It may also encourage extended cognitivists to explore the ways in which affective communication complicates the simple inside-outside opposition around which much of the EMT debate over has revolved.

1.3.1 Proprioceptively extended cognition

The core of the extended-mind thesis is the notion that our cognitive processes are often, or typically, or even invariably interactive across the intracranial/extracranial boundary—that they are, in the other terms typically used for this characteristic, situated, embodied, distributed, or, to use Noë's (2004; Noë and O'Regan 2002; O'Regan and Noë 2001) term for this interactivity in perception, enactive. As David Kirsh (2005: 151) puts it: "Metacognition works, in part, by controlling the interaction of person and world. It is not just a mental control mechanism regulating Cartesian mental performance. It is a component in the dynamic coupling of agent and environment."

Kirsh (ibid.: 153–157) lists five tenets of the thesis that mind is extended, situated, embodied, distributed, or enactive:

[1] We are much more adept at making intelligent decisions by responding interactively to environmental cues and constraints than we are at the kind of purely intracranial thinking ("reasoning") posited by traditional philosophy of mind.

[2] The environments we thus respond to interactively tend to be mainly cultural environments, created specifically for this interaction.

[3] "[H]umans (and other animals) are causally coupled so closely with their environments that cognition is effectively distributed over mind and environment" (ibid.: 154).

[4] "[T]his close causal coupling [with our environments] holds true at different temporal levels (Kirsh, 1999). People interact in a dynamic manner with their environments at frequencies that range from 50 or 100 ms in fast paced games to seconds and minutes such as when we cook, surf the web, or drive a car" (ibid.: 155).

[5] Extended or situated or distributed cognition is not only *coupled* but *coordinated*. "Because people are coupled to their environments at many temporal frequencies, sometimes aware sometimes unaware of the nature of their active perceptual engagement, they should be seen more as managers of their interaction, as coordinators locked in a

system of action reaction, than as purely rational agents evaluating possible actions on the basis of predicted consequences" (ibid.: 157).

Of these five tenets, (3) is obviously the original thesis set forth by Clark and Chalmers (1998); (1), (2), (4), and (5) are later refinements. I want to build my discussion in this section around (5)—very briefly, as this section is a place-holder for a lengthier treatment in §5.4—but with a shift in emphasis. My focus will be not just on *coordination*, but on the *feeling* of coordination—that is, on the "management of interaction" through the qualitative externalization of self out into the environment.

I'm thinking of Connerton's (1989: 95) comment that "we know where the letters are on the typewriter as we know where one of our limbs is." As David Bohm (1992) would put it, we expand our bodily proprioception to include the typewriter or computer keyboard. This is what Andy Clark calls "fluency"; it is the interactive quality he and David Chalmers were looking for in specifying that Otto's use of his notebook must be "automatic." In a longer example, Connerton (ibid.: 91–93) summarizes the detailed observations David Sudnow made of his five-year process of learning to play jazz piano, noting (and at the end quoting Sudnow) that "the difference between disjointedly trying to play jazz and catching on to what successful playing feels like" is "similar to the difference between 'the aphasic's or stutterer's or brain-damaged speaker's or new foreigner's attempts' to construct a smooth sentence, and 'the competent three-year-old's flowing utterance'" (ibid.: 92). Connerton comments:

What does it mean to achieve this flowing utterance? It means that the process of looking for notes, the explicit seeking and finding of recognizable and visually grasped places out there, has become redundant. It means that one has acquired, from a habitual position at the middle of the piano, an incorporated sense of places and distances and pressures. To be able to sit at a piano and get an initial orientation by the slightest touch "anywhere" on the keyboard; to bring your finger precisely to a spot "two feet" to your left, where half an inch off or a different pressure on arrival would have been a mistake; to move another "seventeen inches" and strike another note just as precisely; to move another "twenty-three inches" just as accurately; to execute all these moves rapidly and spontaneously as when, if ordered to touch your ear or your knee, you move your hand to the your ear or your knee by the shortest route and without having to think of them; to be as familiar with a terrain of hands and keyboard whose respective surfaces have become as intimately known as the respective surfaces of your tongue and teeth and palate: to do all this, which is to master a range of skills any competent jazz player has at his command, is to have a habitual knowledge—one might equally say a remembrance—in the hands; it is to have, as Sudnow puts it, "an embodied way of accomplishing distances" which can be accomplished only through "a long course of incorporation." (ibid.: 92–93)

We tend to marvel at this ability in blind pianists, perhaps because we assume that brilliant sighted pianists are *looking* for the right keys and aiming for them visually; following Sudnow, Connerton argues that this is not the case. Talented sighted pianists could play just as well with their eyes closed, because in a sense they don't *play* the piano as an alien object (which is how horrible piano players like me play it); they *feel* it, as if it were a part of their own bodies. They play proprioceptively. They have expanded their affective or proprioceptive "selves" to incorporate it.

The same can obviously be said of operators of vehicles and other equipment. It is much easier to slide the car you drive every day into a tight parallel parking spot than to do the same with a friend's car because you can *feel* your car's body as if it were your own.[12] Operators of forklifts, backhoes, and cranes say they feel their equipment as if it were part of their own bodies. So do fighter pilots. So do players of video games, in a virtual world.

The proprioceptive phenomenon of the phantom limb is interesting in this context. Here is a case where the actual body is diminished but the proprioceptive body remains the same size as before the amputation, and is capable of feeling itches and pains where no physical limb exists. The connection with the interface between the extended mind and the tool arises with the fact that, as Michael Kremer notes, "no amputee with an artificial lower limb can walk on it satisfactorily until the body-image, in other words the phantom, is incorporated into it" (quoted in Sacks 1970/1985: 67). Indeed, Sacks describes one amputee waking up in the morning and finding his phantom leg still asleep, still numb or "anesthetized," and thus finding that he can't walk on his prosthetic leg; he begins to slap his stump vigorously until the phantom limb is, as Sacks (ibid.) wonderfully puts it, "fulgurated." The phantom leg, "asleep," is "retracted" into the existing physical leg, and thus unavailable for externalization into the prosthetic leg; not until the phantom leg "wakes up" can it be externalized, so that the prosthetic leg becomes part of the amputee's proprioceptive body.

There is also the phenomenon of "body English," in which a bowler, a batter, or a javelin thrower feels that the ball, javelin, or other already propelled object remains part of his or her proprioceptive body, and so remains susceptible to proprioceptive "guidance," as if by remote control, through the bending of the body in the direction the object needs to go.

We want to say that this feeling is patently phantasmatic, because bending one's body obviously can't have any material effect on the trajectory of a propelled object; but then the phantom limb phenomenon is just as phantasmatic. So is the feeling a driver has that s/he *is* the car. The real difference between body English and these other extended proprioceptive phenomena is that in body English the object is no longer in actual physical interactive contact with the player, and so "interacts" with the player only visually; in driving, flying, playing the piano, playing video games, and walking on a prosthetic leg, the proprioceptive "phantom" or "phantasm" that extends out and engorges the environmental object interactively facilitates kinesthetic-becoming-affective-becoming-conative-becoming-cognitive processing.

And although body English has no physical effect on a propelled object, it does have other uses for the extended body-becoming-mind. While translating a chainsaw manual into Finnish a few years ago, I noticed that I was moving my body in odd ways at the computer—hunching my right shoulder, for example. I gradually realized that I was acting out the movements described in the manual—running my gloved hand down the log before sawing it to remove snow and debris; rocking the chainsaw up and down to saw through a log; cutting from below to keep the chain from binding, and so on. Since I was translating into Finnish, the body English my proprioceptive memory was generating was a reenactment of actual experiences using a chainsaw in Finland, typically in the winter, in the woods near a friend's cottage. What I found was that these proprioceptive reenactments actually facilitated word recall. I would read in the English original "The chainsaw may buck," think *What's "buck" in Finnish?*, and then mimic the kinesthetics of a chainsaw bucking with my upper body, and it would come to me: *Oh, "potkia," right.* The remembered/imagined Finnish situatedness of my proprioceptive incorporation of the chainsaw supercharged my memory.

What is happening in such cases, I suggest, is that cognition is facilitated not just by the enactive or situated or distributed coupling and coordination of mind and tool (or other environmental object, including a body part) but by the incorporation of the object into an extended proprioceptive body-becoming-mind. Hegel theorizes that extension as a two-step process, with the externalization of mind as tools (extended mind) as *thesis* and the internalization of tools as desire (conative mind) as *antithesis*, and I have followed that model (though I've reversed the order) in my discussion here; however, as I suggested earlier, the synthetic resolution of the thetic and antithetic moments in that dialectic, which Hegel calls "reason," is actually a proprioceptive *circulation*, what is internalized being externalized and what is externalized being internalized.

1.3.2 Mood-dependent cognition

If our cognitive processing is actually enhanced by our tendency (and in certain cases ability) to "personalize" the extracranial objects with which we work and the settings in which we work, by proprioceptively or dialogically projecting affective "self" or "personality" onto them, it would be reasonable to expect that our own affective states when we enter into such "couplings" or "coordinations" would significantly influence the kind of affectivity we project, and thus also, perhaps, influence the effectiveness of the resulting cognitive processing. And indeed the empirical research on state-dependent learning over the last three or four decades seems to confirm that such is the case.

As Eich (1989) reports, there was a directional shift in the empirical study of state-dependent learning in the 1970s and the early 1980s, from an earlier focus on the state-dependent effects of drugs to a new focus on those caused by changes in affect or mood. Bartlett and Santrock (1979) and Tulving (1976, 1979, 1983), for example, developed an "interactive" model of remembering that was based not just on how well a memory was encoded but on the affective circumstances of its encoding and retrieval. Reus, Weingartner, and Post (1979) found that depressed patients were not able to recall feeling good or "up," not out of denial, but as a result of (depressed) mood-dependent memory. Other bodily and affective states that according to these transitional studies significantly influenced memory included hyperactivity (Swanson and Kinsbourne 1976), dissociative identity disorder (Ludwig et al. 1972), myofascial pain (Eich et al. 1985), and epilepsy (Eich 1986).

Eich (1989: 350) also notes that transitional studies of *place*-dependent memory from that same period (e.g., Metzger et al. 1979; Saufley et al. 1985) produced inconsistent results, apparently because the "coupling" or "coordination" of cognition and place or setting must be mediated by mood or other affective orientations:

Fernandez and Glenberg (1985), for example, have conjectured that in order to establish an association between an event and the environment in which it occurs, contiguity alone between the event and the environment may not be sufficient. Rather, it may be necessary that a person perceives the environment as causing or enabling the event to happen, for only then will a change in the environment cause the event to be forgotten. This conjecture, which is reminiscent of Thorndike's (1932) concept of causal belongingness, has been extended by Bower (1985) to encompass moods. By Bower's account, evidence of mood dependent memory is unlikely to materialize unless subjects are convinced that their current emotions are caused by the events that they will later be asked to remember.

These early conjectures are borne out by Eich's own later research. Eich found, for example, that the environmental effects on cognition depend not on environmental *appearances* but on how the learner *feels* about them: "Thus, even when target events are encoded and retrieved in the same physical setting, memory performance suffers if the attending affective states differ" (1995: 293). Eich and Macaulay (2000: 244) explored the effects of experimentally induced "affectively realistic and subjectively convincing states of happiness and sadness" on subjects' ability to recall specific autobiographical events and compared them with the effects of feigned or simulated versions of those states on their recall of similar events, and found that "the mood-congruent effects elicited by simulated moods are qualitatively different from those evoked by induced moods, and that only authentic affects have the power to produce mood-dependent effects." (For reviews of the field since 1989, see Eich and Macaulay 2006; Eich 2007a; Eich 2007b.)

In a study of a different kind, Thompson et al. (2001) investigated "the effect of differing levels of emotional arousal on learning and memory for words in matching and mismatching contexts." They taught experienced skydivers a list of new words in two learning environments, one on the ground and the other while actually skydiving, and then tested for recall in either matching contexts (learned on the ground, recalled on the ground; learned in the air, recalled in the air) or mismatching contexts (learned on the ground, recalled in the air; learned in the air, recalled on the ground). Their assumption that the extreme emotional arousal of the skydiving environment would have a negative effect on the subjects' ability to recall the new words was borne out: though in every case recall was higher in the matching context than in the mismatching context, recall was significantly lower in *both* the matching and mismatching contexts involving actual skydiving. "We propose," they wrote, "that under extremely emotionally arousing circumstances, environmental and/or mood cues are unlikely to become encoded or linked to newly acquired information and thus cannot serve as cues to retrieval."

The study by Thompson and colleagues makes me wonder whether what felt like my relative "impairment" or "impediment" in learning a new numerical series ($3/6 + 1 = 4/7$) in the pool might not have had something to do with increased emotional arousal while swimming. Although swimming laps is far from the intense emotional experience of skydiving—in fact, most lap swimmers would call it boring—there is certainly a sensory intensity stirred up by turbulence in the water, the bubbles from exhalations and hands entering the water, and the general physical activity of stroking, kicking, twisting, and breathing that might adversely affect cognitive capacities; and swimming laps is unquestionably more intense emotionally than, say, sitting at this computer writing this chapter.

Forgas (2002: 5) reviews theories of the influence of affect on judgment, behavior, and cognitive processing:

- the *affect-as-information* model: asking oneself "how do I feel about this?" as a quickie shortcut to a judgment when motivation is too low to warrant more detailed analysis (see Schwarz and Clore 1983; Schwarz 1990; Forgas and Moylan 1987); and
- the *affect-priming* model: affect neither motivates nor behavioristically conditions judgment but "is an integral aspect of cognitive representations about the social world" and so should "automatically prime related ideas and memories, facilitating their use in tasks that require constructive thinking." (See Bower 1981; Clark and Isen 1982; Isen 1984, 1987; Baron 1987; Forgas and Bower 1987.)

The main burden of Forgas' 2002 article, however, is to refine the Affect Infusion Model (Forgas 1995), which he developed specifically in an attempt to integrate the most powerfully predictive aspects of both the affect-as-information model and the affect-priming model (see also Forgas 2007) in terms of four processing strategies in social situations. To summarize:

Direct-access strategies. These are basically habitualized response. As we will see Peirce (1931–1958: 5.475–76; 1998: 409) theorizing in §4.2, the emotional, energetic, and logical interpretants are automatized through frequent interpretive response to a familiar sign or group of signs, so that the interpretive process occurs under the radar of conscious awareness, and the only perceptible affect may be what Wittgenstein (1953, paragraph 151) calls the feeling of "that's easy" or "I know this." Or, to put it in Forgas' terms, in direct-access strategies affect doesn't *infuse* (conscious) cognition; at most it works automatically behind the scenes.

Motivated strategies. Because the cognitive response here is narrowly and preemptively focused or directed by a specific motive or purpose—"All I need to know is whether you are going to be there. Yes? Good. End of discussion, then"—it precludes the need for gathering and sorting new information that typically requires affect-infusion.

Heuristic strategies. These involve a search for and evaluative sifting through new information, and thus some affect-infusion, but the bare minimum: as Forgas (ibid.: 8) notes, heuristic strategies are "most likely when the task is simple, familiar, or of little personal relevance; when cognitive capacity is limited; and when there are no motivational or situational pressures for more detailed processing." Not all heuristic strategies, however, involve affect infusion—only when people orient themselves to the task by asking how they feel about it.

Substantive strategies. This is the fullest and most complex context for affect-infused cognition, requiring individuals to seek out, sift through, select, remember, and interpret new information, and to integrate every step of the process with past experience and knowledge. According to Forgas (ibid.), substantive strategies are likely when "the task is unusual, demanding, complex, or personally relevant; there are no direct access responses available; there are no clear motivational goals to guide processing; and there are adequate time and other processing resources available."

Forgas (ibid.) notes that "the AIM also specifies a range of contextual variables related to the task, the person, and the situation that influence processing choices and thus behaviors." Thus, some individuals may regularly shunt processing, regardless of task or situation, into direct-access (habitualized) or motivated (narrowly and preemptively focused) strategies, and as a result infuse it far less frequently with evaluative affect; others may regularly ramp up processing across all task types and situation types into substantive strategies, and so quite frequently engage the full scale of affect-infused cognition.

Forgas' (1995) AIM was, at the time, the most comprehensive model of affect-infused cognition available; his 2002 paper appeared as the "target article" in a special issue of *Psychological Inquiry* devoted to the AIM and presenting fifteen brief commentaries from leading researchers in the field, many of whom argue convincingly, seven years on, that it isn't nearly comprehensive enough. It fails to take into consideration the effects of interpersonal relationships on affect-infusion (Clark 2002; Perrot and Bodenhausen 2002); it fails to address the embodiment of affective signals (Clore and Tamir 2002); it fails to explore the facilitative impact positive affect tends to have on cognitive flexibility and innovation (Isen 2002); it completely neglects the apparently affectless processes of mood-incongruent evaluation (Martin et al. 2002); and it appears to be overly rigid in its systemic predictions, and so offers explanations that are at odds with research results in various areas (Macaulay and Eich 2002; Manstead and van der Pligt 2002).

1.4 Conclusion

In this chapter we have been rethinking the phenomenology surrounding the founding claim of the extended-mind thesis, from Clark and Chalmers (1998), that mind-tool interaction constitutes extended mind. And I do think that it is undeniable that we often feel proprioceptively "one" with the tools we use, as if the computer we are using or the car we're driving were an extension or an externalization of our own body-becoming-mind—making us what David Hess (1995: 373) calls "low-tech cyborgs."

The Hegelian notion that mind is shaped through internalizations (incorporative imaginings) of tools is likewise powerful and persuasive—especially when combined with the image of tools as externalized mind, so that mind and tools "cycle through" each other. But these cyclical or circulatory externalizations/internalizations are emphatically a phenomenology. There is no question of mind *literally* (if we read that to mean *materially*) arcing out across the space between the thinker's skull and the tool. From a firm intracranialist perspective, therefore, the argument in this chapter doesn't change much. If all these outside-in and inside-out border crossings are basically just phenomenal, just *imagined*, then they are all still intracranial. Even if the phenomenology is crucial to successful use of the tools in question, the extended mind is still, in the dismissive terms of the hard-core materialist, *just in our heads*. The intracranialist can quite calmly assent to the claim that we interact with our environments in ways that *feel* like extended cognition—ways that are attended by experiences of active cognitive contributions from body parts, tools, workspaces, and other environmental features—and then reiterate "But it's all still happening inside each individual human skull."

But then I think it is important to bear in mind that there are limitations on the kinds of claims we can reasonably and realistically make. The more we learn from neuroscientists about the interpretive distortions our nervous systems introduce into perception, and from subatomic physicists about observer effects and other forms of quantum uncertainty, the harder it is to maintain a naive pre-twentieth-century epistemological confidence about materialism: that once the human mind and its distortions have been removed from the perceptual loop, matter can be accurately described. The only epistemologically tenable realism these days has to be saturated in one way or another with idealism—with a recognition that mind cannot be excluded from the study of matter, and therefore that the old Enlightenment goal of understanding nature without human prejudice is no longer scientifically viable, and is of interest only to the intellectual historian.

And yet it still *seems* to us that we can know the reality in which we find ourselves. Triangulating our perceptions and attaining some measure of working certainty about matter still *feels* like a viable project. Naive realism lingers—even in the most unrelenting epistemological skeptics among us—as a powerful phenomenology. And one of the main driving forces behind that phenomenology is the belief that it is *not* just a phenomenology, that it is a materialist realism. Thus we have the paradox of a materialist and a representational realist like Jerry Fodor offering a hypothesis about mind that is almost pure idealism, grounded in ideological preferences for computational models derived from Chomsky and Turing and almost perfectly protected against empirical verification. (Since the Language of Thought is private, our only access to it is through the distorting lens of natural language—well, and through idealist hypotheses.) Thus, too, we have the paradox of a materialist externalist like Andy Clark (2008: xxvi) writing of mind-body-world cycles "quite literally extending the machinery of mind out into the world," and quite literally extending the idealist *metaphor* of a mechanical mind out into the world. Because mind is fundamentally an idealist construct that is far more at home with metaphors than with literal machines and circuits, it seems intuitively appropriate to Clark to describe the mind metaphorically and then attempt to literalize the metaphor materially, at the same time disavowing the phenomenalism (the *feeling* that he is right about mind, and that his rightness about mind is specifically a feeling) on which his claims so integrally rely.

From the perspective of the fractured or failed idealism that I call liar-paradox monism, arguing over whether a tool truly *is* or *is not* mind seems a bit like theologians arguing over the exact nature of the Holy Ghost: pointless, because impossible to prove one way or the other. By the same token, dismissing the proprioceptive sense that our tools are living and thinking entities that work *with* us as "just in the head" is like Plato dismissing actual human life as mere shadows on a cave wall—bad, disposable copies of a transcendental original. In each case, the default or normal or normative state, the founding state for all criterial claims about reality, is one that human beings cannot (reliably) know. Each camp relegates the state that human beings *can* know, namely life on earth (the transcendentalists) or qualia (the materialists), to a despised secondary status as unreliably *reflective* of the normative state.

Of course liar-paradox monism also recognizes that we do have *some* idea of what matter is like beyond the reach of our experiences, because the predictions our experiences lead us to make about it are often thwarted.

As a result, I can personalize my computer phenomenologically, feel as if it is not only alive but a friend, an ally, a co-conspirator, and then get exceedingly frustrated when it gets stuck in a loop and will not let me guide it out of it. Then it doesn't matter how much I scream "No! No! Stop that! What the hell are you doing to me?"—the computer just keeps doggedly doing what it's doing, *as if it had no idea what I was saying.*

This is the fractured or failed part of liar-paradox idealism: my computer, who is my friend, sometimes unaccountably acts like an inanimate object. As a result, I form a belief that it probably *is* an inanimate object, and keep provisionally contrasting that belief with my strong *feeling* that it is alive and friendly and there to help me do my work till I am willing to say, tentatively, that it probably only *seems* to be alive.

This, then, is my hesitant and self-doubting solution to the debate over extended mind: As long as we argue on the basis of the nature of extracranial objects, that debate will be unending. If we can agree that there are limitations on the kinds of claims *humans* can make about the world they live in, maybe we can think through the questions surrounding the extended (body-becoming-)mind and work toward a better understanding of how cognition functions.

2 Language as Cognitive Labels

Although I don't join Andy Clark in believing that mind "literally" (whatever that might mean) extends to tools and other epistemic artifacts, there are some important ways in which the *feeling* that it does—extended mind as quale—enhances our cognitive processes. Since the claim that mind does indeed extend to epistemic artifacts is the core of the EMT, it may seem as if what I have offered so far constitutes a refutation of the EMT. What I am offering instead, however, is an *expansion* of the EMT, with a twist. My brief—one that is beginning to get some traction with philosophers of mind (see Sterelny 2012)—is that the realm in which (body-becoming-) mind most demonstrably extends is sociality, our interactions not with inanimate objects and workspaces but with other people.[1] Specifically, I argue that the primary form taken by the extended body-becoming-mind is *interpersonal communication*: the communication of (affective-becoming-) cognitive labels (chapter 2), speech acts as (affective-becoming-)conative force (chapter 3), qualia as interpretants (chapter 4), and group dynamics as exemplified in the social phenomena of empathy, face, and ritual (chapter 5).

This theory of interpersonal communication as extended body-becoming-mind is offered in opposition to the prevailing rationalist philosophy of language (RPOL), which posits exclusively *propositional* communication between humans: sender S produces a propositional thought T, representing informational content I, which S then translates (using an internal phonological/morphological/syntactic/semantic/pragmatic encoder/decoder) into a coherent utterance U in natural language L; receiver R, also a fluent speaker of L, feeds U into his or her internal phonological/morphological/syntactic/semantic/pragmatic encoder/decoder, which retranslates the somewhat disorderly natural language of U back into the propositional clarity of T as a representation of I. Communication functions through just the two levels: the propositional and private *language of thought* (the LOT), and the public and conventional vehicle into which we translate our Ts as Us in order to convey them to Rs (or from which we translate an R's Us as Ts in order to understand them), namely *natural language*.

Given the radical assaults that have been launched on the RPOL in the last 200+ years—since the German Idealists and Romantics (see Esterhammer 2001 and Robinson 2006: 32–47 for discussion)—it is perhaps to be congratulated upon having survived more or less intact. Some would attribute that survival to *truth*: the RPOL, they might claim, accurately describes how we actually communicate. Since I believe, with Wittgenstein, Austin, Bakhtin, Derrida, and many others, that the RPOL is utterly, irredeemably, and even dangerously false, I attribute its survival to ideology: it is grounded in the Enlightenment ideology of reductionist empirical science, which is grounded in the Christian ideology of a rational Creator, which is grounded in the rationalist mysticism of Plato. Any philosophy with that kind of pedigree is going to seem intuitively right no matter how powerful the arguments are that are launched against it.

I would certainly agree that human communication does transfer information from head to head, and that information idealized as abstract data packets in sentence form can be called propositions. I would add, however, following Austin (1962/1975), that information is not all that is transferred. The broadest category of the transferred contents, I submit, would be qualia (see chapter 4), including not only cognitive qualia but also reticulated and situated perceptual and memory images and various kinds of affective, conative, and kinesthetic force.

To put it schematically, what is communicated through language may sometimes be informational content, but [a] those other qualitative forces always accompany it, [b] not all linguistic communication conveys informational content (phatic utterances are the most obvious example of non-informational linguistic communications), and [c] not all communication is linguistic. I will be discussing (a) and (b) in chapter 3 and (c) in chapter 5; chapter 4 is an excursus making a case for the communicability of qualia. Here in chapter 2 I will explore the RPOL on its own ground, showing that even without the broader contexts of (a), (b), and (c) it too points us in the end to the interpersonal complexity of the middle that it would exclude.

I mentioned in the introduction that Clark (2008: 91) doesn't protest, and even grants them their starting point "for the sake of argument," when Adams and Aizawa (2001, 2008) ground their critique of the EMT in Fodor's (1975) philosophy of language;[2] but Clark (ibid.: 54–56) does challenge

Fodor's language-of-thought hypothesis (LOTH) on two points, which he crystallizes in terms of "representational hybridity." First, as we saw in §1.2.1, he insists that natural languages and other symbolic systems have a massively transformative impact on cognitive processing, so that internal thought and external symbols get mixed up (hybridized); second, he argues that our understanding and use of linguistic and other symbols arises out of, and remains integrally intertwined with, our bodily actions in and interactions with the world. Because "the material structures of language both reflect, and then systematically transform, our thinking and reasoning about the world, . . . our cognitive relation to our own words and language (both as individuals and as a species) defies any simple logic of inner versus outer" (ibid.: 59).

This important critique, which relies on and modifies anti-LOTHarian thinking from Dennett (1991, 1996) to Churchland (1995) and Barsalou (1999), is not particularly ambitious. For Clark our cognitive relation to our own words and language may defy any *simple* logic of inner versus outer; however, his critique doesn't really challenge the bivalent logic of LOT vs. natural language; it merely complicates it. The two may get mixed up, but what is "inside" is still, for Clark, the LOT plus some internalized symbols, and what is "outside" is still "the material structures of language" (whatever that materiality might be when it's at home[3]) with a conventionalized simulacrum of embodied and perhaps extended thought.

In addition, for Clark language remains radically asocial. "Linguistic forms and structures," he writes, "are first encountered as simply objects (additional structure) in our world. But they then form a potent overlay that effectively, and iteratively, reconfigures the space for biological reason and self-control" (ibid.). But "linguistic forms and structures" are not encountered in the world, as objects or anything else, because they don't exist in the world until they are *constructed* by the syntactic imagination. To the extent that they appear to us as objects, they are regularities in the qualitative flow of language that we first feel or sense, second construct as stable structural abstractions, and only third reify as objects. They are never "simply objects" that we encounter—first, second, third, or ever. What we "first encounter" in or as language, in fact, is not tertiary constructs of this sort but *people doing things with words*; and it requires a high capacity for abstraction to move from such encounters with people doing things with words to "objectifying" something in or around or behind those people's words-as-doings as "linguistic forms and structures," indeed as the strangely immaterial "material structures of language." (One strange thing about the RPOL is that the farther the classificational units of linguistic "science" are abstracted from any actual empirical use of language, the more linguistic "scientists" tend to talk about "objective" and "material" structures.)

And once Clark's hypothetical language user has mastered this objectification, the resulting "linguistic forms and structures" in his account become an overlay not for helping us interact more complexly and more effectively with other people, but for "reconfigur[ing] the space for biological reason and self-control"—a space that is again radically asocial, one that may involve tools but doesn't involve other people. For someone as interested as he is in extended mind, Clark is rather surprisingly focused on the cognitive processes of one human being at a time.

My goal in this chapter is to work within the verbal-label conception of language to undermine the bivalent logic of "inner and outer" (intracranial cognition vs. transcranial communication) far more radically than Clark does. To that end, I want first to take another look at the Adams-Aizawa critique of the EMT (§2.1); then to take a run through Fodor's LOTH, on which the Adams-Aizawa critique implicitly rests (§2.2); then to set up a neo-Jamesian scalar or soritic series that traces the emergence of language out of affect-becoming-cognition (§2.3). In chapter 3 I will take another pass through the philosophy of language, but this time in terms not of labels but of bodily force.

2.1 The Adams-Aizawa critique of the EMT

A simplified syllogistic formulation of the Adams-Aizawa critique of the EMT might look as follows:

[1] Cognition originates in the central nervous system of the cognizing human actor.
[2] The objects to which advocates of extended cognition believe cognition extends include the cognizing actor's extracranial body (including the peripheral nervous system) and/or that actor's environment (including tools and other inanimate objects and systems).
[3] The part of information processing that we are willing to call cognition must entail nonderived representations. (If there is a part that doesn't, we are not willing to call it cognition.)
[4] The part of information processing that we are willing to call cognition must not entail derived representations. (If there is a part that does, we are not willing to call it cognition.)
[5] The extracranial objects in (4) are incapable of generating nonderived representations.

[6] Putatively cognitive events that occur in or through the extracranial objects in (4) cannot be classified as cognition.

Note that Adams and Aizawa present both their minor premises, (1) and (2), and their major premises, (3) and (4), as *empirical*: their claims in (1), (3), and (4) reflect their sense of how the cognitive science field has traditionally constructed cognition, and their claim in (2) is specifically a description of how the advocates of extended cognition construct cognition. As they themselves recognize, and indeed insist, these claims are empirical in a displaced sense: they are claims about the empirical characteristics not of cognition but rather of scholarly consensus on the nature of cognition. This is epistemologically a canny move. It ensures that their claims about cognition don't rely (explicitly) upon any *ontology* of cognition, but only on current philosophical *constructions* of cognition. Adams and Aizawa's assertion that "cognition involves non-derived representations, representations that mean what they do independently of other representational or intentional capacities" (ibid.: 30) is thus not intended to form "part of a definition of the cognitive"—they are not (overtly) stipulating a realist description of the cognitive as intracranial—but is simply an "empirical hypothesis" (ibid.: 55). "We do not maintain," they write, "that non-derived representations must be found in the head" (ibid.). But "in addition to our hypothesis that cognition involves non-derived representations, we want to advance the further empirical hypothesis that, as a matter of contingent empirical fact, non-derived representations happen to occur these days only in nervous systems. Insofar as this latter hypothesis is true, we have some non-question-begging, defeasible reason to think that, contrary to what the advocates of extended cognition propose, cognitive processing is by and large to be found within the brain." (ibid.) By "empirical hypothesis," in other words, they mean specifically that their hypotheses about the nature of cognition in the real world that we currently inhabit (excluding for the sake of argument other possible worlds) could serve as a basis for empirical testing, and thus that their claims are, as they say, defeasible: some future scientific study could conceivably disprove their hypothesis, showing that certain extracranial objects (say, neural nets) do indeed generate nonderived representations, or that human interaction with those objects constitutes a cognitive system in its own right.

However, a significant burden of Adams and Aizawa's argument is logical as well. In terms of my syllogistic reduction of their argument, for example, conclusion (5) produces conclusion (6) only in virtue of the claim that the belief reported in minor premise (2) is logically incompatible with major premises (3) and (4). More specifically, the central logical plank in their anti-extracranialist platform is their identification of what they call the "coupling-constitution fallacy," namely that "one cannot simply move from an observation of a causal dependency between cognition and the body and the environment to the conclusion that cognition extends into the body and the environment" (2008: 91).

Now, given minor premise (1), for the specific cases specified in minor premise (2) both conclusion (5) and conclusion (6) would appear to hold. But in Adams and Aizawa's own "contingent empirical" sense, aren't those cases mentioned in (2) unnecessarily restricted? What would the consequences for the EMT be, we might ask, if we were to conceptualize *other people* as a given cognizing actor's tools, and thus part of that actor's "extended cognitive system"? We might then simplistically consider the theoretical problems Adams and Aizawa raise for extended cognition solved: if the "epistemic artifacts" (Sterelny 2004) used by what we can call the *central actor* are other people—what we may call *peripheral actors*—then the "artifacts" too are capable of generating nonderived representations and thus of cognitive thought. Hence, this simplistic critique would run, extended cognition is possible.

For example, in the US-based Verizon Wireless commercials, "Test Man" wanders around the country asking "Can you hear me now?" over his mobile phone, and, when the person on the other end of the line—presumably at some Verizon home office or testing center—responds affirmatively, he says "Good" and keeps walking to the next test spot. If Test Man is the central actor and the unseen and unheard person presumably on the other end of the line is the peripheral actor, Test Man can be imagined as using the other person as a kind of tracking/recording device—but a *human* and therefore cognitive one. For obvious reasons, the interlocutor never says "No, you're breaking up," but if s/he did, we can imagine the two of them entering into the kind of interactive game the rest of us play whenever a mobile phone conversation begins to break up: adjusting our respective positions in space and asking "How about now? Is that better?" This game would involve two actors working together to generate a nonderived representation of the optimum relative locations for their cell phone conversation—arguably both an unambiguous fulfillment of Adams and Aizawa's conditions for a cognitive event in their major premises (1) and (2) and patently "extended" in the double sense they identify: extracranial as both fully embodied and fully interactive. An inanimate tracking/recording device would, as Adams and Aizawa's primary "mark of cognition" predicts, be incapable of playing this game; but two human beings can play it easily, and in the real world do so quite frequently. Even if we accept Adams and Aizawa's argument that cognition doesn't extend out from a central human actor to that actor's epistemic artifacts, then, it would seem fairly simple to make the case that it might extend out from a central human actor to one or more peripheral human actors. Though Adams and Aizawa (2008) don't explicitly address this possibility,[4] it is clear from their account that this suggestion *is* simplistic, and thus arguably frivolous, as, in their view, linguistic communication conveys, and so also operates on, only *derived* representations: "[W]e presuppose that thoughts have nonderived semantic content, but that natural language has merely derived content"[5] (ibid.: 34). Human interaction mediated linguistically or otherwise semiotically communicates not (cognitive) *thoughts* but (noncognitive) *conventionalized representations of thoughts*, and so cannot in itself constitute extended cognition. Although such interaction is probably cognitive, to put that in terms of the fallacy Adams and Aizawa identify, it is a form of *coupled* cognition without *constitution* as extended: each individual human actor, standing at the center of his or her cognitive realm, with a separate (precognitive) body and a separate (noncognitive) environment, interacts cognitively with other similar individual human actors, but because the actors' thoughts remain separate, so too does their cognition.[6]

What's more, Adams and Aizawa note, "normal" or "paradigm" human cognition not only consists of the intracranial production of nonderived representations, but is characterized by specific "mechanisms," such as short-term and long-term memory production and "the differences between the processes inside the first neurons dedicated to sensation and perception" (CNS-based channels of cognition) and "the processes that transpire prior to sensory transduction" (PNS-based and thus precognitive causes of or preparations for cognition) (ibid.: 69). Even though their survey of the relevant literature on these mechanisms yields the disturbing conclusion that there may be "nothing in common to these different types of processes and mechanisms, save perhaps that they all operate upon nonderived representations," and thus that perhaps "there is no such thing as cognitive processing *per se*, but only memory processing, attentional processing, visual processing, linguistic processing, and so forth" (ibid.: 74–75), they also note that the resulting "grab bag of processes" (ibid.: 75) differs substantially from the kind of "general" cognition posited by advocates of extended cognition. Thus, in order for the kind of "transcranial cognition" I imagined in the Verizon Wireless example to qualify as normal or paradigm cognition, for Adams and Aizawa not only would it have to share thoughts; it would also have to consist of the same "grab bag of processes" that characterizes intracranial cognition.

Thus, even though Adams and Aizawa don't envision my Test Man proposal, and therefore don't formalize this rebuttal to it, I might well offer up a syllogistic formalization of it for them:

[1] The Verizon Wireless Test Man and his interlocutor work together over the phone to determine reception strength at a series of locations.
[2] Some cognitivists might characterize their collaboration as an example of extended cognition.
[3] Cognition consists of thoughts (nonderived representations) and processes (remembering, paying attention, perceiving, verbalizing, and so on) whose origin and destination are intracranial.
[4] Transcranial human communication proceeds by means of language or other sign systems capable of bearing only derived content (no thoughts, only secondary representations of thoughts) and lacking shared processes for remembering, paying attention, perceiving, verbalizing, and so on.
[5] The telephone interactions between the Verizon Wireless Test Man and his interlocutor offer examples of coupled cognition (two separate cognitive agents interacting) without constituting extended cognition.

The weak link in that syllogism, I suggest, is major premise (4); in a sense, this entire book is a series of critiques of the thinking behind it. Transcranial human communication, Adams and Aizawa insist, is "merely derived" and therefore noncognitive; as they themselves recognize, this solution is "not entirely unproblematic" (ibid.: 34). The philosophical tradition from which they borrow the solution is not merely the naturalized semantics (causal model of mental content, reductive representationalism) that they specifically mention,[7] but, more broadly, the work coming out of Fodor's (1975) language-of-thought hypothesis.

2.2 Natural language and the language of thought

Fodor's (1975) language-of-thought hypothesis (LOTH) postulates an idealized "Mentalese" or language of thought that *constitutes* thought and forms the genetic foundation for natural language. For Fodor the LOT is a computational system of representations consisting entirely of a combinatorial syntax and semantics—no pragmatics (which is to say no situated interactivity), and, as Clark notes, no action-oriented embodiment. The LOT is completely cut off from interaction with the world (objects and people); it tokens specific representations syntactically and semantically in the sense of performing logical operations on idealized referents. (In the LOT, the word "cat" refers not to actual felines in the world, but to the Platonic image or form of a cat.) Thinking, while constrained by semantic relations with these ideal referents, largely consists of syntactic operations—a notion that Fodor borrows from the transformational-generative grammar of Noam Chomsky (1957, 1965), who, along with Alan Turing, is one of the godfathers of the LOTH. As Piccinini (2004) shows in some detail, the LOTH was one of the most influential instantiations of a Computational Theory of Mind (CTM) based on the notion—wildly popular among philosophers of mind, linguists, and others from the 1940s to the 1980s—that the human brain was a kind of computing mechanism, or else functioned enough like one to be usefully describable in computational terms.

In a sense, the "naturalized semantics" on which Adams and Aizawa expressly base their conception of intracraniality is a latecomer to the LOTH. First developed as a revision to the LOTH by Fred Dretske (1981, 1986), who directed Adams' dissertation, it was subsequently adopted and further developed by Fodor (1987, 1990, 1998). It is a semantics not of "natural language" but specifically of the LOT. *Natural* language is taken by this philosophical tradition to be inherently and indeed doubly *unnatural*: one step removed from the LOT (which as Fodor conceives it is produced directly by neurons) and so two steps removed from nature. Nature is material and objective, and is studied by materialists, objectivists, empiricists, scientists; "natural" language as it is used in "natural" contexts is conventional and artificial, and is studied by cultural theorists. (In the mid 1970s linguists were still self-styled scientists studying the abstract syntactic structures of a LOT-like *langue* or the abstract syntactic transformations of a vaguely psychologized LOT-like "competence," not natural language as it is used in natural contexts.) The notion that something humans do—communicate with one another—might be considered "nature" was and is anathema to this Enlightenment mentality, for which nature is by definition the nonhuman—that which has not yet been transformed by human culture.[8] Nature is neural pathways; the LOT that those pathways produce is one order of depravation away from nature; because "natural language" (Saussure's *parole*, Chomsky's performance) is a second order away, it is so depraved as not to be worth studying at all. What Dennis Stampe, Fred Dretske, Jerry Fodor, and Adams and Aizawa mean by "naturalized semantics" is the attempt to reduce the LOT back to the nature from which it arose—to understand LOT semantics in terms of relationalities (or what Fodor calls "asymmetric dependencies") found in nature, such as causality, resemblance, correlation, teleological function, and structural isomorphism. The "meaning" of smoke as naturally caused by fire is the methodological ideal.

The semantics of natural relationalities like that between fire and smoke is also the ideal form of nonderivation that for Fodor and his followers is found in only slightly less natural form in the LOT. The semantic relationship between an arrow and directionality is utterly conventional, thus derived; in order to learn to *follow* an arrow, to go in the direction the arrow points, we must learn to manipulate semiotic conventions. The semantic relationship between smoke and the fire that causes it, by contrast, is not conventional, and thus radically nonderived; it doesn't depend for its functionality on human sign systems; it *just is*. In fact virtually no one would contest the distinction between derived and nonderived representations at these extremes. Where LOT theorists enter into contested territory is in their insistence that the LOT is non-natural (because human) but closer to nature (because directly generated by the brain) than it is to natural language and other conventional sign systems—contra the Wittgensteinian tradition, which attributes most or all mental content to the internalization of natural language. Because for these thinkers the LOT occupies a precarious middle ground between nature and culture (more cultural than fire giving off smoke, more natural than arrows pointing the way), they are determined to minimize its cultural aspects and to assimilate it as far as is possible to nature, or to something very like nature. As we saw in §1.2.1, Clark (2008: 54–55) finds Fodor (1998: 72) admitting in passing that the LOT has bits and pieces of conventionalized natural language incorporated into it, and Adams and Aizawa are careful to reiterate that intracranial cognition is *mostly* nonderived. Still, for LOT theorists, the LOT, *for all practical purposes*, generates and operates on nonderived content, and wherever it doesn't do so it should ideally be repatriated to its true homeland in nature—that is to say, it should be semantically "(re)naturalized."

Now, the LOTH is, as its name suggests, a hypothesis. Like the EMT, and like the Adams-Aizawa anti-EMT, it is not so much an epistemologically plausible depiction of empirical reality as it is a model devised to bring some sort of provisional order to the complexity that is human thought. And just as the EMT as Clark and Chalmers (1998) present it works only if we posit the kind of total access to everyone's thoughts and attitudes that is possible only in hypotheticals—if we assume that we can watch Otto not only taking his notebook out of his shoulder bag but also endorsing its contents—so too does the LOTH require for proper functioning complete imaginary access to the LOT, which by Fodor's own definition is private and absolutely inaccessible to any outsider observer. Our only real-world access to the LOT, according to this ideal-world hypothesis, is through natural language, which inevitably distorts the LOT, rendering "access" to it illusory. In the ideal world of the hypothetical, however, *God* has access to things that are inaccessible to humans; and the perspective of the LOTH is precisely a God's-eye view, adopted provisionally by the thought experimenter.

As long as one doesn't mind Platonism, of course, there is nothing wrong with this kind of hypothesizing. The LOTH does conceive natural language as an imitation of the LOT, with the depravation of form and content that for Plato attends every new level of imitation; and Plato's reassuring transcendental and monotheistic theology, a strong precursor to and influence on the Hellenized Judaism that spawned Christianity, makes it seem both entirely natural and powerfully reassuring to situate the philosopher of mind squarely in the center of God's eye.

As a philosophy of language, however, as I hope to show explicitly in this chapter and implicitly in the next, it is woefully inadequate, and Adams and Aizawa's reliance on it in their critique of the EMT effectively vitiates that critique.

2.3 The fuzzy logic of thought and language

"To date," Adams and Aizawa write, "most discussions of the bounds of cognition have centered on a stark contrast. Either cognition is all in the brain or it extends into the body, or into the body and external environment. It is, however, possible to provide a rough arrangement of theories of the bounds of cognition along a spectrum of increasingly broad boundaries, from a core of neurons within the brain at one end of the spectrum to all sorts of extracorporeal tools with which we interact at the other end. Setting out such a spectrum provides a helpful first step in better appreciating the issues" (2008: 17). What the last sentence means for Adams and Aizawa is that laying out the spectrum from a "core of neurons" to "extracorporeal tools" spatially will help us identify the specific point(s) at which the binarizing line(s) between the cognitive and the noncognitive can or should be drawn. For example, at the early end, as the sensory nerves feed sense data upstream into the CNS, Adams and Aizawa note that for orthodox cognitive psychology "cognition begins somewhere after transduction." They continue: "Exactly where, we suppose, is up for grabs. Various considerations, however, suggest that cognitive processing could begin quite soon after transduction" (ibid.: 18). At the other end, "still farther

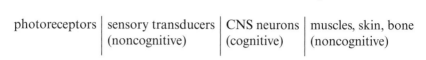

| photoreceptors | sensory transducers (noncognitive) | CNS neurons (cognitive) | muscles, skin, bone (noncognitive) |

Figure 2.1

out on the extended cognition spectrum, one might also think that muscles, skin, and bone are cognitive processors and that cognitive processing takes place in the muscles" (ibid.: 19). Advocates of extended cognition, Adams and Aizawa grant, may think this way. "But surely, says orthodoxy, cognizing must end at the neuromuscular junction. When considered in terms of the nature of the biological processes involved, it is outlandish to suppose that neuronal processes and muscular processes equally support cognitive processes" (ibid.). See figure 2.1.

I want to suggest that a similar spectrum may be found in the interactions of thought and language—and that, in imposing their customary binary opposition (the "stark contrast") between cognitive and noncognitive on this spectrum of thought and language, without even spatializing it first, Adams and Aizawa do less than justice to the complexity of the intertwined phenomena. Having spatialized the spectrum of thought and language, however, I propose to offer an analysis that proceeds not through binarization in terms of cognition and noncognition, but rather through fuzzy logic. As is well known, fuzzy logic offers an elegant solution to the *sorites* paradox by positing a continuous scale or spectrum of logical states between binary poles like "heap" and "nonheap," or, in this case, "derived" and "nonderived." From within a fuzzy-logic analytic, in fact, the *sorites* series seems paradoxical or "vague" only because a bivalent logic is fundamentally ill-suited to real-world complexities like those of thought and language. The counterintuitive notion that thought is cognitive and language is not seems to me an obvious casualty of the excessive simplicity of a bivalent logic in the study of human cognition. What I want to suggest in this section is that thought *emerges* out of precognitive or subcognitive processes, and *becomes language* and other transcranial and therefore arguably postcognitive processes, in a series of scalar transformations that Adams and Aizawa and the naturalized-semantics tradition want to reduce to a simple binary opposition, but that might be far more accurately and usefully described in terms of fuzzy hedges—"precognitive anticipations of thought," "semicognitive thought-like processes," "complex feeling-thought mixtures," "preconscious thought," "nonconceptual thought,"

Language as Cognitive Labels

"walks like a thought, quacks like a thought," "probably thought," "thought plus something else that doesn't necessarily disqualify it as thought," and so on.

The specific spectrum I want to offer is taken from present-day neo-Jamesian neurophysiology, as articulated specifically by Antonio Damasio (1994, 1999, 2003), David Dornsife Chair in Neuroscience, Professor of Psychology and Neurology, and director of the Brain and Creativity Institute at the University of Southern California. His model of the emergence of mind out of "body" is specifically representationalist, but on a series of evolutionary levels (2003: 30ff).[9] For Damasio, the drives, motivations, and appetites represent ("map") various metabolic and reflexive states; the emotions map the appetites and other body states; the feelings map emotions and other body states; and mind or "cognition" narrowly conceived—logical, analytical, computational, "rational" thought—maps feelings as well as proprioceptive, enteroceptive, and other bodily information. Damasio's (1994) somatic-marker hypothesis is specifically an explanatory by-product of the homeostatic emergence of thought out of the social feelings (the need to regulate one's social environment homeostatically by thinking about feelings) and the organizing power the feeling-based autonomic nervous system continues to wield over thought. In Damasio's terms, therefore, the emergence of mind out of body is specifically not "cognitive" in the narrow rationalist sense but, rather, affective-becoming-cognitive—that "becoming" signaling the claim that human cognition never quite separates from affect.[10]

The *sorites* series that follows has been criticized on the grounds that, while (as I show) the boundary between derived and nonderived representations is fuzzy, that doesn't vitiate the distinction. I agree, in principle: there is an important distinction to be made between the thinking that humans do as the production and manipulation of nonderived representations and the thinking that streetlamps don't do (because they are incapable of producing nonderived representations). This *sorites* series is not intended to undo that distinction. What it is intended to undo is, rather, the naturalized-semantics view, championed by Adams and Aizawa against Clark (and not protested by Clark), that *natural language consists entirely of derived representations* and therefore doesn't constitute thought, and that natural language therefore cannot be a channel or circuit of extended mind. Language is spread all over the gray middle area that is most powerfully fractalized by the series, and so, as Adams and Aizawa themselves seem to intuit, is revealed by the series as an extremely weak candidate for the *non distributio medii* that would make it pure conventionalized symbols or labels. As the series also shows language emerging out of nonverbal communication and issuing into meaningful social interaction—especially conative pressure on others to act in certain ways—it tends to expand that fractalized middle ground to encompass large swaths of human sociality, thought, and feeling, all of which, I will show, is part of the fuzzy middle between derived and nonderived representations. To the extent that the LOTH is an "empirical" hypothesis—based on the assumption that neuroscience will eventually prove that all thought is fundamentally nonderived computation, and that everything that is not nonderived computation is not thought—the series provides empirical evidence against it.

The soritic or scalar model begins as follows: I will continue it in §3.0, §3.4, and §5.4:

At first [a] I'm irritated, but I haven't noticed it yet. Presumably I have not yet represented ("mapped") my irritation in or by a thought. Intuitively, in other words, almost no one would be inclined to identity this affective state as "cognitive." It is at best precognitive, part of what Damasio (2004: 30) calls "the innate and automated equipment of life governance—the homeostasis machine." Since I haven't noticed it, it isn't even a quale yet, but because emotional states typically emerge gradually into consciousness we might want to call it a prequale, or a prequale-becoming-qualitative. Note also that the generation of "higher" (increasingly "cognitive") maps (b, c) of these lower levels remains partly automated as well: we don't always *decide* to think a thought; often it arises out of the preconscious functioning of the "homeostasis machine."

Aizawa and Adams take issue with Daniel Dennett's argument that "our intentionality is highly derived, and in just the same way that the intentionality of our robots (and even our books and maps) is derived" (Dennett 1990: 62, quoted by Adams and Aizawa (2008: 42)), just because, as they summarize Dennett's argument, "DNA encodes instructions from which symbols in the brain are built" (ibid.: 44). This is not, however, the kind of conventionalized derivativity that makes natural language problematic for LOT theory. Adams and Aizawa could easily insist that primary emotions—anger and fear, for example—are "hard-wired" into our brains, and thus genetically derived, without undermining their Fodorian position in the slightest. Genetic derivations don't come from other people—are not publicly traded, as it were—and so are not contaminated by the secondariness of conventionality. But then what about the research cited by Griffiths and Scarantino (2009: 438–440) showing the high degree to which the so-called primary emotions constitute a performative interactive display aimed at the (re)negotiation of social relationships? According to those findings, our specific rhetorical and performative needs in specific social situations tend to *shape* the emotions our bodies experience. Those findings are controversial, of course, but they should serve to indicate at least the possibility that social interaction influences prequalitative/preconscious affective body states, and thus that derivativity, though perhaps it doesn't go all the way down, goes down a lot further than the intracranialists would like to believe.

The account of my emotional state in (a) constitutes the prelinguistic foundation for an alternative model of the "language of thought." Rather than being "innate," like Fodor's LOT, thought in the affective-becoming-cognitive model emerges out of homeostatic processing, which is physiologically innate but which in individual organisms assumes its specific forms and functionalities in interaction with its environment, and is gradually mixed with (a > b) affective pressures and (b > c) verbal labels that circulate through us from other people.

Next [b] I start *feeling* my irritation—becoming affectively aware of it. Have I yet represented my body state with a thought? Probably not, though this is debatable. In William James' (1890: 2.448–2.4450) terms, a feeling is a secondary representation of an emotion (possesses aboutness), and therefore is functionally analogous to cognition narrowly conceived. But is it nonderived? If Adams and Aizawa were to challenge the research Griffiths and Scarantino cite and argue that primary emotions are purely nonderived, would they make the same claim for our ability to *feel* those primary emotions—specifically, for our ability to feel those emotions *as* anger or *as* fear, which is to say to differentiate among them affectively? And what about the more complex social feelings (jealousy, guilt, shame, embarrassment), which Griffiths and Scarantino (2009: 441–442, 449) problematically but indicatively call "higher cognitive emotions"?

The crucial derivativity-related question in (b) would be "Where does our affective 'knowledge' of emotional states come from?" It is, I take it, radically counterintuitive to claim that we are born with that ability to distinguish, even at a precognitive affective level, between different emotional states—that feeling-based differentiations among body states are innate. We *learn* to feel different emotions—and we learn to make those affective distinctions as we learn language, in our first two or three years of life. Our caretakers and older peers may not always verbally instruct us in such differentiations—"Are you feeling *angry*, sweetie?"—but it would seem beyond dispute that we learn to distinguish affectively (feelingly) among emotional states in interaction with others, and that those interactions often involve verbal or other semiotic labels. And if our rhetorical and performative social needs tend to shape our emotional states, they are even more likely to shape the qualitative interpretations ("representations") we place on those states.

Now [c] I cognize my feeling, and say to myself—in these words, but without voicing them aloud—"Hey, I'm feeling angry." This is of course a *bona fide* thought, a mental representation of a body state, but since it is specifically a *verbalized* mental representation, its derivativity status is unclear. Given that Fodor (1998: 72) admits that bits and pieces of natural language tend to get mixed up in the LOT, would Adams and Aizawa want to insist that (c) is actually one of those bits and pieces that have been successfully incorporated into the LOT, and so is technically no longer derived? Or would that incorporation still have to be identified as a form of derivation? Does the "true" LOT have to be kept pure or pristine by continuing to distinguish between "truly" private and nonderived thoughts and the internalized flotsam and jetsam of our social interactions? If so, then the boundary between nonderived thought and derived language would have to be drawn between (b) and (c). But of course, as we have seen, that seam is problematic too—at least it is if we accept the Jamesian notion that feelings are socially derived preverbal "labels" (representations) placed on emotional states.

But again I submit that the problem with the LOT model is its dualism: the boundary between the language of thought and natural language *has* to be drawn somewhere. In the soritic emerging-gradually-out-of-something-else model that I am calling body-becoming-mind or affective-becoming-cognitive, it is easier to live with fluid boundaries. If my social interactions shaped my emotions in (a) and the preverbal affective "labels" I placed on those emotions in (b), in (c) we clearly see verbalized thought emerging out of what Clark calls "hybrid representations"—organismic homeostatic processing mixed with conventionalized linguistic interactions with other humans.

Now, even though I can see that no one else is around, [d] I mutter out loud to myself the same words I expressed silently inside my head in (c): "Hey, I'm feeling angry." This is now "natural language," and therefore according to Adams and Aizawa "merely derived content"; but it is difficult to see a significant or pressing ontological difference between (c), which they might be willing to identify as the first nonderived representation or "thought" or "cognitive event," and (d).

Now you walk into the room, and, still amazed at my discovery, [e] I repeat my words to you: "Hey, I'm feeling angry." Adams and Aizawa could

Language as Cognitive Labels 83

arguably be imagined as wanting to make the seam between (d) and (e) the boundary where my nonderived representation becomes "merely derived content," because now it is addressed to another person—i.e., that "merely derived content" is not "merely derived" for me as the speaker, but is merely packaged for you as the listener. There is, after all, a significant difference between an utterance addressed to an "inner" listener who has total access to my thoughts and an "outer" listener who doesn't. Still, this is such a subtle shading of a difference that it is hard to imagine that Adams and Aizawa would want to draw the definitive boundary between cognition and noncognition precisely here.

The series can be continued, though somewhat controversially. If "Hey, I'm feeling angry" is a thought when (e) I express it aloud to you, why is it not a thought when [f_1] you hear it echoing inside your own head? Because, as Adams and Aizawa will want to insist, now it is *definitely* derived. "It"—the uttered words, and perhaps their meaning, carried on the aural signal—crosses the airspace between my mouth and your ears and undergoes a transformation. "It" begins in my head as *mine*, my own, part of my self-description; once "it" enters your head, "it" becomes from your perspective *his* (Doug Robinson's), a third-person account, part of that other person's self-description. In orthodox cognitivist terms, my words are a derived representation of my thought, even if they resound in your head; inside your head, they form an alien (doubly derived) object, like a rock, that is not assimilated into your cognition but is merely examined objectively. This would imply that it is not (c–e) "natural language" that bears "merely derived content," but (f) "natural language as received by a listener."

But is this an accurate depiction of what happens to another person's words in your head? Do they really not mix with your own inner words and preverbalized thoughts? Don't they, in fact, often become difficult to distinguish from your own? Phenomenologically speaking, it isn't enough to hang a sign saying "Doug Robinson said these words" on a heard utterance; we have to *keep* hanging that sign, over and over, or we easily forget, and blithely assimilate Doug Robinson's words into our own repertoire of things to say. How often do we not only tell someone else's story as our own, but actually believe that it happened to us? How often do we go back to some favorite thinker's work and discover there not only some idea that we have spent the last fifteen years presenting as our own, but nearly the exact wording that we have been using? An RPOL account of these beliefs in the originality (nonderivation) of these borrowed words and phrases and ideas will want to discount them as false memories, but the falsity of those memories is much easier to establish in rationalist theory than it is in psychological reality. Our undergraduate students are not the only ones who paraphrase incautiously, risking accusations of plagiarism; we professors are highly susceptible to that danger ourselves, and must maintain a high degree of cautionary arousal while paraphrasing to avoid assimilating another person's words into our own without proper attribution. I believe we all have an intuitive enough sense of just how commonly we "borrow" or entirely appropriate someone else's words and ideas and images as to provide, in Adams and Aizawa's terms, a "contingent empirical" justification for the extension of the cognitive spectrum from (d, e) my utterance to (f) your hearing of the utterance.[11]

Suppose further that, hearing my words, you suddenly realize that you too are angry. Hearing me say "Hey, I'm feeling angry," (f_1) you identify with my "I"—grammatically, after all, that pronoun is called a "shifter," and it is extremely difficult for toddlers to learn to negotiate the I-you binary that Adams and Aizawa implicitly place at the core of their radical intracranialism—and [g_1] realize that it is true. "I" *am* feeling angry. Only now the "I" is inside your head, and refers to your own body state as you feel it.

This appeal to fuzzy logic should suggest one problem with the blanket binary opposition between private thoughts that are nonderived and therefore cognitive and public utterances that are derived and therefore noncognitive: any attempt we make to bifurcate the soritic or scalar spectrum from (a) not being aware of irritation (pre-thought) to (g) becoming aware of our own irritation through the medium of someone else's declaration (post-thought) into discrete chunks labeled "cognition" and "noncognition" is going to be artificial and ultimately arbitrary. Somewhere along the spectrum we will intuitively want to insist that at least one binary transition has occurred, and perhaps two—pre-thought becoming thought, and perhaps then ceasing to be thought. But where?

So far we have hovered rather timidly in the vicinity of Clark's (2008: 54–56) critique of Fodor's LOTH as insufficiently attentive to the embodied interactivity of the LOT, and the representational hybridity (inner-outer/nonderived-derived mixing) that results. Now let's move decisively past that critique and consider some ways in which language functions not simply to label and organize our internalized and externalized worlds but to circulate *social force* from body to body through speech acts.

3 Language as Conative Force

In chapter 2, language consisted of verbal labels that help us organize our experience cognitively, especially understood in terms of the transcranial transferability of those labels and their transformative cognitive effect on each individual's understanding of the world. As I began to suggest in the introduction, however, this is an extremely narrow conception of language, and one that, as we've seen (§2.0), has been philosophically under assault at least since the German Romantics and Idealists, and most strenuously so since the 1955 William James lectures at Harvard that became Austin 1962/1975. In this chapter we will be exploring speech acts not as cognitive labels but as a channel of communicable (transferrable) bodily force—a conative force that energizes/mobilizes other bodies.

To begin, recall the soritic or scalar series launched in §2.3:

[a] I'm irritated, but don't feel it yet.
[b] I begin to feel my irritation.
[c] I say to myself subvocally, "Hey, I'm feeling angry."
[d] I mutter out loud, though no one hears me, "Hey, I'm feeling angry."
[e] You walk into the room, and I say to you "Hey, I'm feeling angry."
[f_1] You hear me say it.
[g_1] You realize that it's true, "I'm feeling angry"—but the "I" refers to you.

Imagine now that you and I are a couple, and instead of (f_1) internalizing my words and (g_1) realizing that you're feeling angry too, [f_2] you take my words as an accusation, a speech act, and [g_2] that feeling of being accused and attacked *makes* you angry. Austin argues that language doesn't just *represent* or "constate" reality (convey information with "constative" utterances) but performs actions, and so *changes* reality (with "performative" utterances such as "I now pronounce you man and wife" or "I sentence you to five years in jail," or ultimately, Austin realizes halfway through his lectures, all language). In response to (g_2), "constativists"—the RPOL proponents whose hegemony among philosophers of mind and language Austin was explicitly seeking to undermine, who believed that language consists entirely of labels and label-based statements conveying propositional information about the world—would almost certainly want to "correct" your misreading of my utterance: I wasn't *trying* to anger you; I was simply stating my own anger verbally. Rationally speaking, therefore, you shouldn't feel accused; you frankly have no right to your anger. This constativist correction may be true in some cases—but not *a priori*. Indeed, you may even be right. If I am self-aware enough, I may give some consideration to your accusation that my declaration was actually an accusation, and realize that for the past few days or weeks [h_1] I have indeed been feeling not just angry but angry *at you*, that you did something that angered me days ago, that I have been trying hard to feel all right about it but failing, and that unconsciously my declaration *was* intended to make you feel bad about what you did. My intention in (e), we might say, was affective-becoming-conative(-becoming-cognitive), but it doesn't actually become cognitive until ($f_2 > g_2$) your reaction prompts (h_1) my self-realization.

But it is even more complicated than that. Say [f_3] I secretly *wanted* to irritate you—my (e) saying to you "Hey, I'm feeling angry" was a deliberate (fully affective-becoming-conative-becoming-cognitive) provocation—but [g_3] you don't bite. You just smile consolingly and give me a loving pat on the cheek. According to Austin, my (f_3) attempt to irritate you is an *illocutionary* act (what I'm attempting to do *in* saying something) and my (g_2) success in actually irritating you is a *perlocutionary* act (what I actually do *by* saying something). But clearly I can't perform the perlocutionary act of irritating you unless you collaborate in that act with me and *respond* with irritation; in Austin's terms, (g_3) would be a failed perlocutionary act.

But how exactly is it possible for *my* act to fail through something *you* do (or don't do)?

To supplement that scalar series schematically, then:

[a] I'm irritated, but don't feel it yet.
[b] I begin to feel my irritation.
[c] I say to myself, subvocally, "Hey, I'm feeling angry."
[d] I mutter out loud, though no one hears me, "Hey, I'm feeling angry."
[e] You walk into the room, and I say to you "Hey, I'm feeling angry."

| [f_1] You hear me say it. | [f_2] You hear me accusing you of something. | [f_3] I *secretly wanted* to irritate you; my saying to you "Hey, I'm feeling angry" is a deliberate provocation. |

[g₁] You realize that it's true, "I am feeling angry"—but the "I" refers to you.

[g₂] The accusation you hear in my utterance makes you angry.

[g₃] But you don't let yourself be provoked.

[h₁] I think about it and realize that you're right: I *am* angry at you.

Now, the problem that the success or failure of *my* perlocutionary act depends on *your* reaction to it gave Austin considerable trouble; indeed, in a sense, it is the central issue—which he fails to resolve—in the second half of his book, beginning at the end of lecture VIII and continuing through the end of lecture XI. He summarizes the issue (somewhat problematically) at the beginning of lecture XII: "The total speech act in the total speech situation is the *only actual* phenomenon which, in the last resort, we are engaged in elucidating" (ibid.: 148). Note there, first of all, Austin's equation of "the total speech act in the total speech situation" with phenomenal *actuality*: understood phenomenologically, what human beings do, feel, and think while communicating *is* real, actual, and thus "natural." This is a very different kind of naturalization from the naturalized semantics of LOT theory. Whereas the LOT theorists were determined to reduce language to neural events and other dependencies found in material nature, Austin is interested in the qualitative phenomena of *conative force* (pressure to behave and believe in certain ways) experienced in and through specific socially situated (inter)actions.

But note also that "the total speech act in the total speech situation" consists of both illocutionary acts and perlocutionary acts, both supposedly performed by individuals (the former as what I am trying to do with words, the latter what I am actually doing *to you* with words), and the actional and situational totality Austin (ibid.: 110) describes is ultimately too complex to reduce to the actions of individuals: "For clearly *any*, or almost any, perlocutionary act is liable to be brought off, in sufficiently special circumstances, by the issuing, with or without calculation, of any utterance whatsoever."

Stanley Cavell (2003: xix) problematically argues against taking Austin at his word here. [a] This "uncharacteristic outburst," he says, "is not to be trusted," because, while [b] illocutions "can name what they do," [c] perlocutions cannot. If they could, [d] speech would be a form of magic:

I could say "I irritate you" and you would instantly feel irritated, or I could say "I make you laugh" and you would find yourself laughing irresistibly. The argument in (b > c > d) is valid, of course, but I submit that it doesn't validate (a). The problem is Austin's careless juxtaposition "with or without calculation." Cavell takes him to be saying (and wants us to mistrust his saying) that a perlocutionary act can be brought off *with* calculation, which is obviously wrong, impossible, and ignores what I take to be the true direction Austin is going with this idea, which is that any illocutionary act can be *taken* by a listener (*without* the speaker's calculation) to be performing any perlocutionary act—or rather, since the idea of a perlocutionary *act* is misleading, having any perlocutionary *effect*. Here, it seems to me, Austin is cutting himself loose from the analytical framework he has been building, which would link specific illocutions to specific perlocutions in some neat causal or otherwise tightly unidirectional relationship, and concluding that we really only try to perform *illocutionary* acts, and perlocutions are the unpredictable and uncontrollable effects of what we do. Any illocutionary act may thus have any kind of perlocutionary effect imaginable, depending on how listeners respond.

I argued on pages 95–99 of Robinson 2003 that the solution to Austin's quandary must be to expand our conception of the speech actor from a single individual to the whole group—that the "total speech act in the total speech situation" can include both a successful illocutionary act and a failed perlocutionary act only if the total speech act is performed by the collective, not by any one individual. That expanded conception drew heavily on Sawyer's (2001) notion of the group mind, but also on Bakhtin (1934–1935/1981) and others of his circle, among them V. N. Voloshinov: "In point of fact, *the word is a two-sided act*. It is determined equally by *whose* word it is and *for whom* it is meant. As word, it is precisely *the product of the reciprocal relationship between speaker and listener, addresser and addressee*. . . . I give myself verbal shape from another's point of view" (1930/1973: 86). I argued that there are many such group speech acts—intimidating, insulting, warning, persuading, and so on—but also implied that in some nontrivial sense *every* speech act is performed by the group mind. Even the classic illocutionary act of promising (see Searle 1969) depends for its success not just on the promiser's fulfillment of that promise but on the audience's "periperformative" (Sedgwick 2003: 70–72) witnessing of the promise, which acts as both collective guidance and enforcement.

My argumentative trajectory in the present chapter will take us through four conceptualizations of speech acts, presented as complications of Austin—even though the second, developed as it was behind the Iron Curtain during the violent, precarious, and intellectually isolated period of Stalin's purges in the late 1920s and early 1930s, could not have had foreknowledge of Austin.

In §3.1 I will explore Jacques Derrida's reframing of Austin on speech acts in terms of *the reperformability of the performative* (§3.1.1) and *the displacement of force* (§3.1.2). Derrida's coinage for the former, "iterability," is specifically a phenomenology of social interaction. In the latter, he traces the ways in which the communicative (inter)acts that reiterate or reperform the performative are channeled not propositionally but through bodily force.

In §3.2, I turn back to Mikhail Bakhtin in the specific context of a series of rethinkings of the notion that speech acts are performed by groups rather than individuals as part of the project of linguistic unification, or what Derrida calls the "policing" of speech acts, aimed at stabilization—but always partly having a destabilizing effect as well. Those rethinkings will be aimed not at overturning the theory of the group speech act, but rather at complicating the liberal assumptions about consensus among equals on which that theory implicitly rested, through examinations of social power differentials.

In §3.3 I broach the reading of Austin offered by the French sociologist Pierre Bourdieu, who suggests that the success of any speech act is conditioned socially, collectively, and specifically by the state power. I challenge this notion, showing how Bourdieu's own theory of *habitus* offers a more powerful model for the study of the social conditioning of speech acts than this insistence on state power, with examples drawn from (§3.3.1) laughter as the perlocutionary effect of stand-up comedy (and other organized entertainment) and (§3.3.2) persuasion-becoming-belief (*pistis*) as theorized by Aristotle in the *Rhetoric*.

In §3.4, I move into the revisionary model of speech acts offered by John Searle (1975) that is generally called "indirect speech acts"—especially as they are channeled nonverbally, through body language and other affective communication.

3.1 Derrida on iterability and the displacement of force

Derrida didn't devote a great deal of attention to the Anglo-American philosophical tradition, but one of his most famous articles, "Signature event context," is a deconstruction of Austin 1962/1975 that is best known for its take on Austin's inclination to call a certain kind of literary or dramatic speech act "*parasitic* upon its normal use" (Austin 1962/1975: 22), leading to Derrida's development of the (arche)concept of iterability (for which see §3.1.1 below).

Derrida begins his reading of Austin with a four-step appreciation of speech-act theory that underscores the thematics with which he opens the piece but to which we will turn second (§3.1.2), namely the thematics of language as the transfer of force through bodies. The four appreciative steps are: [a] speech acts are acts of communication that [b] "do not designate the transference or passage of a thought-content, but, in some way, the communication of an original movement (to be defined within a *general theory of action*), an operation and the production of an effect" (1962/1975: 13)—that is, speech acts seem to step us back from the representational disembodiment of written signs to something closer to the kinesthetic transfer or displacement of force. [c] The performative (the quintessential speech act in the first seven lectures of Austin's book) "does not describe something that exists outside of language and prior to it. It produces or transforms a situation, it effects" (ibid.). Hence, [d] "Austin was obliged to free the analysis of the performative from the authority of the truth *value*, from the true/false opposition, at least in its classical form, and to substitute for it at times the value of force, of difference of force (*illocutionary* or *perlocutionary force*)" (ibid.).

"In this line of thought," Derrida adds parenthetically, "which is nothing less than Nietzschean, this in particular [namely (d)] strikes me as moving in the direction of Nietzsche himself, who often acknowledged a certain affinity for a vein of English thought" (ibid.). Derrida also praises Austin for his "analysis which is patient, open, aporetical, in constant transformation, often more fruitful in the acknowledgment of impasses than in its positions" (ibid.: 14)—high praise from the master of aporetic discourse.

Derrida (1972/1988) became something of a *cause célèbre* when John Searle (1977) rather patronizingly "corrected" his "misreading" of Austin, and Derrida (1977/1988) responded with a crushing 100-page devastation of Searle's intervention. This so-called Searle-Derrida debate has seemed to many a signal encounter between the Anglo-American and the Continental philosophical traditions, and others have felt inspired to weigh in on it as well, including some more judicious views to the effect that Derrida missed one or another important point in Austin, or that Derrida didn't know either Austin's other writings or the Anglo-American philosophical tradition that Austin was working in and to a large extent against ("dismantling" is Austin's own word for what he was trying to do to that tradition) and so didn't really do justice to Austin.

Stanley Cavell (1995), for example, who attended Austin's 1955 William James Lectures as a grad student, somewhat more cautiously and circumspectly argues that, in "excluding" the performance of performatives as "parasitic" upon "serious" uses, Austin really is just temporarily setting them aside in this particular context, the lectures of *How To Do Things With Words*, having dealt with that complexity elsewhere (in Austin 1961). And it is certainly true that Austin dealt extensively with those complexities in that earlier article, and that the passage in *How To Do Things With Words* in which he excludes performances of performatives as "parasitic" can usefully be read as a temporary and above all strategic exclusion. Austin there says specifically that "language in such circumstances is in special ways—intelligibly—used not *seriously*, but in many ways *parasitic* upon its normal use—ways which fall under the doctrine of the *etiolations* of language" (1962/1975: 22). "In such circumstances," "in special ways," "intelligibly," "in many ways": this does all sound as if Austin is not throwing performances of performances "in a ditch," as Derrida says, but merely setting them aside for more complex discussion later.

However, note how Austin's (ibid.: 104) language changes when he returns to this issue in the second half of the book:

To take this farther, let us be quite clear that the expression "use of language" can cover other matters even more diverse than the illocutionary and perlocutionary acts and obviously quite diverse from any with which we are here concerned. For example, we may speak of the "use of language" *for* something, e.g. for joking; and we may use "in" in a way different from the illocutionary "in," as when we say "in saying 'p' I was joking" or "acting a part" or "writing poetry"; or again we may speak of "a poetical use of language" as distinct from "the use of language in poetry." These references to "use of language" have nothing to do with the illocutionary act. For example, if I say "Go and catch a falling star," it may be quite clear what both the meaning and the force of my utterance is, but still wholly unresolved which of these other kinds of things I may be doing. There are aetiolations, parasitic uses, etc., various "not serious" and "not full normal" uses. The normal conditions of reference may be suspended, or no attempt made to make you do anything, as Walt Whitman does not seriously incite the eagle of liberty to soar.

It seems relatively uncontroversial to observe there that Austin is no longer merely *postponing* discussion of these matters, or merely *strategically* or *temporarily* excluding performances of performatives. He is constructing a stable axiomatics of "normal" vs. "not full normal" uses of the performative or speech act. Joking, acting a part, and writing poetry *"have nothing to do with the illocutionary act"*—presumably because in them "no attempt [is being] made to make you do anything." That Austin is just flat wrong about this should be evident. Of course one can perform illocutionary acts in or by joking, acting a part, or writing poetry! Walt Whitman may not be seriously inciting the eagle of liberty to soar, but he is doing *something*—for example, inciting the citizens of a democratic country to behave democratically, to expand the behavioral role of democratic ideals and values in their own lives. The illocutionary acts performed in or by joking or acting a part or writing poetry may be implicit or indirect, but they are illocutionary acts nonetheless. I can hint politely at some error a friend has made by joking about it, or joking around it, or joking past it, or even joking irrelevantly, or by imitating some moment in a movie or popular TV show, replaying the part of some character, so that my friend will recognize the allusion and understand it to be an *invocative implicature* or *invocature* (for which see chapter 13 of Robinson 2003).

Above all, it seems to me that Austin here is *unaware* that he is wrong—that his thinking is still in process about these matters, that this is something he hasn't quite worked out yet—and thus that Derrida is right and Cavell is wrong.

Readers who cringe at the thought of being immersed in Jacques Derrida's argumentation or prose style longer than is necessary should note that the core of my cooptation of Derrida-on-Austin for a radical expansion of the EMT is to be found in §3.1.2, and that they can skip ahead to that section without losing too much of the argument.

3.1.1 Iterability

One way of reading Derrida's "Signature event context" (1972/1988) would be to see in it a continuation and an expansion of what Derrida takes to be Austin's knock-down argument against the RPOL. This reading strategy might proceed by advancing and developing Austin's notion that, rather than transmitting stable packets of "thought-content," the speech actor transmits *force* (on which more in §3.1.2). Still, Derrida writes, Austin keeps butting up against the same problem, or against three problems, (a-c), that according to Derrida have common origins, specifically in the exclusion of writing, the exclusion of the *"graphematic in general"* (ibid.: 14)—that is to say, in the exclusion of the structure of iterability that he posits as the condition of all verbal communication.

[a] Although Austin's performative utterance has no referential content for the utterer to intend, that utterer nevertheless has to be physically *present* at the performing of the performative: a successful performative requires "consciousness, the conscious presence of the intention of the speaking subject in the totality of his speech act" (ibid.). This is, of course, the classic

definition of face-to-face encounters, taking its guarantee of meaning from the physical presence of the conscious intending speaker—and it is precisely that which Derrida is going to want to undermine in the name of writing.

[b] While Austin salutarily grounds his definition of the performative in the risk of its failure—he insists on "recognizing that the possibility of the negative (in this case, of infelicities) is in fact a structural possibility, that failure is an essential risk of the operations under consideration"—he simultaneously attempts to regulate that risk by excluding it as "accidental, exterior, one which teaches us nothing about the linguistic phenomenon being considered" (ibid.: 15). Austin "does not ponder the consequences issuing from the fact that a possibility—a possible risk—is *always* possible, and is in some sense a necessary possibility" (ibid.).[1]

[c] The weightiest problem for Derrida is Austin's exclusion of certain quoted or performed performatives as "parasitic" on "serious" ones. If an actor dressed up as a minister on stage says "I now pronounce you man and wife" to two other actors dressed up as a bride and a groom, the performative utterance does *not* perform the action of marrying the couple. It's only a line in a play: not "serious."

Now, obviously (c) is a significant impasse for Austin, one that he really should have been able to traverse: a performative is *"in a peculiar way* hollow or void if said by an actor on the stage, or if introduced in a poem, or spoken in soliloquy" (Austin 1962/1875: 22), which is to say that an utterance-as-*performance* becomes *"parasitic* upon its normal use" (ibid.) when it is *performed*. Does this mean that performatives can be performed only once—that they are somehow hollowed out or voided (rendered "empty schemata") by repeat performances? Or does it mean that performatives can be performed only on a certain *level* of experience, in what Goffman (1974) calls a certain *frame* of experience, and are hollowed out when raised to a higher level or rekeyed for a higher frame? And how can that one single experiential frame be preemptively bounded, so that performances aren't accidentally rendered hollow or void or parasitic by stepping inadvertently across some ill-drawn line?

Many solutions to Austin's dilemma have been developed in the half-century since he posed it—among them Searle's (1975) indirect speech acts, Grice's (1975/1989) conversational implicature, and Goffman's (1974) frame analysis—but in fact the obvious and indeed commonsensical solution is the one offered by Derrida himself. In response to Searle's (1977: 204) remark that "we do not, for example, hold the actor responsible today for the promise he made on stage last night the way we normally hold people responsible for their promises," Derrida replies that "it would not be the actor who should be held responsible but rather the speaker committed by the promise *in the scene*, that is, the character" (1977/1988: 89). Thus, the minister *in the play* says "I now pronounce you man and wife" and the bride and groom *in the play* are thereby married. The performative performed on stage is in no way hollow or void; it just operates in its own fictional frame.

In his original deconstruction of Austin, though, Derrida (1972/1988) takes a different tack. He argues that Austin's "structural parasitism," the performability of any performative, is part of the "general iterability" of all language and thus a performative's "internal and positive condition of possibility": "For, ultimately, isn't it true that what Austin excludes as anomaly, exception, 'non-serious,' *citation* (on stage, in a poem, or a soliloquy) is the determined modification of a general citationality—or rather, a general iterability—without which there would not even be a 'successful' performative?" (ibid.: 17). Reperformances of performatives *in a new frame*, in other words, are ultimately just a special case of reperformances in general, which are of the very essence of performance, of performability, and so also of the performative.

Here is where Derrida uploads his graphematic concept based on writing to an absent addressee into the speech-act situation from which writing was originally (normatively) excluded: the fact that the written text can be infinitely reread, and that those rereadings radically rupture the face-to-face context that is traditionally taken as normative for communication, here becomes the infinite (and necessary) (re)performability of the speech act, of the performative, and thus also of the "speech act" in a broader sense, the act of doing things with words. Iterability becomes the "again-ness" of all language: the fact, to put it as simply as is possible, that everything in language, including written, spoken, and gestural signs, comes to us with a history—and indeed must come to us with a history in order to be understandable and thus *communicable*. The completely new word or phrase or gesture, the sign with no ties whatsoever to anything we've ever heard or seen or known (to the extent that we can even imagine such a thing), would be incomprehensible, because it would not have accreted "readability" or performability through a thousand or a hundred thousand repetitions.

But iterability is also more, as Derrida theorizes it, than mere repetition, mere accretive history as repetition. It is also a *transformative* history. "Let us not forget," Derrida (1988: 119) writes, "that 'iterability' does not signify simply, as Searle seems to think, repeatability of the same, but rather alterability of this same idealized in the singularity of the event, for instance, in this or that speech act." What is iteratively accreted is not a vast collection of identical units or perfect copies of the same thing; rather, every (re)iteration of "the same" introduces some slight difference or deviation. The reason there is no "pure" performative is that in order for an utterance to "perform" it must have been repeat-performed over and over, each time slightly differently.

The "minister in real life" who utters the ritual performative phrase "I now pronounce you husband and wife" to a "bride and groom in real life," and thereby marries them, has said that phrase hundreds of times, each time with a slightly different intonation, with a slightly different degree of intensity or attentiveness or focus, and above all to a different couple. We are not machines. Relationships, situations, body language, and a hundred different prompts and signals all condition how we say things to each other. And the bridal couple and the assembled congregation have heard the phrase uttered in other weddings, perhaps by this same minister, perhaps by others, perhaps in different versions ("I now pronounce you husband and wife," "I now pronounce you man and wife," "I now pronounce you husband and husband," and so on), almost certainly to different couples. Sometimes something went wrong, or felt wrong, or felt vaguely *off*. Sometimes the officiant was feeling ill, or had a hangover; sometimes a baby cried through the whole ceremony; sometimes the entire room was filled with the smell of burning dust. We have "attended" weddings vicariously at the movies, on television, in plays, and in friends' stories, and not only have we been able to respond complexly to the dramas being enacted in and through the fictional weddings on the basis of our experience of other weddings; we have learned by "attending" those playacted or recounted weddings to respond more complexly to weddings and marriages in our various real-life frames as well. Each time, despite those differences, the utterance of that ritual performative was perceived by the people present as transforming the couple into a *married* couple, whether the two people were married in a fictional or a nonfictional frame. Everyone present comes to each new wedding ceremony with an iterative history not only of previous performances of the "I now pronounce you husband and wife" performative but also of the social consequences of those performances—the marital histories of the couples so transformed. Having seen other couples transformed into married couples by past performances of the ritual performative, they are primed to see this new couple so transformed as well; but each time is slightly different, and takes its ritual power from its difference-in-sameness, sameness-in-difference, slicing each midway and inserting the other into the cut.

Let us consider the three explanatory models involved here:

[1] In the communicative world posited by the RPOL (and attacked by Austin and Derrida), propositional thoughts are encoded in the sender's head without slippage and decoded in the receiver's head without slippage.
  [1_{BS}] The constative speech-act tradition launched by Benveniste (1966/1973) and Searle (1969) attempts to rescue speech-act theory from (2) for (1) by restoring the speech act to abstract ideality.
[2] In the communicative world explored by Austin, there is slippage between performatives and their uptake, or between illocutionary force and perlocutionary effect; but the slippage is accidental, or, in Austin's words, "an infernal shame" (ibid.: 23). Things don't go according to plan, and that leads to what Austin calls "infelicities," including misfires (misinvocations, misexecutions, misapplications, flaws, and hitches) and abuses (especially insincerities), but also this strange category called "parasitic" speech acts.
[3] In the communicative world theorized by Derrida, the slippage is not accidental but a condition of possibility for communication.

In a sense, both (1_{BS}) and (3) are attempts to rescue us from the randomness of (2)—(1_{BS}) by idealizing the speech act as a *stable* mental structure (i.e., not interactive in the social world), (3) by idealizing iterability as an *unstable* mental structure (unstable because it *is* interactive in the social world). Actually for Derrida iterability is a (re)stabilizing-*cum*-destabilizing mental interactivity: every communicative act partially destabilizes communication, and we react to that destabilization by attempting to restabilize it through a new (re)iteration, but that restabilization itself inevitably has a partially destabilizing effect as well. The (re)iterative or (re)performative act is designed to (re)stabilize communication, but the gap between bodies that the (re)stabilizing speech act has to cross deflects and destabilizes it too.

There are, however, two problems with my account here. One comes from Derrida: his theory of iterability, he would want to insist, is not exactly an idealization, because "the iterability of the mark does not leave any of the philosophical oppositions which govern the idealizing abstraction intact (for instance, serious/non-serious, literal/metaphorical or sarcastic, ordinary/parasitical, strict/non-strict, etc.). Iterability blurs *a priori* the dividing-line that passes between these opposed terms, 'corrupting' it if you like, contaminating it parasitically, qua limit" (1977/1988: 70). Derrida's argument in (3) that there is a *pattern* or an *order* to what Austin sees as randomness strongly resembles idealization, but the product of that operation is not ideality but a fractured or partly failed quest for order. And indeed that quest is itself *constitutive* of the affective-becoming-conative impulse that generates the cognitive process called idealization: "[T]he unique character of this structure of iterability, or rather of this chain, since iterability can be supplemented by a variety of terms (such as *difference*, grapheme, trace, etc.), lies in the fact that, comprising identity *and* difference, repetition *and* alteration, etc., it renders the *project* of idealization possible without lending '*itself*' to any pure, simple, and idealizable conceptualization" (ibid.: 71). (For an articulation of something like this position as liar-paradox monism, see the appendix.)

The other problem is that Derrida doesn't stop to interrogate the linkage he sets up between the repeated partial failure of the ideal unification of the performative and what he calls the "conditions of possibility" of communication. His assumption that the performative *must* partially fail in order for communication to be possible seems to grow out of his understanding of writing, or "graphematics in general," according to which a written message communicates not despite but *in virtue of* the spatiotemporal slippage between the writing and the reading. I would argue that (3) in the tabulation above has at least three possible instantiations:

[3a] (Re)stabilization is a recurring and never entirely successful response to the inevitability of destabilization. Destabilization may be endemic to the fact of biological individuation—the fact that we occupy different bodies, and can never experience the world from exactly the same location or in exactly the same way as anyone else—but is nevertheless an unfortunate *limitation* on our desire to impose order on social interaction.

[3b] The account in (3a) is accurate with regard to what Austin calls "infelicities" (misfires and abuses); but the type of speech act that is "used not seriously, but in ways *parasitic* upon its normal use" (Austin 1962/1975: 22)—which Austin doesn't classify as an infelicity but dismisses as not germane to a theory of speech acts, and on which Derrida builds his theory of iterability—offers a powerful *exception* to (3a). Without the destabilizations produced by infelicities, our communication would be more successful; without "parasitic" or reperformative or reiterative destabilizations, we could not communicate at all.

[3c] Without communicative destabilization *in general*, we could not communicate at all. Iterability is not an exception to the rule; it is the rule, albeit a rule that works through (and indeed marks the possibility of) the proliferation of exceptions, limitations, reformulations, etc.

Or, more succinctly: In (3a) destabilization is an unsettling fact of life to which we attempt to respond, restabilizingly; in (3b) destabilization *in infelicities* is an unsettling fact of life to which we attempt to respond, restabilizingly, but *in reperformances* it is what makes communication possible; and in (3c) *all* destabilization is what makes communication possible.

Of these, (3a) maps something like a transitional position between (2) and (3bc), assigning communicative destabilization of all sorts a less random role than it plays in (2) but a less constitutive role in the chain of iterability than it plays in (3c); and (3b) would map a transitional position between (3a) and (3c). But which position is Derrida's?

Judging from Derrida's rhetoric, we might be inclined to name (3c); looking closely at his specific claims, we might lean more strongly toward (3b). He does not in fact explicitly make *all* communicative destabilizations constitutive of the possibility of communication; for him what is expressly constitutive of that possibility is iterability alone. In the passage I quoted earlier, for example, he asks "Isn't it true that what Austin excludes as anomaly, exception, 'non-serious,' *citation* (on stage, in a poem, or a soliloquy) is the determined modification of a general citationality—or rather, a general iterability—without which there would not even be a 'successful' performative?" (ibid.: 17). Or, as he asks a few lines later, "would a performative utterance be possible if a citational doubling [*doublure*] did not come to split and dissociate from itself the pure singularity of the event?" The "pure singularity of the event" would invoke the idealized model of communication offered by (1) the RPOL; the "citational doubling" that fractures and separates itself from that singularity is, for Derrida, the descent from the RPOL's transcendental model to the world of actual human communication. Intuitively, the fact that an utterance can be reprised, reperformed, or reiterated in a new context, by a new speech actor, for a new audience, in what Goffman (1974) would call a new frame, and without *a priori* limitations on the rhetorical creativity that may brought to such a reframing, does indeed seem to offer an entirely appropriate explanation of the shift from idealized abstractions to socially situated interactivity, and thus of the possibility of real-world communication.

But it is typical of Derrida's argumentative strategies—and, as I suggested above, itself an instance of iterability—that in his hands a single exception to a rule tends to proliferate and insinuate itself into this nook and that cranny of a system or a situation until it becomes not quite the rule, not quite the new norm, not quite the ideal, but an entity occupying something like the honorific status previously accorded to the rule, the norm, or the ideal. And in fact in section i, where Derrida deals not specifically with Austin's theory of *mis*fires, *mis*invocations, *mis*executions, *mis*applications, and so on, but rather with Searle's (1977) repeated accusations that Derrida has *mis*understood Austin, *mis*read or *mis*stated Austin's claims, he notes that the "mis" is itself an instance or iteration of iterability, and argues that "to account for the possibility of such *mis*ses in general is, to put it still in Sarl's [Searle's] code, the *crux*, the *crucial* difficulty of the theory of speech acts" (1977/1988: 40). Searle (1969: 55) himself seems to have recognized precisely this difficulty, in restricting his inquiry to *ideal* speech acts alone, to "the center of the concept of promising," and excluding the "marginal, fringe, and partially defective promises" that Austin called misfires from consideration altogether. Unlike Searle, Derrida insists that speech-act theory *find a way* to "account for the possibility of such *mis*ses in general."

Clearly, however, Derrida's insistence that speech-act theory be able to *explain* the possibility of *mis*ses does not amount to an announcement that *mis*ses are *constitutive* of communication. It would be entirely possible for Derrida to argue that speech acts are conative responses to misfires, and are themselves susceptible to misfires—that would constitute an account of "the possibility of such *mis*ses in general"—and then to add that the other problematic category that Austin dismisses, "parasitic" speech acts, works in a different way: as a constitutive "condition of possibility" for communication.

In any case, I submit that Derrida's explicit claims about reperformability as this sort of constitutive condition of possibility for communication are intuitively easy to accept, but the implicit claims that arguably derive from his explicit claims—namely that *misfires* make communication possible too—are more problematic and less intuitively acceptable. Without a high degree of stability in our verbal exchanges, we could not understand each other; without a certain degree of instability in those exchanges, we would have nothing to say that would be worth saying. Iterability or "the alterability of the same" makes human verbal communication in all its nuanced complexity possible. But exactly what is enabled by misfires? Aren't they just mistakes?

Derrida doesn't make this case expressly, but if we juxtapose the now-famous theorizations of iterability with the largely forgotten opening pages of "Signature event context" we may draw the conclusion that for Derrida, at some level, the speech-act importance of misfires and other infelicities and abuses is that they are communicative acts in their own right, and so wield conative *force*—and that it is the reticulatory displacement of that force through a group that makes misfires part of the constitutive "conditions of possibility" for communication. What makes communication possible, in other words, is not simply that every performative is a reperformance of past performances; it is also and especially the fact that every performative *does* something to other people.

"For example," Austin (1962/1975: 28) writes in his early discussion of misfires, "at a party, you say, when picking sides, 'I pick George': George grunts 'I'm not playing.' Has George been picked?" Your illocutionary act of *picking* is in jeopardy, obviously, and from your point of view the coherence of the entire speech situation may be teetering on the brink, but that very anxiety about your ability to complete your speech act perlocutionarily is itself the perlocutionary effect of George's illocutionary act of *refusing*. In that obvious sense, a misfire is a performance, a performative, and specifically in George's case both an affirmative or confirmative reperformance of past performances of *grumpily refusing to cooperate* and an antagonistic reperformance of past performances of *willingly and cheerfully agreeing to be picked*. At a deeper level, however, just as by *picking* George you mobilize and organize his behavior—he now has to play the game—so too does George's refusal to let his behavior be so mobilized organize the behavior of everyone else at the party. His grumpy refusenik affect is a potentially disruptive force, an affective-becoming-conative wet blanket that must be dealt with.

To put this distinction in simplified bivalent terms: it is our biological *separateness* that makes iterability constitutive of the possibility of communication, but it is our affective-becoming-conative *connectedness* that makes misfires constitutive of that possibility. Because we move through the world in different skinbags, because I cannot see through your eyes or digest your food, every reperformance of a performative intermixes difference, deviation, into repetition of "the same"; but because the extended body-becoming-mind collectively feels and responds to misfires as a disruptive force, every failed performative contributes to communication just as powerfully, and indeed just as constructively, as the successful ones.

3.1.2 The displacement of force

Because Derrida's deconstruction of Austin revolves around writing and the absent reader and interrogates the assumption that face-to-face encounters in which bodies are physically present to each other are the primal scene of communication, it is often read as a celebration of disembodiment, of radical abstraction. In fact quite the opposite is true. Derrida begins and ends his article with *kinesthetic* communication, noting that "one can, for instance, *communicate a movement* or that a tremor [*ébranlement*], a shock, a displacement of force can be communicated—that is, propagated, transmitted" (1972/1988: 1). No semantic or conceptual content is communicated here; the communication of a movement, a shock, a force is not apparently a linguistic exchange, or even, more broadly, a semiotic event. And, as I have been hinting, this transfer not of *information* but of *force* from body to body is, for Derrida, Austin's implicit model of the speech act. Speech acts are performed by bodies, for bodies, and on bodies. Doing things to other people with words, Austin's (1962/1975: 12) definition of the speech act, is a communication of *force* to those people's bodies.

This is obviously a radically productive shift away from the conception of language as verbal labels that Andy Clark shares with his critics. But the important issues for an application of Austin's theory to the extended body-becoming-mind are ones that Derrida himself doesn't raise: [a] what kind of force *is* displaced or propagated or transmitted through speech acts, and, barring the kinds of collisions that displace force in a car crash or a billiards game, [b] exactly how does that force leap the air space between bodies?

Suppose I *irritate* you—my speech act does something to you, causes a state change in your body. The perlocutionary effect of my speech act in or on your body is affective. Does that mean that (a) the illocutionary force of my speech act is also affective, and that (b) the channel or medium by which it is communicated from my body to yours is affective too?

Or suppose I *warn* you not to step out into traffic, and you heed my warning, check your step, and avoid being hit by a bus. The perlocutionary effect of my speech act on your body is kinesthetic. Does that mean that (a) the illocutionary force of my speech act is also kinesthetic, and that (b) the channel or medium by which it is communicated is kinesthetic as well?

Or suppose I *pronounce* you and another person husband and wife; once I utter those words, you two are married. The perlocutionary effect of my speech act is institutional: it ushers the two of you into the institution of matrimony. It would seem to go without saying that (a) the illocutionary force of my speech act is institutional. But what does that mean, exactly? And (b) what would it mean for it to be communicated by an "institutional" channel or medium?

I could continue to list speech acts for pages, asking of each the same two questions. Instead let me suggest the generalization that I began to adumbrate at the end of the previous section: the illocutionary force of any speech act is *conative*, in the sense that it mobilizes or energizes or "volitionalizes" the target body-becoming-mind to act. I warn you, and you stop short of being hit by the oncoming bus: that is conation in its purest form. To the extent that the irritated person simply *is* irritated, that is affect, an emotional interpretant; to the extent that that affective state motivates the irritated person to react in some way (to say something, to move away, to make an irritated face), that is conation, an energetic interpretant. Just-married people do now exist in a new institutional state; but surely that state energizes them to *feel* differently about themselves and their partners in relation to the rest of the world (an emotional interpretant), and to *act* differently in those same relationships (an energetic interpretant), which would be affect-becoming-conation. As Peirce notes (see §4.2 for discussion), emotional interpretants (Firsts) and energetic interpretants (Seconds) tend to issue into the Thirdness of logical interpretants, which would be cognition—*thinking* differently about the changed situation. But I submit that the core of the force transferred by the speech act is conative. It puts pressure on its targets to behave differently. It (re-)mobilizes their will to act.

The communicative channel by which this conative force is transferred from body to body is the topic of chapter 5. I argue there that it is at base affective, mediated by the mirror-neuron system; but obviously, as shared affect issues into reticulated conative pressures, it is affective-becoming-conative; and as those pressures issue into the verbalized form of a *speech* act, the communicative channel is affective-becoming-conative-becoming-cognitive.

More broadly, too, if we imagine (§3.1.1) performativity-as-iterability too as transmitting some sort of affective-becoming-conative force, and thus as something more than the clever mind game to which it has been reduced in some poststructuralist quarters, we may ask ourselves (a) just what the force is that is manifested in or through specific (re)iterations of the performative, and (b) what that force is exerted on or against. Derrida calls iterability the "alterability of this [repeated] same idealized in the singularity of the event, for instance, in this or that speech act" (1988: 119). What is the force channeled into and through and by "alteration"? Derrida, again, doesn't address this question, but to anticipate the discussion of Bakhtin that follows in the next section, I would speculate that the "incoming" iteration—the performative performed by someone else that I take over and alter in my own "outgoing" reiteration—offers some kind of resistance to my alteration, so that iterability as alterability as the partial overcoming of that resistance entails some small modicum of force. But where, and how, and against what or whom is that force exerted? Or should we read "idealized in the singularity of the event" to mean *disembodied*, abstracted out of the realm of the displacement of force from body to body? What is idealized for Derrida is in fact not the force but alterability, which suggests that a specific displacement of "altering" or transformative/iterative force *is* the idealization he means. But is force-as-idealization a metaphorical force? By "idealization" does Derrida mean a "tokening" or instantiation of alterability, so that any kind of alteration will count as an idealization?

3.2 Bakhtin on internal dialogism

Toward the last of the 80,000 or so words Derrida wrote on the subject of communication as iterability, he returned to the imagery of force and thus of body:

If I speak of great stability, it is in order to emphasize that this semantic level is neither originary, nor ahistorical, nor simple, nor self-identical in any of its elements, nor even entirely semantic or significant. Such stabilization is relative, even if it is sometimes so great as to seem immutable and permanent. It is the momentary result of a whole history of relations of force (intra- and extrasemantic, intra- and extradiscursive, intra- and extraliterary or -philosophical, intra- and extraacademic, etc.). In order for this history to have taken place, in its turbulence and in its stases, in order for relations of force, of tensions, or of wars to have taken place, in order for hegemonies to have imposed themselves during a determinate period, there must have been a certain play in all these structures, hence a certain instability or non-self-identity, nontransparency. (1988: 145)

This, clearly, is iterability writ large, and writ specifically through the body politic—iterability as the driving historical principle, stabilizing and destabilizing, behind the complex societal relations of force that turbulently shape and never perfectly regulate whole populations, complexly iterative relations of embodied social force.

This vision of iterability is strikingly reminiscent of Mikhail Bakhtin's (1934–1935/1981) argument that "unitary language" is a precarious idealizing regime that is forcibly and repressively *maintained* in a sea of heteroglossia[2]:

Unitary language constitutes the theoretical expression of the historical processes of linguistic unification and centralization, an expression of the centripetal forces of language. A unitary language is not something given [дан *dan*[3]] but is always in essence posited [задан *zadan*]—and at every moment of its linguistic life it is opposed to the realities of heteroglossia. But at the same time it makes its real presence felt as a force for overcoming this heteroglossia, imposing specific limits to it, guaranteeing a certain maximum of mutual understanding and crystalizing into a real, although still relative, unity—the unity of the reigning conversational (everyday) and literary language, "correct language." (ibid.: 270)

In theory a unitary language is the fantasy object of the RPOL: whether we speak of Saussure's *langue*, Chomsky's competence, or Fodor's LOT, each is the imaginary structural or systemic state of perfection from which all actual language use (*parole*, performance, natural language) is taken to be a sad and confused falling away. Here Bakhtin, like Derrida, is arguing that unitary languages are not entirely fantasized. They do exist in the social world of language use, "an expression of the centripetal forces of language," or what Derrida calls the stabilizing effects of an iterative relation of forces; but they must be created, maintained, policed, shored up against the entropic or centrifugal or destabilizing impulses also constantly at work in language and society, which Bakhtin calls "heteroglossia" and Derrida calls the "play" in the iterative structures. "A common unitary language," Bakhtin continues, "is a system of linguistic norms. But these norms do not constitute an abstract imperative; they are rather the generative forces of linguistic life, forces that struggle to overcome the heteroglossia of language, forces that unite and centralize verbal-ideological thought, creating within a heteroglot national language the firm, stable linguistic nucleus of an officially recognized literary language, or else defending an already formed language from the pressure of growing heteroglossia." Bakhtin insists that he is interested not in a reductionist understanding of language as a minimal system of "elementary forms (linguistic symbols)" derived by idealization (abstraction) from the complexity of actual communication, but rather in "language conceived as ideologically saturated, language as a world view, even as a concrete opinion, insuring a *maximum* of mutual understanding in all spheres of ideological life" (ibid.: 271).

This latter conception of language is in fact Bakhtin's vision of language as extended body-becoming-mind. Ideological saturation is specifically the saturation of each individual language user's sense of language, orientation toward language, use of language, with the forceful *voices of other people*, the voices of everyone else who has used the language—with the *vocal forces of collectivity*. This is what Bakhtin calls "internal dialogism," the saturation of "the word" (слово *slovo*, which his English translators often render as "discourse") with other people's words: "The word is born in a dialogue as a living rejoinder within it; the word is shaped in dialogic interaction with an alien word that is already in the object. A word forms a concept of its own object in a dialogic way" (ibid.: 279). In other words, every word anyone ever speaks or writes is saturated not only with alien vocalizations of that word but with the past dialogues in which those alien vocalizations were uttered.

But the word's internal dialogism is not mere saturation with the forces of vocal pastness; it is also an anticipatory orientation to the forces of vocal futurity, a directedness toward an "answer-word" that powerfully shapes the form it takes. "The word in living conversation," Bakhtin (ibid.: 280) writes, "is directly, blatantly, oriented toward a future answer-word: it provokes an answer, anticipates it and structures itself in the answer's direction. Forming itself in an atmosphere of the already spoken, the word is at the same time determined by that which has not yet been said but which is needed and in fact anticipated by the answering word." Other people's voices flow into and through every word we speak, every speech act we perform, from the past and the future: we (re)iterate/(re)perform and thus alter the words we have heard other people speak, the speech acts whose force other people have channeled to us; and as we project or imagine our interlocutor(s) responding to the speech act we are getting ready to perform, we internalize that imagined response, build it too into the imminent speech act. As remembered speech acts surge through us from the past *and* anticipated speech acts reach back from the future into the present of a spoken or written exchange, then, our locutions become internalizations not just of the dialogue we are currently in but also of dialogues in which we have participated in the past and in which we expect to participate in the future.

Now, Adams and Aizawa would almost certainly want to describe "remembering" and "anticipating" as intracranial cognitive processes—and in important ways they are. But Bakhtin's focus on *voice*—and specifically *tone* of voice as the qualitative First that is typically dropped out of Peirce's tone-token-type triad (see §4.3 and §A2.1.3 for discussion)—suggests that "remembering" and "anticipating" are also transcranial forms of connectivity. Not only are dialogized *words* internalized (remembered and anticipated) and reproduced as new (derived, conventional) *words*; for Bakhtin, *accented* words are *re-accented*, *tonalized* words are *retonalized*.[4] Those accents and tonalizations are embodied channels of conative force—transmitted to us transcranially by other people, felt by us intracranially—to which we add our own transformative modicum of counterforce. In other words, for Bakhtin the word is not an abstract data packet that is represented propositionally in the LOT and translated into or out of natural language; it is a bodily force in which the voices of many people collide, clash, vie for control. "As a living, socio-ideological concrete thing, as heteroglot opinion," Bakhtin (ibid.: 293) writes, "language, for the individual consciousness, lies on the borderline between oneself and the other. The word in language is half someone else's. It becomes 'one's own' only when the speaker populates it with his own intention, his own accent, when he appropriates the word, adapting it to his own semantic and expressive intention." Or again: "Language is not a neutral medium that passes freely and easily into the private property of the speaker's intentions; it is populated—overpopulated—with the intentions of others. Expropriating it, forcing it to submit to one's own intentions and accents, is a difficult and complicated process" (ibid.: 294).

Notice the metaphors of force there. For Bakhtin, the word is an alien territory that the speaker attacks and subdues militarily. Bakhtin's verb for "(over)populate" is (пере)населить *(pere)naselit'* "(over)settle," from село *selo* "village"; his verb for "appropriate" or "expropriate" is овладеть *ovladet'* "seize," from владеть *vladet'* "possess, own," from the root влад *vlad*, related to power, sovereignty, rule, command; his noun for "forcing [something/someone] to submit" is подчинение *podchinenie* "subjugation, subordination," from чин *chin* "rank, order." Bakhtin's conception of internal dialogism is sometimes taken to be a form of liberal consensus, the collaboration of equals in the creation of a group speech act—indeed, my theory of the group speech act on pages 95–99 of Robinson 2003 was explicitly grounded in something like this understanding of Bakhtin's thinking—but this passage makes it clear that the process is considerably more conflictual than is often thought.

The internalized conflict or strife adumbrated in this metaphorics would, in fact, appear to be the conative force at work behind Bakhtin's understanding of linguistic unification, as it is perhaps behind Derrida's somatopolitical iteration of iterability in terms of the (de)stabilizing relations of forces disseminated throughout a social field. Bakhtin's conception of linguistic unification as a social project (задан *zadan*) imposed on a language means specifically pressure put on language *users* to unify their usages—pressure or force that is channeled through "expropriative" or "subjugative" tonal iterations.

The kind of tonal force that I suggest is for Bakhtin the disseminatory channel of linguistic unification might be illustrated with an utterance like "No, I'm sorry, I don't have any, or, as Jimmy would say, 'I ain't got none'"—said with a slight tone of disdain, or humorous condescension, and perhaps with one eyebrow raised almost imperceptibly. This jibe at "bad grammar"—at a deviation from educated white middle-class English as the standard of linguistic unity—is embodied, channeled through tone of voice and a twitch of the lips and one eyebrow, and so is officially invisible, a kind of communicative Stealth bomber, and above all plausibly deniable. "What, you thought I was making fun of Jimmy? Heavens no. I find his English—well, sort of attractive. Colorful. I would never make *fun* of it." After all, I'm just *quoting*. I'm just *repeating what Jimmy says*. But of course the affective jibe finds its target nevertheless. It acts conatively on the listener "intracranially" (as an internalized form of transcranial communication, as in g_1, above) so as to discourage lower-class usages, to stigmatize them and the people who use them as deviant(s). Enough such tonal iterations of linguistic regulation and whole populations will toe the line. At the very least they will *feel guilty* whenever they say "ain't" or use a double negative, and apologize to their hearers for using "bad grammar"; and that means that they will introject kinesthetic force as a push toward linguistic unity into their own deviance, in the form of tonal shame and/or verbal apology, and thus also, even in their failure to comply, will participate in the unification project.

But of course, as Bakhtin also insists, counterhegemonic impulses toward heteroglossia (Russian разноречие, *raznorechie* "different-speechedness"—Bakhtin's own coinage) persist. Or as Derrida would gloss that, "there must have been a certain play in all these structures, hence a certain instability or non-self-identity, nontransparency." It is easy enough to mock snide authoritarian retonalizations with your own snide anti-authoritarian retonalizations: "You gotta love it: 'Sort of *attractive*'! 'Colorful!'"

3.3 Bourdieu on *habitus*

One final complication to this "group speech act" model might be gleaned from the reading of Austin's claim that "*any*, or almost any, perlocutionary act is liable to be brought off, in sufficiently special circumstances, by the issuing, with or without calculation, of any utterance whatsoever" offered by the French sociologist Pierre Bourdieu (1982/1991). In essence Bourdieu argues that the conative "bring-off" or trigger of a perlocutionary act lies not in the individual actor's illocutionary intentions, as Stanley Cavell too noted, but in the "sufficiently special circumstances," the "total speech situation," which Bourdieu identifies as social *habitus*. Intimidation, for example, "can only be exerted on a person predisposed (in his habitus) to feel it, whereas others will ignore it" (ibid.: 51). The trigger for intimidation, both for intimidating and for being intimidated, is pulled not by "the speech act itself" (however that might be reductively idealized) but by the social *habitus* supporting and conditioning the speech act.

Note that in Bourdieu's formulation *habitus* is at once [a] an "external" social situation or scene, organized in culturally coherent patterns and [b] an "internal" social orientation—for Bourdieu a person is "predisposed (*in his habitus*)"—that guides the individual's behavior conatively as "reason" might have done in a more primitive explanatory model. (See Dennett 1991; Robinson 2001.) *Habitus* is specifically the collective organization of behavior that the individual internalizes (and continually reiterates) as a conative (guiding/motivating) force. One of the things *habitus* organizes conatively inside the individual, in fact, is the action-oriented interpretation of the external social scene—not only what the current situation or context is, not only how it is supposed to be interpreted, but also how it is supposed to be used to guide behavioral (including cognitive) choices. Austin's error, as Bourdieu argues, lay in looking for the power of words in the words themselves rather than in the social uses of words, the social conditions in which words are *assigned* that power: "The language of authority never governs without the collaboration of those it governs, without the help of the social mechanisms capable of producing this complicity, based on misrecognition, which is the basis of all authority" (ibid.: 113).

The "social mechanisms capable of producing this complicity" are, clearly, transmitted from body to body by/as *habitus*—which is to say also that they *are themselves habitus*, the socially conditioned/conditioning agent(s) or carrier(s) of social conditions.[5] Social *habitus* conditions the collaboration of the powerless in the wielding of social power, the "being intimidated" of those intimidated by intimidators, and also conditions the collaboration of the powerful in the dissemination of collaboration in the wielding of power, the "intimidating" of those who intimidate intimidatees.

What Bourdieu neglects to mention, however, is that one powerful mobile agent of the social *habitus* that effects this collaborative conditioning is itself the speech act. For example, the speech act of intimidating *helps condition* the intimidatee to respond properly (submissively) to intimidation. It's not, in other words, that any given utterance "contains" its own perlocutionary effect, as Austin seems to have hoped at first and then reluctantly decided simply wasn't the case; nor is it that perlocutionary effect is ideally disconnected from illocutionary force, utterly determined by the listener's response and so out of the speaker's control, as Austin suspected was the case but was reluctant to argue. Nor is it simply that groups of people perform speech acts collaboratively, collectively, as I argued on pages 95–99 of Robinson 2003. It is also that speech acts are attempts to *condition* listeners to respond properly to them, to respond with the socially expected perlocutionary effects—and that, in actualizing the proper response, in effectuating the desired conditioning, perlocutionary effects too condition speakers to ritualize the speech acts that "work," to go on iterating socially effective speech acts along socially effective lines.

This modification of Bourdieu's model suggests that the speech act operates as a channel of habitualizing power *through* the embodied mimeticisms and mirrorings of social interaction. (For discussion, see §5.1.)

3.3.1 Complicating *habitus* 1: Laughter

Take the perlocutionary effect of laughter. How do we "make someone laugh"? Obviously, as Cavell noted, not by the social magic of saying "Laugh!" or "I make you laugh!" Nor, as Austin too would insist, just by saying something that we consider funny. But neither is producing the perlocutionary effect of laughter entirely random. Having noticed what makes a person laugh once, we may be able to mimic that laughter-inducing act deliberately, making that same person laugh on a later occasion by successfully reenacting the perlocutionary trigger of laughter, and, perhaps, extending the perlocutionary act to other laughers as well, generalizing the laughter-inducing act iteratively to appeal to larger and larger audiences. Comedians cannot be "naturally" funny, because comic speech acts are not natural events; they are social actions, developed through close conative attention to the dynamics of embodied social mimeticism, which is to say, attention not only to the buttons that *must* be pushed to make people laugh, but also to the slow iterative and interactive process of helping people develop new buttons that *can* be pushed to make them laugh.

But that mimeticism is more than comics learning what makes people laugh and conditioning people to find *them* funny; it is also bi- and multidirectional, laughers learning to laugh at comic speech acts by modeling their responses on other laughers' embodied response to the laugh-inducing act, laughers mimicking each other mirroring the comic. This is why comedy is so much funnier in a group—why, in fact, some people report that they cannot laugh at a funny movie or television show (let alone comic novel or humor book) when they are alone in a room. They need the reinforcing multidirectional mimeticism of group laughter—in an audience at an actual comedy show or in a darkened movie theater, or with friends and family in the living room—in order to reproduce for the comic speech act the proper perlocutionary effect of laughter. And it may well be that laughing at comic speech acts while alone in a room becomes possible through the reiteration of the multidirectional mimeticism of crowd laughter spun in what Damasio (1999: 80) calls the "as-if body loop" of the imagination. Indeed, the function of a laugh track, or of the laughter of a studio audience recorded around the sound stage where a sitcom is being taped, is to use the data compression of an audio channel to create an imagined full-bodied response, and thus to condition home viewers to produce the desired perlocutionary effect as well. Because we hear people laughing even when we can't see or perhaps feel them laughing, we use the auditory body loop to generate an as-if body loop of being in the presence of people laughing, and so may feel more disposed to join in the laughter.[6]

3.3.2 Complicating *habitus* 2: Persuasion

Or take an example from the history of philosophy: Aristotle's use of *pistis* in the *Rhetoric*. *Pistis* is of course his central term in the handbook, the keyword that most pithily sums up what he is attempting to do in the *Rhetoric*: it is not only "persuasion" but "means of persuasion," and thus "proof" or "argument." To the extent that the book is a practical guide to persuading people, therefore, it is about *pisteis* as the specific argumentative strategies and devices (speech acts) that the rhetor should learn to use to that end. This plural noun *pisteis* appears throughout the *Rhetoric* in just this sense, and is translated with great semantic consistency as "proofs" by Freese (1926), as "proofs [persuasion]" by Cooper (1932), and as "modes of persuasion" or "means of persuasion" or "means of effecting persuasion" by Roberts (1984). (Kennedy 1991/2007 loan-translates it as *pisteis*, often with explanatory notes.)

But *pistis* is not only persuasion; it is also belief, the *result* of persuasion. This semantic duality obviously makes things a bit difficult for translators attempting to render the term more or less consistently into English, which lacks a single term that would cover both the illocutionary act of persuading and the perlocutionary effect of being persuaded. Even in English, however, we should be in a position to note that persuading is a speech act that cannot be performed by a single individual: *I* cannot persuade *you* unless *you* are persuaded. If I claim that I have persuaded you but you insist that you remain unpersuaded, at best we have an is-so/is-not situation, and at worst one of us is lying. In that sense the Greek *pistis* is more conducive to a complex sociological understanding of believing and persuading than the English tendency to separate the verbs by speaker and hearer.

In *Rhetoric* 1.1.3 (1354a15) Aristotle calls the enthymeme the *sōma tēs pisteōs*, the *body* of believing/persuading. One might translate that expansively as the body of the group speech act by which persuasion becomes belief. Jeffrey Walker (2000: 84–85) reminds us that the root of *enthumēma* is *thumos* "heart," which he identifies as "the seat of affect," so the best translation of *enthumēma* may be not the loan translation "enthymeme" or the descriptive "truncated or popular syllogism," but *encouragement*: "It is indeed its rootedness in *thumos* and the *pathē* [emotions] that gives an *enthumēma*, or indeed any argument whatsoever, its value and its relevance for the audience the rhetor wishes to persuade; and it is the enthymeme's simultaneous embodiment of a heterogeneous set of *pisteis*, combining the 'assurances' of *logos* (as apodictic propositional reasoning) with those of *pathos* and *ēthos*, that makes it a powerful 'encouragement' to belief and action." As we saw in §1.3.1, encouragement is affect-becoming-conation, but both the affect and the conation are specifically *interactive*, involved in the reticulation of affective motivation from body to body. But as the enthymeme is far more than body—it is encouragement-becoming-understanding, body-becoming-mind—so too is the *sōma tēs pisteōs* far more than enthymemes: it is the reticulatory body-becoming-mind of the community of language users that makes enthymemes meaningful summations of this or that aspect of experience. People *feel* the meanings of enthymemes, and are able to use them and recognize them with the deep and undeniable feeling that the good ones do refer to reality and the bad ones don't, because the linguistic and cultural values that structure their world—structure "truth" and "reality" and "identity" for them—are reticulated through the group body-becoming-mind in the form of persuasive-becoming-encouraging-becoming-believing (affective-becoming-conative-becoming-cognitive) speech acts. Anything that we currently believe—including things like "2 + 2 = 4" and "'to persuade' is a verb meaning 'to change someone's belief so as to conform to your own'" and "it's important to be fair" and "the sun rises every morning" and "the sun doesn't so much 'rise' as emerge into view as the earth rotates in space" and "my family loves me" and so on—was once something that we had to be persuaded of; but because the persuasion wasn't necessarily always propositional, we may think of many beliefs as "natural," as things we have somehow simply registered objectively as facts. We were persuaded in those cases too, but the persuasion happened on a "lower" level of the body-becoming-mind. We were persuaded affectively, through pressures placed on us to conform to group assumptions and norms. The body of persuasion-becoming-belief in those cases is so bodily that we hardly even notice it happening; but it is still an event in an entelechial body-becoming-mind that *can* be articulated in propositional form.

Griffiths and Scarantino call this approach to human social interaction transactionalist, noting that "emotion is a form of skillful engagement with the social environment that involves a dynamic process of negotiation mediated by reciprocal feedback between emoter and interactants" (2009: 446). This "reciprocal feedback" is bodily, primarily affective, and tends to occur below the level of conscious awareness; the "negotiation" Griffiths and Scarantino refer to is not conducted in the give and take of a verbal conversation. But group speech acts are *accompanied* and rendered possible by this sort of affective communication, this "reciprocal feedback," which can seem to make a club full of laughers into a single body-becoming-mind.

But again, although persuading/believing is in some sense always a collaborative group speech act, the fact that the collaboration often occurs across power differentials—a more powerful speaker attempting to persuade less powerful listeners, a less powerful speaker attempting to persuade more powerful listeners—reminds us not to assimilate the group speech act to liberal models of social negotiation. It is the speaker's job to *persuade* the audience—to convert the audience to a point of view that may or may not be in their best interests but certainly is in the best interests of the speaker and the group(s) s/he represents. Persuasion-becoming-believing is a channeling of conative force that seeks to condition its social targets to collaborate in the local (intracranial) implementation of that force.

Specifically, Aristotle says that the rhetor's job description involves the *dunamis peri hekaston tou theōrēsai to endekhomenon pithanon* (1.2.1, 1357b26), which might be translated literally as "the ability in each case to see/observe the available persuasivity." The usual translation of *to endekhomenon pithanon* is the "available means of persuasion," which would tend to assimilate what the rhetor is "seeing" or "observing" (and mobilizing for persuasive purposes) to the *pisteis*, which is to say to arguments, proofs, persuasive strategies and structures and set pieces of all kinds; but this is misleading, because there is really nothing about persuasive strategies that is "seeable" or "observable." The rhetor *knows* them: s/he doesn't have to *see* them. *Pisteis* are to be mastered, internalized, produced; what is to be seen *peri hekaston*, observed in each specific rhetorical situation, is something else, something external enough to be studied from across a room. And *Rhetoric* 1.2 suggests that this external something is what Susan Miller (2008: 51) calls the "interactive phenomenology" of human social life that makes persuasion possible: the "atechnic arguments" that rhetors find already existing in people's conversations, confessions, contracts, testimonials, and the like (1.2.2), our tendency to believe or trust or allow ourselves to be persuaded by certain kinds of socially accepted people (1.2.4), the emotions felt by an audience (1.2.5), specialized real-world knowledge (1.2.7), enthymemes and examples (1.2.8–10), people's opinions (1.2.11 and 1.2.13), the kinds of things we tend to debate (1.2.12), and signs and probabilities (1.2.14–18). Rhetoric is the attempt to persuade others; its success rests on the rhetor's ability to *condition* his or her audience to be persuaded. And that conditioning consists in the ability to "see" or "observe" (or read) in the audience what they are thinking (atechnic arguments, real-world knowledge, enthymemes, examples, opinions, controversial issues, signs, probabilities) and feeling (social valuations and emotions), and channel them strategically through directive speech acts.

Of course, the fact that it is not only possible to resist this conditioning but possible to resist it *because* it is conditioning—to sit stony-faced through a sitcom with a laugh track, annoyed that the producers are working so hard to make you laugh, or to refuse to be persuaded *because* the speaker is so persuasive ("slick" or "glib")—makes it clear that this is not a conditioned reflex, which is to say, not a simple mechanical cause of laughter or belief or whatever, and thus also that the model I am building is not behaviorist. The conformative power of crowd behavior is so strong that we *have* to resist it if we don't want to be affected by it—which is to say that it does affect us, somatically, no matter what, and quite often all we can do by way of resistance is to block its somatic effects before they issue into action. And even that minimal resistance isn't always possible. Sometimes we laugh at a movie that is much too stupid to laugh at, that we tell ourselves we couldn't possibly find funny. But this kind of overwhelmingly perlocutionary-effective illocutionary force doesn't mean that a stimulus mechanically *caused* us to respond; it simply means that our resistance was inadequate to the task. It also doesn't mean that our bodies are statically structured to respond mechanically to certain stimuli. Our bodily responses to stimuli are acquired dispositions, are in fact sociobiologically iterative, arising out of millions of mimetic/adaptive interactions with similar social stimuli in the past (often in the evolutionary past), and are continually being iteratively reconditioned in and through and by and for our experiences with movies, with television shows, with other media events, with written texts, with other people in audiences, and in ordinary conversation.

It does mean, however, that certain perlocutionary effects are more or less *predictable* responses to certain illocutionary acts—never perfectly predictable, as the entertainment industry knows well, but predictable nonetheless, or the entertainment industry could not exist. Certain plot and character elements, combined with certain visual and auditory tracks, are likely to make audiences laugh, cry, or feel anxious or relieved because they have done so before. The repetition of those elements is likely not only to work again, but also to continue to condition audiences to respond in the expected way, and thus to *ensure* that it will work again. Politicians, televangelists, teachers, parents, and other manipulators also know how to "push the right buttons" and thus produce in their manipulatees the desired perlocutionary effects—with some resistance, of course, but for the most part not only submissively but willingly: the manipulatees *decide* (or at least feel nonconsciously disposed) to go along with the manipulation, in many cases even when they recognize that it is manipulation.

3.4 Indirect speech acts

Let's look back at the soritic series as we left it in §3.0:

[a] I'm irritated, but don't feel it yet.
[b] I begin to feel my irritation.
[c] I say to myself, subvocally, "Hey, I'm feeling angry."
[d] I mutter out loud, though no one hears me, "Hey, I'm feeling angry."
[e] You walk into the room, and I say to you "Hey, I'm feeling angry."

[f$_1$] You hear me say it.	[f$_2$] You hear me accusing you of something.	[f$_3$] I *secretly wanted* to irritate you; my saying to you "Hey, I'm feeling angry" is a deliberate provocation.
[g$_1$] You realize that it's true, "I am feeling angry"—but the "I" refers to you.	[g$_2$] The accusation you hear in my utterance makes you angry.	[g$_3$] But you don't let yourself be provoked.
[h$_1$] I think about it and realize that you're right: I *am* angry at you.		

Now consider the speech-act exchanges (f_2-g_2-h_1) and (f_3-g_3) and ask yourself this question: How do we *know* what speech act someone else is performing? This brings us back to the problematic of Clark and Chalmers (1998) *knowing* that Otto is endorsing his notebook's contents, and therefore using it automatically, through extended mind. I argued in §0.2 that Otto endorsing the notebook's contents is not an observable act, in contrast with Otto pulling the notebook out of his shoulder bag; but what if it is one? What if it could be one? Could there be subtle but clearly recognizable body-language "tells" that indicate visually to the attentive observer the act of endorsing?

What I realize in (h_1) is that you read my speech act more accurately than I did myself. How did you do that? In (f_3) I tried to keep my desire to irritate you secret, but it seemed to me in (g_3) that you had read my hidden intentions correctly and simply refused to play my game. How did you read me? For that matter, how did I know that you had read me correctly and decided to deflect my provocation with niceness, rather than, say, simply failing to pick up my carefully concealed signals? How do we successfully *identify* speech acts?

One of the avenues Austin pursued in attempting to answer this question ran through the speech act that announces or names itself—the autodeictic or "explicit" (or what came to be known as the "direct") speech act. For example, (g_2) might well take [g_{2dir1}] the fully verbalized form of you saying "I accuse you of being emotionally dishonest," overtly announcing its status as an accusation. But what about speech acts that don't expressly name themselves? Searle (1975) speaks of "indirect" speech acts, which are nonautodeictic, and the question with which I opened the preceding paragraph could usefully be reframed in his terms as "How do we know what *indirect* speech act someone else is performing?"

You could, for example, perform the accusatory speech act in (g_2) by saying [g_{2dir2}] "Oh. I see." Obviously, now you are no longer *telling* me that (g_{2dir2}) is actually [$g_{2dir2/indir1}$] an indirect accusatory speech act; but our social experience tells us that if I know you well enough, I am fairly likely to read your speech act correctly anyway. On what basis do I attribute an indirect accusation to such a determinedly noncommittal locution—and how could I possibly do so accurately? The direct speech act it apparently performs is what Austin (1962/1975: 151) called an "expositive" (the speech-act version of the constative utterance that simply conveys information): it expositively conveys the information that you "see," or understand. But when you say (g_{2dir2}) "Oh. I see," I *know* you're doing more than conveying that information. I know, say, that you're also angry. I may not know *why* you're angry (but you can be sure that I will be racing cognitively through a series of alternative explanations, testing them against what I know about you and remember about our relationship), but I do know that you *are* angry. How do I know?

The obvious answer—though it doesn't seem to be obvious to the "constative"[7] speech-act tradition coming out of Searle (1969) and others, who tend to ignore this aspect of the speech act—is that I read your body language. I say (e) "Hey, I'm feeling angry," and you raise your eyebrows, cross your arms, lean back pointedly, and say, with clipped tones, narrowed eyes, a flat gaze, and a tight mouth, ($g_{2dir2/indir1}$) "Oh. I see." Your body language tells me you're angry. Or I say (e) "Hey, I'm feeling angry," and you let your eyes go soft, lean toward me, touch my arm, and say, in a sympathizing tone, [$g_{3dir2/indir2}$] "Oh. I see." Your body language tells me that you are not taking my anger personally, and in fact are reacting sympathetically and supportively.

Or imagine that you do utter (g_{2dir1}) the autodeictic locution that announces your speech act as an accusation, "I accuse you of being emotionally dishonest," but say it not [$g_{2dir1/indir1}$] with your eyes flashing, your arms waving, your feet pacing, but [$g_{2dir1/indir2}$] in a tender, cajoling tone, while stroking my cheek and hair. These two stagings of (g_{2dir1}) could be analytically *reduced* to "the same" speech act, of course, by imposing a hierarchy according to which the direct (autodeictic) speech act is the *true core* of the speech act and the bodily staging is mere emotional (connotative) coloring; but it should be undeniable even to the constative speech-act theorist that the body language in ($g_{2dir/indir2}$) superadds to (g_{2dir}) an indirect speech act of *suggesting*, or *cajoling*, or even *seducing*—and that what Austin calls the "total speech act in the total speech situation" is therefore significantly different in ($g_{2dir1/indir1}$) and ($g_{2dir1/indir2}$).

Indeed, if one were to insist on reducing the total speech act in the total speech situation to a single simple speech act, the socially situated and kinesically signaled indirect speech act would seem to be a more realistic candidate for such a reduction than the direct one. In Peircean terms (see chapter 4), my emotional interpretant (feeling) and energetic interpretant (vicarious participation in your body movements) lead me to construct a logical interpretant that tells me what speech act you're "really" performing. My reading of ($g_{2dir1/indir2}$) your sweet, loving body language may tell me that (g_{2dir1}) your direct speech act "I accuse you of being emotionally dishonest" is accusatory in name only; that the *true* speech act you're performing is cajoling. My reading of your body language may tell me that your direct speech act (g_{2dir2}) "Oh. I see" is expositive in name only; that ($g_{2dir2/indir1}$) the "true" speech act you're performing is accusatory (and that you really are angry).

Language as Conative Force 117

But even reduction to the "true" indirect speech act is inadequate. For one thing, we can *feel* more complexity than this. (An explication of this ability to feel other people's body language *and* the body states that the body language displays is the burden of chapter 5.) In my affective response to ($g_{2dir2/indir1}$) "Oh. I see" I can feel in my body the physical and emotional exertion in your body that goes into suppressing the direct speech act of, say, (g_{2dir1}) "I accuse you of being emotionally dishonest." When you stage (g_{2dir1}) with tender, loving body language, I can feel not only that your total speech act isn't "really" accusatory, but that your choice of words in the direct (locutionary) speech act "I accuse you of being emotionally dishonest" adds significant displaced-accusatory nuance. You aren't just *soothing* me, say; you are *cajoling* me. Even though you're being sweet about it, you probably do want me to start thinking about my emotional dishonesty. The fact that you stage ($g_{2dir2/indir1}$) your anger with the superficially neutral or noncommittal direct speech act "Oh. I see" hints at a considerably more tangled skein than either reduction, to the direct expositive or to the indirect accusation, can capture. Read psychoanalytically, your total speech act is likely to be extremely complex and highly layered, with multiple baffles and misdirections protecting its full complexity even from you yourself; untying its Gordian knot entirely may require considerably subtler emotional and energetic interpretants, and probably a nonverbal-becoming-verbal follow-up as well:

[$g_{2dir2/indir1}$] "Oh. I see." <raised eyebrows, crossed arms, postural withdrawal, clipped tone of voice, narrowed eyes, flat gaze, tight mouth>
[h_2]   "What?" <look and tone of hurt innocence>
[i]   "Nothing" <same body language as in ($g_{2dir2/indir1}$)>
[j]   "Come on, don't be that way. Tell me!"

Or:

[$g_{2dir2/indir1}$] "Oh. I see." <raised eyebrows, crossed arms, postural withdrawal, clipped tone of voice, narrowed eyes, flat gaze, tight mouth>
[h_2]   "What?" <look and tone of hurt innocence>
[i]   "You know perfectly well what!" <same body language as in (g_{2indir}), except your eyes flash briefly>
[j]   "I don't, I swear!" <same hurt innocent look and tone as in (h_2), buttressed with a tonal escalation designed to establish sincerity>

In the verbal exchange that ensues, in which (let's say) our respective intentions and interpretations are fully explicated and critiqued (if such an explicatory fullness is in fact possible), it may well turn out that [k_1] I was right in (j), that (i) your assumption that I knew why you were angry was unfounded—you've misread something I said or did—but I may also come eventually to realize that [k_2] you're right, I should have realized what was going on, and it was only my unfathomable obtuseness that kept me in the dark. In this latter case, again, you seem to have known something about me that I myself didn't know.

So again, the overriding epistemological question is: Did you really know what I was thinking and feeling before I did? Or is your apparent knowing just another seeming, another quale, like the feeling that mind extends to epistemic artifacts?

3.5 Conclusions

We appear to have come to an impasse. It seems to us that we can (sometimes) read other people's minds, even relatively accurately, but we don't have a convincing model for our ability to do so. The rationalist philosophy of language (RPOL) that we explored in chapter 2 holds that all communication between humans is linguistic and propositional, which is to say, label-based: the sender of a message puts a series of conventionally ordered verbal labels on a thought; the recipient of the message "decodes" those labels and understands what the sender is saying. This chapter has been dedicated to the possibility that there are other channels of communication, especially some sort of affective-becoming-conative *force* that is often directly verbalized as speech acts, but, as indirect speech acts suggest, need not be verbalized in order to be transmitted. By what communicative channel or channels, then, is that force transferred from head to head, or from body to body? What other form of transcraniality is there, other than the label-based linguistic channel posited by the RPOL?

Before we consider some research-based answers to that question, we need to take a slight philosophical detour into the problem of the transferability or shareability of qualia. If the RPOL prevails, qualia don't need to be transferred from person to person: they can either be *represented* propositionally in language or "quined" (Dennett 1988) as nonexistent. The challenge I have offered to the RPOL here in this chapter requires that some sort of experiential "mind" or body-becoming-mind be communicable from person to person without the propositional label-based communication made possible by natural language. Exploring that possibility is the burden of chapter 4.

4 Qualia as Interpretants

Daniel Dennett (1988, 1991: 368–411) famously proposes that we "quine" (deny the existence of) qualia: to his mind they are mere fleeting figments or fictions that have no place in a properly *materialist* explanation of consciousness. This is a radical, some would say excessive, solution to what has been called the explanatory gap between materialism and qualia (Levine 1983) or the Hard Problem of Consciousness (Chalmers 1995/1997): simply deny the existence of the nonphysical phenomena that seem to pose the problem. I deal with that gap or Hard Problem in the appendix; for now, let us begin with the response Owen Flanagan (1992) offers to Dennett's proposal: "Those who would quine qualia are bothered by the fact that they seem mysterious—essentially private, ineffable, and not subject to third-person evaluation. Qualia are none of these things."

At first glance this response to Dennett is even more radical than Dennett's original proposal. Could qualia truly be *none* of these things? It is clear how "effable" qualia are; philosophers have been "effing" (namely, theorizing) them for a century and a half. But how are they neither private nor "not subject to third-person evaluation"? Flanagan's sentence that seems designed to provide an answer to my question reads "When a person says, 'I believe that snow is white,' there is almost never any doubt that she is in a state of belief rather than a state of desire" (ibid.: 67–68). Why, because she specifically *said* "I believe"? This is part of what Flanagan means—he later (ibid.: 70) discusses the detectability of qualia in other people through verbal reports—but he also suggests that "there really is a certain way it feels to be believing something, and that way of feeling is different from the way it feels to be desiring something" (ibid.: 68). I think that's true, but I submit that it's a rather problematic basis for the claim that qualia are "subject to third-person evaluation." Flanagan seems to be arguing, or at least implying, that [a] we recognize other people's qualitative states because [b] we experience those states ourselves and as a result

[c] recognize *classes* of qualia, like "beliefy feels" and "desirey feels"—but how does that work, exactly? The interpretive move from (b) to (a) there is iffy: What is it in or about other people that makes it possible for us reliably to recognize their qualitative states as part of specific classes of qualitative states that we ourselves have experienced?

Answering that question is in one sense the task of the book in its entirety. The tentative answer that I began developing in chapter 3, and will expand further in chapter 5, is that social animals possess an affective-becoming-conative channel of communication whose entelechy in humans does seem to reach its *telos* in the cognitive channels of natural language, but which doesn't always complete that entelechy even in humans (let alone in other animals). And I want to suggest here that the basic *unit* of that communication—let us say the basic unit of the full entelechy of affective-becoming-conative-becoming-cognitive communication—is the quale.

Of course, my suggestion in chapter 1 that we harbor qualia that seem (to us) to prove that our bodies and tools and workspaces contribute actively to cognition will almost certainly fail to constitute adequate proof of extension for materialists—even those materialists who hold back from the kind of radical denial of qualia that Dennett proposes. Even if a materialist reader of chapter 1 were willing to agree that mind is made up of qualia—that while neurons constitute the brain, qualia constitute the mind—that reader would still be likely to protest that in the mind's interactions with extracranial objects qualia have nowhere to go, and thus that mind-as-qualia does not (cannot) extend. If qualia are mental representations—and I think it should be relatively uncontroversial that they are—then all parties to the extended-mind debate might be said to agree, even to stipulate (see Clark 2008), that paper and pencil neither generate nor channel nor store qualia. At most they are a blank screen onto which we project qualia; the qualia that we thus project don't actually make the leap across space "into" them.

My brief in this chapter is that qualia *can* be shared—that Flanagan is right, and they are not the private figments they have often taken to be; that they can be communicated transcranially; and that, as we saw in chapter 2, they carry transcraniality with them. I propose to make that case here by a rather roundabout route, however, first (§4.1) tracing the history of the conceptualization of qualia; second (§4.2) exploring the strong parallels between Peirce's theorization of qualia and his theorization of the interpretant; third (§4.3) examining two other Peircean concepts that seem to cover something like the same conceptual ground as qualia and interpretants, tones and qualisigns; fourth (§4.4) considering the complementary possibilities that all qualia are or are not interpretants, and that all interpretants are or are not qualia; and fifth (§4.5) speculating that, to the extent that qualia are not only interpretants but *shared* interpretants, they collectively organize mind into a conative force that serves as our primary channel of social regulation.

4.1 Peirce on qualia

One quale, two or more qualia: this philosophical term, originally derived from a Latin word meaning "what sort," describes mental events, states, or experiences that have a certain "quality" or "qualitative feel" to them. The way a quale is usually defined, there is *something it is like* to have one (Nagel 1974: 437). Qualia collectively, moment by moment, constitute my feeling that I am alive, and that I am the person who bears my name and lives at my address. The "narrative" (first-person, coherently sequenced) experience of being or having a self is often attributed to the feeling that all the qualia that pass through my consciousness or awareness are *my* qualia. Obviously the ability to generate such a sense of self depends heavily not just on the ability to build one's qualia into a coherent story but also on some rough memory of the qualia that have gone before. Psychological disorders like depersonalization are sometimes described as a breakdown in the organization of qualitative experience around a first-person perspective, in the production out of the steady flow of qualia of a feeling of being a coherent self: the depersonalized sufferer doesn't feel like a person, doesn't feel alive, or feels trapped in some other person's life. Qualia are sometimes adduced as what differentiates us from computers (or zombies), which, the argument goes, may simulate human cognitive and even affective life uncannily, but don't *feel* alive, or anything else.

Philosophical theories of the quale are often traced to C. I. Lewis (1929), but while the two histories of the concept of the quale that we have, Crane 2000 and Keeley 2009, disagree on many things, they agree in tracing the philosophical history of the quale back to the work of Charles Sanders Peirce. Crane insists that Peirce first theorized the quale in 1866 in a set of notes entitled "Quale-consciousness"; as Keeley notes, however, the editors of volume 6 of the *Collected Papers* (Peirce 1931–1958) somewhat circuitously date those notes to 1898,[1] and the 1866 text in which Peirce first mentioned qualia was lecture IX of his Lowell Lectures on "The Logic of Science; or, Induction and Hypothesis." Noting that Peirce's use of the term in 1866 is entirely congruent with its rather casual appearances in two contemporary translations from ancient Greek (Thomas Taylor's 1812 commentary on Aristotle's *Categories* and Benjamin Jowett's 1875 *Meno*), Keeley (ibid.: 78) suggests that this is an indication that "'*quale*,' while a foreign term—it is often italicized—was nonetheless in common use in the English-speaking intellectual world." Keeley (ibid.: 77) also notes that "what we have in all of these early appearances of the term is a sense that fits the *OED* definition: 'The quality of a thing; a thing having certain qualities,' perhaps with an emphasis on the second part of this definition."

As I say, however, Crane and Keeley agree that the modern technical sense of the term arises out of an intellectual-historical trajectory from Peirce to Lewis. Both Crane and Keeley also note that Peirce's ideas were transmitted to Lewis through William James and Josiah Royce, two of Lewis' professors at Harvard, who were both heavily influenced by Peirce.[2] James published two articles on "spatial qualia" (1879a, 1879b) only thirteen years after Peirce's 1866 Lowell Lectures, and incorporated much of that work into chapter 20 of his *Principles* (1890/1950: 2.154): "No single *quale* of sensation can, by itself, amount to a consciousness of *position*." Royce (1898/2005), while not referring to qualia by that name, built his theory of community around the idea of social communication among entities (human and nonhuman, animate and nonanimate) who share the same apperceptive span (see Peltz 2007), a conception that seems to point to the possibility of shared qualia.[3] In addition, Keeley traces an explosion of philosophical and scientific quale theories in the decades following Peirce's 1866 Lowell Lectures, various scholars identifying as qualia [a] our feelings of pleasure (approbation) and pain (disapprobation) (Ward 1883; Stout 1888; Whittaker 1890; Stanley 1892; Nichols 1892); [b] our experience of space, including the two early papers on "spatial qualia" by William James (1879a, 1879b) and the "Perception of space" chapter in James (1890/1950) mentioned above (see also James 1887a, 1887b); [c] the phenomenality of emotion (Irons 1897a, 1897b; Rogers 1904); and [d] the experience of effort (Dewey 1897). In this history, clearly, James and Royce were only the Harvard scholars whose Peirce-influenced thinking about qualia had the greatest impact on C. I. Lewis.

The primary burden of Peirce's 1898 lecture notes is that the qualeconsciousness of his title is "entirely simple," because it has "but one quality, but one element" (1934–1958: 6.231); that it is "all that it is in and for itself" (ibid.); that "the Now is one, and but one" (ibid.); that "it is essentially solitary and celibate, a dweller in the desert" (ibid.: 6.234); and also, strikingly, that it follows from this unity principle "that there is no check upon the utmost variety and diversity of *quale*-consciousness as it appears to the comparing intellect" (ibid.: 6.236), so that quale-consciousness is "a chaos of fortuitously wandering atoms" (ibid.: 6.237). It is, Peirce insists, precisely because each quale is a perfect simple unity that this chaos prevails (ibid.: 6.235). "Whatever is absolutely simple must be absolutely free; for a law over it must apply to some common feature of it. And if it has no features, no law can seize upon it" (ibid.: 6.236). "This is the logic," he concludes, "by which the unity of *quale*-consciousness, implying simplicity, and through simplicity, freedom, necessarily results in endless multiplicity and variety. All that is a perfectly ostensive result of logic and involves no paradox whatsoever. . . ." (ibid.: 6.237; ellipsis Peirce's).

The reason Peirce's claims seem paradoxical, obviously, is that what he means by quale-consciousness is simultaneously *the quale that is now* (which is all that any quale ever is, he insists, and all that quale-consciousness ever is at any given moment) and the infinite variety of such now-qualia as they appear to "the comparing consciousness" or "the comparing intellect," which he defines as a kind of metaquale: "All the operations of the intellect consist in taking composite photographs of *quale*-consciousnesses. Instead of introducing any unity, they only introduce conflict that was not in the *quale*-consciousness itself" (ibid.: 6.233). Insofar as Peirce's notes are themselves an operation of the intellect that seeks to introduce the *idea* of quale-consciousness as unity, this is somewhat problematic; presumably he means that any individual's intellectual metaquale perceives in her or his own occurrent quale-consciousness only conflict, not unity, and that his own summative philosophical remarks therefore constitute a kind of intellectual metametaquale that restores to quale-consciousness the unity of which the comparing intellect's original occurrent metaquale deprived it.

The pure singularity of quale-consciousness, Peirce notes, entails that it can never be double: "If *quale*-consciousness were double, it would be like a case of double consciousness. One might pronounce the object to be blue that the other said was not blue and the principle of contradiction would only assert that one judge must be set above these two. But where would be the strife requiring a judge if the *quale*-consciousness were double?" (ibid.: 6.232). One is tempted to protest that a *logical* constraint like "the principle of contradiction" hardly seems applicable to human consciousness,[4] or to offer as a counterexample a split-brain patient reaching two hands into the closet and bringing out one whole separate outfit for the day in each hand—but of course it remains open to question whether this individual has one separate and simultaneous quale-consciousness for each hand's (and brain hemisphere's) sartorial choice, and thus whether his or her quale-consciousness is double. It may well be that the split-brain patient's mind generates a single dominant quale-consciousness, associated with just one hand's choice, and is utterly surprised (a new *sequential* quale rather than a simultaneous one) to find that the other hand holds a separate and apparently "qualitatively" unplanned outfit.[5]

I have, however, begun summarizing Peirce's argument in the middle. He begins, in an argumentative move that has since become *de rigeur*, with color qualia, and specifically with a certain kind of color-blindness, and then adds: "The *quale*-consciousness is not confined to simple sensations. There is a peculiar *quale* to *purple*, though it be only a mixture of red and blue. There is a distinctive *quale* to every combination of sensations so far as it is really synthesized—a distinctive quale to every work of art—a distinctive *quale* to this moment as it is to me—a peculiar *quale* to every day and every week—a peculiar *quale* to my whole personal consciousness. I appeal to your introspection to bear me out" (ibid.: 6.223).

Flanagan (1992: 64) takes issue with Peirce's notion that there is "a peculiar *quale* to every day and every week," noting that the "summary judgments about what a day or a week has been like and how it has gone for us" are almost certainly not qualia. Peirce (1934–1958: 6.228) himself notes that qualia "*are* united so far as they are brought into one *quale*-consciousness at all; and that is why different personalities are formed. Of course, each personality is based upon a 'bundle of habits,' as the saying is that a man is a bundle of habits. But a bundle of habits would not have the unity of self-consciousness. That *unity* must be given as a centre for the habits."

Flanagan's (1992: 64) point of agreement with Peirce that I want to highlight, however, is this: "Like Peirce, I see no principled reason for restricting the concept of qualia to the feels of sensations. 'Qualia' picks out the types of qualitative experience. Not all qualia are sensational. Conscious moods, emotions, beliefs, desires, possibly even what it is like to be me have distinct qualitative character." This is the notion that Strawson takes up in arguing for what he calls "the experience of thinking" or "understanding-experience": "When people today talk of experience, of experiential qualitative content, EQ content for short, they standardly have in mind only things like sensations and sensory images, emotional feelings, and moods considered (so far as they can be) just in respect of their noncognitive felt character. . . . This is unfortunate, because there is also EQ content that is not sensory-affective content. There is *cognitive EQ content*, or *cognitive experience*, as I will call it," which "saturates everything—swimming and digging as much as philosophizing" (1994: 339–340). Strawson proposes, however, to "limit my attention to the cognitive experience involved in comprehendingly entertaining propositions in reading, writing, listening, or thinking" (ibid.: 340).

I find Strawson's account persuasive, and have adopted his expansion of Peirce's model in this book. I do, however, have one small concern: Strawson draws a distinction between cognitive EQ content and sensory-affective EQ content, presumably in virtue of the intuitive fact that experiencing thinking is qualitatively different from sensing pain or seeing a sunset or feeling an emotion. This formulation may give the (I think erroneous) impression that Strawson is dualizing qualia along roughly Cartesian mind-body lines, into the "bodily" realm of sensory-affective EQ content and the "mental" realm of cognitive EQ content. The fact that what he calls cognitive EQ content saturates "swimming and digging as much as philosophizing" suggests instead that the specifically cognitive qualia he is theorizing are in no way isolated from bodily experience. Rather, in apparently distinguishing cognitive EQ content from sensory-affective EQ content he is actually *adding* the former to the latter, integrating or incorporating cognitive qualia into the processing realm previously thought to involve sensory and affective qualia alone.

What Strawson seems to be arguing, in fact, is that cognitive qualia are, to use Peirce's vocabulary, cognitive photographs of cognitive events—and, similarly, that sensory qualia are sensory photographs of sensory events, and affective qualia are affective photographs of affective events. In a sense the notion that cognitive qualia are photographs of cognitive events reverses Peirce, for whom cognition essentially consists of taking photographs of qualia; but then it seems to me that the two-stage models both Peirce and Strawson employ are simplistic. After all, isn't *every* mental photograph arguably a new quale? If so, then the cognitive event that per Peirce is a photograph of a quale is a quale of a quale; and the cognitive quale that per Strawson is a photograph of a cognitive event, which is in turn (grandfathering Peirce back in) a photograph of a quale, is a quale of a quale of a quale. My introspection at least suggests that we can *sense* a pain (have a pain-quale), *feel* ourselves sensing that pain-quale, *think* about the feeling of sensing the pain-quale, and *feel* ourselves thinking about the feeling of sensing the pain-quale. Isn't there in fact something that it is like to have a sensation of pain? This would in a sense be a metaquale of pain; but it would seem to me difficult to deny that it is also another quale. Noticing the metaquale of pain would be a metametaquale of pain, whether internally verbalized or not, and therefore whether one wanted to consider it "thinking" or not; but again there is something that it is like to have a metaquale of pain, making the metametaquale of noticing it yet another quale. And one can notice oneself noticing the metaquale of pain, and so on. Even without conscious *attention* to this qualitative "noticing," and thus without awareness in the fully directed sense, there is a *feeling* of thinking as there is a feeling of emoting or sensing.

And this would be my second point: "feeling" in the Jamesian tradition (richly fed, as we shall see, by Peirce) is not restricted to wallowing in emotion, but rather is precisely the kind of experiential qualitative content that Strawson is working to theorize.[6] We can feel pain, and we can feel ourselves feeling the pain, and when we *think* about the feeling of feeling the pain, there is a feeling-like experiential quality to our thinking as well. We can feel hungry, and feel a desire to find some food, and feel irritation that there's nothing in the fridge or the cupboards that we want to eat, and feel an inclination to jump in the car and drive to the store to buy a snack, then feel a concern that the long-awaited cable guy might come while we're gone.

Finally, if all of these qualia are alike *feelings*, we should bear in mind that any hierarchical talk of qualia, metaqualia, and metametaqualia is merely an explanatory model imposed on qualia after the qualitative fact by the "comparing intellect"—and not, say, an accurate representation of some layered qualitative structure. As they are experienced in occurrent consciousness, all qualia are just qualia.

4.2 Peirce on interpretants

To my knowledge, Peirce himself never drew a connection between qualia and interpretants; what I want to offer here, therefore, is not so much a genetic argument as it is a speculative exploration of perceived similarities.

Still, as Keeley (2009: 79) notes, "the Quale is a foundational concept in Peirce's categories"—something that is easily missed, given the little he wrote about it. Keeley's (ibid.: 87n13) tentative suggestion is that the quale is at the heart of Peirce's understanding of Firstness; and indeed there is a telling moment in Peirce's 1898 lecture notes on quale-consciousness, seemingly presenting the quale as a feeling-based First, that clearly anticipates his theorization of the interpretant nine years later, in 1907, suggesting that he was already beginning to move, in his ruminations on quale-consciousness, toward his mature (post-1906) formulation of the interpretant.[7] (See table 4.1.)

Table 4.1

[1898]	[1907]
I say then that this unity [of quale-consciousness] is logical in this sense, that to feel, to be immediately conscious, so far as possible, without any action and reaction nor any reflection, logically supposes one consciousness and not two nor more. (Peirce 1931–1958: 6.230)[8]	In all cases it includes feelings; for there must, at least, be a sense of comprehending the meaning of the sign. If it includes more than mere feeling, it must evoke some kind of effort. It may include something besides, which, for the present, may be vaguely called 'thought'. I term these three kinds of interpretants the 'emotional', the 'energetic', and the 'logical' interpretants. (Peirce 1998: 409)

The congruence between these two triads amounts to a great deal more than the kind of structural isomorphism one expects from Peirce's three Universes, the First as "immediate" abstract potential as thesis, the Second as "dynamic" unpredictable real-world interactions as antithesis, the Third as a "final" synthesis of the two. The two triads are in fact virtually identical: in each, the First is feeling, the Second is effort or action (and reaction), and the Third is reflection or thought. (Note also, in the interpretant quotation from 1907, the "sense of comprehending the meaning of the sign": this I take to be precisely Strawson's (1994) understanding-experience, a quale of comprehension.) The difference between the two triads, obviously, is that Peirce associates the interpretant with the full triad and the quale only with the First of "feeling" or "immediate consciousness," "without any action and reaction nor any reflection."

Here is a fuller 1907 formulation of the emotional, energetic, and logical interpretants:

The first proper significate effect of a sign is a feeling produced by it. There is almost always a feeling which we come to interpret as evidence that we comprehend the proper effect of the sign, although the foundation of truth in this is frequently very slight. This "emotional interpretant," as I call it, may amount to much more than that feeling of recognition; and in some cases, it is the only proper significate effect that the sign produces. Thus, the performance of a piece of concerted music is a sign. It conveys, and is intended to convey, the composer's musical ideas; but these usually consist merely of a series of feelings. If a sign produces any further proper significate effect, it will do so through the mediation of the emotional interpretant, and such further effect will always involve an effort. I call it the energetic interpretant. The effort may be a muscular one, as it is in the case of the command to ground arms; but it is much more usually an exertion upon the Inner World, a mental effort.

It never can be the meaning of an intellectual concept, since it is a single act, [while] such a concept is of a general nature. But what further kind of effect can there be?

In advance of ascertaining the nature of this effect, it will be convenient to adopt a designation for it, and I will call it the *logical interpretant*, without as yet determining whether this term shall extend to anything beside the meaning of a general concept, though certainly closely related to that, or not. Shall we say that this effect may be a thought, that is to say, a mental sign? No doubt, it may be so; only, if this sign be of an intellectual kind—as it would have to be—it must itself have a logical interpretant; so that it cannot be the *ultimate* logical interpretant of the concept. It can be proved that the only mental effect that can be so produced and that is not a sign but is of a general application is a *habit-change*; meaning by a habit-change a modification of a person's tendencies toward action, resulting from previous experiences or from previous exertions of his will or acts, or from a complexus of both kinds of cause. It excludes natural dispositions, as the term "habit" does, when it is accurately used; but it includes beside associations, what may be called "transsociations," or alterations of association, and even includes *dissociation*, which has usually been looked upon by psychologists (I believe mistakenly), as of deeply contrary nature to association. (Peirce 1931–1958: 5.475–476)

The first thing to note here is that Peirce's wording ("This 'emotional interpretant,' as I call it, may amount to much more than that feeling of recognition; and in some cases, it is the only proper significate effect that the sign produces") suggests that he may have inadvertently left out a "not"—that is, that he may have meant "may *not* amount to much more than that feeling of recognition" or "may amount to *not* much more than that feeling of recognition." Not only is the standard collocation of "amount to much more" "*doesn't* amount to much more"; following that phrase up with "and in some cases, it is the *only* proper significate effect that the sign produces" implies an idiomatic movement from "*little* more" to "indeed *nothing* more." The putative move from "*much* more" (what, exactly?) to "indeed nothing more" would seem unidiomatic and anti-conventional enough to be virtually incoherent.

In any case, I submit that what Peirce is suggesting here is that the emotional interpretant is for all practical purposes *just* "that feeling of recognition," just the "sense of comprehending the meaning of the sign," or what Strawson might call a recognition-experience. The only real difference between this theorization of the emotional interpretant and his earlier theorization of the quale is that the latter is grammatically intransitive, lacking an object: to experience a quale is "to feel, to be immediately conscious," while the emotional interpretant is a transitive feeling, a feeling *of* something. But of course Peirce recognizes that qualia are experiences of things as well, stating outright that they are experiences of colors and other sensory objects and suggesting more vaguely that they are also experiences of an unspecified class of nonsensory objects—including, as later exfoliators of his ideas will insist, affective events (Flanagan) and cognitive events (Strawson).

The emotional interpretant as a feeling of recognition directed at affective events seems to be what Peirce is hinting at in his suggestion that "the performance of a piece of concerted music is a sign. It conveys, and is intended to convey, the composer's musical ideas; but these usually consist merely of a series of feelings." If we take this literally, the music is *merely* a vehicle by which the composer's feelings are made available to the audience, who, in Tolstoy's (1898/1932) famous trope, are "infected" with them (see chapters 1 and 2 of Robinson 2008 for discussion); the concertgoer's emotional interpretant would thus be not much more than the feeling of being infected by the composer's affect, and the concertgoer's interpretation of the music would be not much more than that emotional interpretant.

But this is, of course, a fairly simplistic conception of music, or of what it is like to listen to music. The most generous construction of Peirce's characterization would be that he actually means not that "the composer's musical ideas . . . usually consist merely of a series of feelings," but rather that this is all the emotional interpretant hears in music: its affective tonality, "happy" or "sad" or "lively" or whatever. Lerdahl and Jackendoff (1996: 3) imagine an ideal construct called "the inexperienced listener" with something like the Firstness or immediacy of perception that might lead him or her to construct the *music itself* as little more than a series of feelings: "A listener without sufficient exposure to an idiom will not be able to organize in any rich way the sounds he perceives." "However," they add, "once he becomes familiar with the idiom, the kind of organization that he attributes to a given piece will not be arbitrary but will be highly constrained in specific ways." Becoming familiar with the idiom ultimately transforms this inexperienced listener into an experienced one:

We will now elaborate the notion of "the musical intuitions of the experienced listener." By this we mean not just his conscious grasp of musical structure; an acculturated listener need never have studied music. Rather we are referring to the largely unconscious knowledge (the "musical intuition") that the listener brings to his hearing—a knowledge that enables him to organize and make coherent the surface patterns of pitch, attack, duration, intensity, timbre, and so forth. Such a listener is able to identify a previously unknown piece as an example of the idiom, to recognize elements of a piece as typical or anomalous, to identify a performer's error as possibly producing an "ungrammatical" configuration, to recognize various kinds of structural repetitions and variations, and, generally, to comprehend a piece within the idiom. (ibid.)

And they add a Peircean teleological touch: "It is useful to make a second idealization about the listener's intuition. Instead of describing the listener's real-time mental processes, we will be concerned only with the final state of his understanding" (ibid.: 3–4). In other words, there may be inexperienced listeners who, guided by the emotional interpretant alone, hear music purely as a series of feelings, but even they will *tend* to move toward greater musical experience, bringing the energetic and possibly even the logical interpretant into play.[9]

And as soon as we imagine the concertgoer as what Lerdahl and Jackendoff call a "sophisticated listener"—a reviewer, a musicologist, a music theorist—things become more complicated still. Now those structural and performative elements that the logical interpretant was able to "organize and make coherent" for the experienced listener—melodies, harmonies, tonalities; prosodic features such as timbre, pitch, duration, intensity; performative qualities such as timing and attack; for the music theorist, ecstatic math—are habitualized by the logical interpretant and then registered by the emotional interpretant, which is the sophisticated listener's only indication that the logical interpretant has been at work on the music. The sophisticated listener doesn't need conscious awareness of the full interpretant triad to construct this particular performance in terms of these qualities, because extended exposure and study have habitualized the affective, kinesthetic-becoming-conative, and cognitive processing of structure and performativity down into preconscious processing that is merely "qualed" by the emotional interpretant—the feeling the sophisticated listener has of recognition and comprehension, or what Strawson would call understanding-experience. A sophisticated listener writing a review of this particular performance, or even just discussing it with friends over drinks after the concert, may have to remobilize this or that interpretant, or even the full triad, in order to facilitate analysis of this or that surprising element (deviation from habitualized expectations), but vast tracts of the work done in the experienced listener by the logical·interpretant come to the sophisticated listener's occurrent cognitive consciousness preprocessed.

Peirce is vague on the energetic interpretant; in the case of the concertgoer we can imagine as examples the tapping foot or finger and nodding head that beat time and so channel a kinesthetic feel for the music. Think of how we often determine the meter of a line of poetry: we may at First vaguely *feel* that it is a familiar verse form (the emotional interpretant for Peirce not yet entailing the inner or outer voicing of a verbal label like "iambic pentameter"), but to give our vague feeling specificity we may Secondarily bang it out, nodding our head and tapping a foot as we chant the line with exaggerated stress, or perhaps tapping a finger on each printed syllable as we chant *duh-DA duh-DA duh-DA duh-DA duh-DA*. That would be what Peirce calls a "muscular" enactment of the energetic interpretant; but he also means by that Second the kind of mental effort that we might describe, using Strawson's terms, as the experience of *trying* to understand. The experienced listener of classical (tonal) music at a concert of atonal music may experience the effort to follow along comprehendingly as an energetic interpretant; Peirce's suggestion that the concertgoer might ride along on the comforting affective states detected by the emotional interpretant might be more accurate of the marginally experienced listener at a performance of some familiar classical favorite, like Vivaldi's *Four Seasons* or Beethoven's *Pastoral Symphony*.

Hearing or reading a poem, one may first *feel* that it is a familiar verse form (emotional interpretant), tap one's finger on the syllables of a single line while voicing the words with exaggerated stress (energetic interpretant), and then say "iambic pentameter" (logical interpretant); but, as Peirce suggests, that process can also be habitualized, so that, as I noted above, one simply has a quale registering the logical interpretant's conclusion. Habit, Peirce notes, is the "essence of the logical interpretant" (1931–1958: 5.486). What Peirce calls the "sense of comprehending the meaning of the sign" would be the quale as emotional interpretant registering the habitualized logical interpretant—something Peirce doesn't quite theorize here. Wittgenstein (1953, paragraph 151) has a discussion of the feeling of "now I can go on" that can be adduced to push Peirce's formulation two steps further:

Or he watches and says "Yes, I know *that* series"—and continues it, just as he would have done if A had written down the series 1, 3, 5, 7, 9.—Or he says nothing at all and simply continues the series. Perhaps he had what may be called the sensation [*Empfindung*, which can also be translated 'feeling'] 'that's easy!'. (Such a sensation is, for example, that of a light quick intake of breath, as when one is slightly startled.)

Arguably there the three alternatives Wittgenstein considers would correspond to the three steps of Peirce's mature interpretant triad, but each alternative would be a matter of registering the action of an habitualized logical interpretant: "the sensation 'that's easy'" an emotional interpretant, saying nothing and simply continuing the series (on paper?) an energetic interpretant, and saying "Yes, I know *that* series" a new logical interpretant registering the old logical interpretant.

4.3 Peirce's tones and qualisigns as qualia

Peirce also has two triads for types of sign that seem to incorporate or explain qualia without specifically mentioning them: the tone-token-type triad and the qualisign-sinsign-legisign triad. Unsurprisingly, perhaps, in view of Keeley's suggestion that the quale for Peirce *is* Firstness, in each of these two triads the First (tone or qualisign) is something like a quale—though it is not absolutely clear that a tone or a qualisign is a quale, or even that a tone is a First. In "Prolegomena to an apology for pragmaticism" from 1906, Peirce writes:

> A common mode of estimating the amount of matter in a MS. or printed book is to count the number of words. There will ordinarily be about twenty *the*'s on a page, and of course they will count as twenty words. In another sense of the word "word," however, there is but one word "the" in the English language; and it is impossible that this word should lie visibly on a page or be heard in any voice, for the reason that it is not a Single thing or Single event. It does not exist; it only determines things that do exist. Such a definitely significant Form, I propose to term a *Type*. A Single event which happens once and whose identity is limited to that one happening or a Single object or thing which is in some single place at any one instant of time, such event or thing being significant only as occurring just when and where it does, such as this or that word on a single line of a single page of a single copy of a book, I will venture to call a *Token*. An indefinite significant character such as a tone of voice can neither be called a Type nor a Token. I propose to call such a Sign a *Tone*. (1931–1958: 4.537)

While Peirce doesn't specifically assign tones, tokens, and types to his three Universes, it is reasonably clear in that passage that a tone must be a First, a token must be a Second, and a type must be a Third; and the editors of the *Collected Papers* (ibid.: 4.537n‡) note that "the type, token and tone are the legisigns, sinsigns and qualisigns discussed in 2.243f and form division (1) in the note to 536," which does make the association of tone with Firstness, token with Secondness, and type with Thirdness clear.

Perhaps because of the relatively short shrift Peirce gives it, tone has tended to drop out of the tone-token-type triad, which tends to be referred to by philosophers as the type-token distinction.[10] The bare-bones description "an indefinite significant character such as a tone of voice"—even if we gloss "character" with the more technical term "quality"[11]—gives us far less to work with than Peirce's 1898 discussion of qualia, let alone his repeated and extensive discussions of interpretants.

But there may be other reasons as well for the neglect Peircean tone has received at the hands of philosophers. We may speculate, for example, that it may have been difficult for Peirce himself, as it was for later scholars, to distinguish tone or tonality as a specific *quality* of the sign, or as the sign in its qualitative Firstness—as a qualisign—from the interpretants that construct a certain "indefinite . . . character" as "significant." Imagine a conversational exchange in which you say "So, are you going?" and I say "Um . . . what did that tone signify?" You may well deny having tonalized your words in any kind of significant way: "I just said, 'So, are you going?'," tonalizing "just said" pointedly to signify something like "I intended to convey only the locutionary meanings of those words, you idiot." How then do we analyze your tone of voice as semantically and pragmatically significant? Traditionally there have been four explanatory scenarios:

[1] You're dissembling. You know you tonalized the words in a way that you suspected I wouldn't like, and now are simply covering your tracks.
[2] Your words were significantly tonalized by some preconscious affective self in you (Dennett 1991 would call it a "demon"). You weren't aware of having done so, but with a little guided introspection you can come to recognize that the source of the tonalization was indeed inside your head (or body).
[3] You really didn't tonalize the words in any kind of tendentious way. The tone that I think I hear in your voice is something that I brought to the conversation myself: I infused my interpretation of your utterance with my own affect.
[4] I'm dissembling. There never was the tone I claim to have heard; I am deliberately pretending to have heard something that wasn't there.

In (1) and (2) tone is a sign, your qualisign; in (3), and possibly (4), tone is an interpretant, or an artifact of my (emotional) interpretant. Another way of putting that would be to say that in (1) and (2) tone is a quality of the message as *sent* (intended); in (3) a tone is a quality of the message as *received* (interpreted). Or again: tone for you in (1) and (2) is outgoing or expressive quality; tone for me in (3) is incoming or perceptual quality.

And if it were easier to distinguish intended/expressive/outgoing quality from interpreted/perceptual/incoming quality, we might be able to say with some certainty that tone in (1) and (2) is a quality of the sign and tone in (3) is a quality of the interpretant. That might further allow us to equate or associate tone-as-interpretant with the quale and distinguish both from tone-as-qualisign.

The problem is that both tonalizations and tone-interpretations tend to occur below our conscious awareness, in the realm of affect, which makes adjudication between outgoing and incoming tonalities difficult, and more a matter of negotiation, even persuasion—which is basically what (2) and (3) are about—than one of objective recognition of the truth.

After all, consider what typically happens when we get into a you-say/I-say disagreement with a significant other over tone—I say it's (1), you say it's (4). We talk and talk, defensively and/or aggressively, each of us trying to persuade the other, until we realize that the argument is fruitless or one of us gives in. If you give in, our mutual conclusion may be the glorious triumph (for me) and humiliating defeat (for you) of (1); if I give in, it may be the glorious triumph (for you) and humiliating defeat (for me) of (4). But it may also, more conciliatorily, be (2)—you weren't aware of tonalizing the utterance as I claim you did, but you did anyway—or (3)—I wasn't aware of projecting my own affect onto your utterance as tone, but I did anyway. In either of those cases, the "truth" is not so much an objective fact simply registered by the "guilty" party as it is a joint rhetorical construct, a persuasive image of the truth that is insistently offered by one of us and finally accepted/adopted as valid by the other. We collaborate on the "unearthing" of the "truth." It is a *negotiated* truth—truth by consensus; truth by committee.

And in practice that ultimately means that your tone-as-qualisign in (2) is saturated with my emotional-energetic-logical interpretant triad, and my tone-as-interpretant in (3) is saturated with your qualisign-sinsign-legisign triad. I *feel* that I'm right about your tonalization (emotional interpretant), and so put considerable effort (energetic interpretant) into finding just the right arguments (logical interpretant) to convince you; when I succeed, you accept (take over) my interpretants as your sign. Because my interpretants, put into embodied (emotionally and energetically charged) words, become signs for *you* to interpret, there is already a mutual interflowing of signs and interpretants even before you agree; your agreement simply allows one set of signs-becoming-interpretants or interpretants-becoming-signs to be collectively pronounced the "truth." In the numbered section of "Prolegomena to an apology for pragmaticism" immediately preceding his theorization of the tone-token-type triad, after all, Peirce (1931–1958: 4.536) himself defines the interpretant as "that which the Sign produces in the Quasi-mind that is the Interpreter by determining the latter to a feeling, to an exertion, or to a Sign, which determination is the Interpretant," suggesting not only that the sign works in the interpreter *in the capacity of* the interpretant but that you and I are quasi-minds through which signs travel en route to becoming interpretants and through which interpretants travel en route to becoming signs. Signs produce interpretants that tend teleologically to "determine" the quasimind that is the interpreter to a logical interpretant as a new sign.

Hence, I'm suggesting, the difficulty Peirce had in theorizing tone as a quality of the sign *apart* from the action of various interpretants. Signs and their interpretants are not so much object and subject—members of radically different ontological categories—as they are a *reticulation*, transient and interchangeable values distributed or dissipated through a communicative economy.

4.4 Qualia as interpretants

What are we to make, then, of the manifest parallels between Peirce's theorizations of qualia and interpretants? Are all interpretants qualia? Are all qualia interpretants? Do interpretants inevitably have the phenomenality that we associate with qualia? Are qualia inevitably involved integrally with interpretation?

The first issue that must be settled arises out of the fact that Peirce explicitly associates quale-consciousness with feelings (or immediate consciousness) "without any action and reaction nor any reflection," which would tend to suggest that a quale, if it is an interpretant at all, can only ever be an emotional interpretant. But then the early work done by Dewey (1897) and others on qualia in terms of "the phenomenal feeling of effort one experiences while trying to concentrate on a symphony or trying to solve a math problem (known as 'moral' effort) or in trying to hold one's hand in a flame ('muscular' effort)" (Keeley 2009: 85) would seem to militate against this sort of restriction of qualia to emotional interpretants. The qualia of moral and muscular effort are strongly reminiscent of the energetic interpretant. And what the late nineteenth century called "moral" effort further anticipates Strawson's notion of cognitive experience strongly enough to warrant exploration of linkages between qualia and logical interpretants as well.

And certainly my remarks in §4.1 on metaqualia and metametaqualia should suggest that something like the triadic (affective > conative > cognitive) stair-stepping of interpretants may well be at work in qualia as well. If we imagine a recovering alcoholic walking down the street and noticing that he is approaching the door to a familiar bar, and First [emotional interpretant] feeling awash in pleasant memories of drinking with buddies in that bar, then Second [energetic interpretant] setting up an inward mental resistance to those memories, and finally Third [logical interpretant] walking determinedly on past the door, perhaps muttering "I *won't* take a drink today," it would be difficult not to call *all* of those interpretants qualia. The main difference between a qualia-based reading and an interpretant-based reading of that scene, in fact, would lie in whether the front door to the bar is taken as an *experience* (the door as a kinesthetic pathway that you traverse in order to have a few drinks with friends) or as a *sign* of that experience—and in Peircean terms that is a difference without a difference. To the extent that the experience is organized as meaningful, it *is* (being taken as) a sign.

The second important issue is: would this association of qualia with interpretants work with all qualia? Or would it be pushing the parallels too far to say that all qualia are in fact interpretants? Possibly the latter. Qualia may or may not all be *representations*; even those who agree that they are may not be willing to think of them as *interpretive* representations. There are, I think, at least three possibilities here:

[1] All qualia are interpretants. Even "outgoing" qualia attached to expressive events guide interpretation, and so qualify as interpretants. (Though in Robinson 2003 I rename interpretants that are attached to expressive events and so designed to guide interpretation in the audience "intendants.")
[2] Only those qualia attached to sensory or conceptual signs (thoughts, concepts, percepts, ideas, impressions, words, rules, schemas, images, memories, phantasms, dreams, etc.) with semantic properties requiring interpretation (content, reference, truth conditions, truth value, etc.) qualify as interpretants.
[3] No qualia are interpretants. Interpretants are conceptual representations that lack phenomenality; qualia are experiential phenomena that lack conceptuality.

Of these, (3) seems an extreme position likely to win the support only of those inclined to treat qualia as harmless but vaguely mystical figments that do no cognitive work, and that can therefore be either dismissed as nonexistent or discounted as evanescent mental will-o'-the-wisps not worthy of philosophical scrutiny. Daniel Dennett (1988, 1991), obviously, is a likely candidate here. But in view of Boghossian's rigid and apparently influential division of representations into the conceptual and the phenomenal ("Mental states appear to come in two *distinct* kinds" (1995: 94, emphasis added)), it may be that this option only seems extreme to a phenomenalist interested in the overlap between those binary poles.

Perhaps the strict reductive representationalist will gravitate to (2), which reflects a certain lingering suspicion toward qualia that are not *transparently* (Tye 2000: 45–51; see also Dretske 1993, Harman 1990, Lycan 1996, and Tye 1996) representational, i.e., not defined in terms of their accuracy or inaccuracy in revealing the veridical truth about their objects, and so not easily reducible to intentional content. To the extent that [2a] the interpretant can be construed as guaranteeing transparency and thus reducibility, equating some qualia with interpretants and dismissing all others might be accepted as a reasonable paraphrase of the reductive representationalist position. To the extent that [2b] the interpretant is construed as introducing interpretive uncertainty into the process and thus problematizing reduction, on the other hand, interpretants as a target model for the theorization of qualia could well be ruled irrelevant to the discussion, leaving (3) as the reductive representationalist's only option.

The phenomenalist will gravitate toward (1), but may do so with some trepidation, inasmuch as that sweeping claim seems to reduce the multifarious forms what-it's-likeness can take in qualia to a single explanatory or interpretive relationality that feels suspiciously akin to (2a) reductive representationalism. Even insisting on (2b) the interpretant as a channel of interpretive indeterminacy might not mollify this complainant, as even indeterminate interpretation seems too confining a straitjacket for qualia.

But think of a sensation of pain. Strawson (1994: 177) says of the widespread notion that intentionality is "the fundamental mark of the mental" that "sensations are among the clearest examples of mental phenomena, and they are not necessarily about anything at all. Sensations of pain, for example, are not about anything in the relevant sense." If that is true, a sensation of pain is a quale but not an interpretant. To qualify as an interpretant, a quale must be an interpretive representation; if we deny sensation representationality right out of the gate, it doesn't stand a chance.

It seems tautological to say that sensations of pain are sensations *of pain*, and thus in the relevant sense *about* pain as well, because phenomenologically speaking the sensation *is* the pain. If we have a pain and take a painkiller that effectively kills the pain, we say that we have no pain; we don't say that we "have" a pain but can't "feel" it. A pain that we don't feel while the painkiller is working is like a belief "we" "have" while we're dreamlessly asleep (Strawson 1994: 167–168); in experiential actuality, which is the only actuality we know, it ceases to exist. If the pain returns once the pill wears off we may want to say that it continued to exist, "dormant," or was rendered temporarily potential rather than actual, while we weren't feeling it; but this would be a cognitive inference akin to the one that our brains use to generate the motion illusion—to process a series of static images so that they seem (phenomenologically) to be moving.[12]

But surely in the medical sense pain is also a symptom of some physiological cause, which it would thus be "about." (In the shamanistic sense it may be a symptom of some supernatural cause.) If you go to a doctor with a pain, s/he is almost certainly not going to assume from the start that the sensation of pain you describe is "not about anything"; that conclusion might occur to the doctor, but only as a last resort after s/he had run tests that ruled out every possible physiological cause. And even then s/he would be likely to take the "pain" you describe to be a symptom of something else, like hypochondria, or a desire for attention—and would continue to worry that there was something that s/he was overlooking, some rare medical condition that s/he simply hadn't thought to test for.

Or imagine that one day you notice a warmth in your left knee. You realize that you've been feeling it, or almost feeling it, for several days now. What is it? Is it a pain? Not really. So far it's just a warmth. But you know enough about physiology to know that a warmth in a joint is not an auspicious sign. You follow the sensation as it develops over the next day or two. By the third day it is definitely a pain, and you call the doctor. At every stage of this process your sensory quale is a representation of some X whose identity remains an enigma, and which, you assume, must eventually yield to accurate (successful) interpretation.

To put it in Peircean terms, a pain may lack symbolicity (representational conventionality) and iconicity (resemblance to its referent), but most of us would certainly assume it possesses indexicality—that it *indicates* some sort of physiological trauma or illness as its cause. Peirce thinks of the index as a "natural" sign; as we saw in §2.2, Jerry Fodor would call the relationship between the pain and its cause a natural "asymmetrical dependency." Pain also tends to be *locally* indexical: a warmth-becoming-pain in the knee tends to attract interpretive attention specifically to the knee.

But of course this reference to interpretive attention may lead some readers to invoke the distinction between the interpretandum-as-object and the interpretans-as-subject. It is possible that by "sensations of pain . . . are not about anything *in the relevant sense*" Strawson means that a sensation of pain is not itself an interpretant but a sign that *produces* an interpretant in "the Quasi-mind that is the interpreter by determining the latter to a feeling, to an exertion, or to a Sign." But as we saw in §4.3, splitting the sign-as-object off from the interpretant-as-subject is an extremely problematic undertaking; I suggested there that signs and their interpretants are not objects and the subjectivity brought to bear on those objects but rather "a *reticulation*, transient and interchangeable values distributed through a communicative economy." This would make the movement from [a] sensations as pre-indexical signs to [b] the interpretations of sensations that reframe them as indices-becoming-interpretants not (a >>> b) a two-step process but (a-becoming-b) an entelechy, a single "thing" in metamorphosis.

Nor, of course, does this discussion of the sensation of pain exhaust the list of qualia that might be proposed as non-interpretants—far from it.[13] Rather than attempt to exhaust that list, I propose to offer an axiom for consideration: *Interpretancy is a function of a persistent and socially organized human desire to make things make sense*. Every quale is potentially an interpretant, I want to suggest, not because it *is* one in its deepest ontological heart of hearts, but because as social animals humans are inveterate interpreters—because we are conditioned culturally to *impose* interpretancy on all experience, or as much of it as we are humanly able.

In light of the foregoing axiom, I would venture a correction of Strawson (1994: 181): "Intentionality is not a supernaturally unbreakable string that connects X's thought to S. It is just a matter of routine causation as it affects a certain sort of representational system." Actually, I submit, it is a matter not of causation but of *interpretation*, as human actors impose it on events within a certain sort of representational system. Intentionality is *ascribed* to events in that system, by the individuals and groups who care about it and its consequences. The emotional > energetic > logical or affective > conative > cognitive trajectory of Peirce's mature interpretant triad reflects the socially situated human interpreter's restless quest for understanding, for an embodied pathway through to the explanatory resting place ("finality") offered by thought. (Presumably Strawson's claim that a sensation of pain is not about anything in particular comes out of the tradition in the philosophy of mind that wants to treat aboutness as a *property* of a representation. A medical diagnosis that *imposes* aboutness on a sensation, via a verbal report or the results of testing, would thus not qualify as *recognizing* what the sensation is about. A corollary of my Peircean pragmaticist axiom that *interpretancy is a function of a persistent and socially organized human desire to make things make sense*, however, would be that *aboutness is a function of interpretancy*, rendering the medical diagnosis that imposes aboutness on a sensation of pain a typical instance of the interpretive orientation that generates all aboutness.)

Another consideration for the phenomenalist who is a bit sourly contemplating the prospect of "reducing" qualia to interpretants: the (2a) reductive transparency of the quale-as-interpretant that I imagined as marginally acceptable to the strict representationalist would in Peirce's terms only be entailed by the *logical* interpretant (and then only potentially).

Recognizing the wealth of complexity entailed by the emotional and energetic interpretants may make the quale-as-interpretant thesis more attractive to the reluctant phenomenalist (and, by the same token, of course, far less attractive to the reductive representationalist). The sensation-of-pain quale in the warmth-in-the-knee example, after all, is not one; it is many, indeed a potentially infinite series of them, emotional interpretants trying to feel their way to the "true meaning" of that warmth, energetic interpretants prodding and palpating and bending the knee, both physically and proprioceptively, in search of an effective interpretation. The logical interpretant "Yeah, it's a pain, better call the doctor" (or, again, the doctor pronouncing a diagnosis) is the *telos* of that qualitative entelechy—what Peirce would call the final interpretant, a Third—but it doesn't exhaust the qualitative significance or force of the entelechial sequence itself.

4.5 Collective organization, regulatory force

This is not a consideration Peirce raises, but it seems axiomatic that for interpretants to structure interpretation they must both be collectively organized and wield regulatory force. As we saw in §3.2, language is the most obvious example here. If I say to you "Look at that cat," you and I will have to have convergent interpretants for each of those words and their relationships to their referents ("joint attention" or "common ground"); if we don't, we will not be able to communicate with each other. As for Bakhtin on linguistic unification and Derrida on stability, "organization" here is more the rough-and-tumble, trial-and-error sort than any kind of pure or perfect transcendental order. Convergence doesn't entail absolute identity, as "regulatory force" doesn't entail perfect or total control; considerable play in the system is possible without jeopardizing the potential for good enough communication. Metaphorical extensions of "look" and "cat"—e.g., "look" as involving the mind's eye rather than the body's eyes, "cat" as referring to a human being with certain properties—don't derail communication, so long as metaphorical implicatures (Grice 1975/1989) are either conventionalized or capable of being worked out. Emotional colorations and connotations could vary quite widely—you and I may have had radically different kinds of emotional relationships with cats, so that, say, you find them cold and aloof and I find them warm and cuddly—without jeopardizing communication significantly. The speech of toddlers and foreigners is fraught with communicational difficulties precisely because it is not yet adequately collectivized or regulated—but again, some degree of regulatory collective organization, even if it is not sufficient for easy or immediate understanding, will allow conversational participants to form and test hypotheses (working or provisional interpretants) and so move toward a rough mutual understanding.

The same would apply to other areas of interpretation as well. In Peirce's example of the concert, you and I may walk out with very different emotional assessments of the music—"liking" vs. "not liking"—but if we didn't have some degree of basic agreement on what is slow music and what is fast, what is light and playful music and what is loud and bombastic, what is "classical" and what is "modern" and what is "popular" music, it would probably never occur to anyone to *hold* concerts. If those convergent assumptions are not inherent "in the music" "itself"—and only a very naive realist believes that they are—they must be organized by the culture and somehow regulatorily reticulated through the group.

A useful model for this group dynamic might be what Ilya Prigogine calls the "dissipative structure" or (in later conceptual expansions of his term) "dissipative system," a self-organizing system that maintains a rough and constantly shifting stability by adapting to changing internal and external environmental conditions and dissipating entropy. Prigogine's model is thermodynamic in its origins, but he himself tentatively extended it to biological systems (Prigogine 1973); for group communication to "count" even as a biological system or ecology it would have to reticulate the regulatory force through the group well below the level of conscious control or planning. The kind of social ecology I'm imagining here, in other words, is not a rational regime but a self-organizing affective-becoming-conative system. How that system might work—how qualia might be transmitted neurologically[14]—is the topic of §5.1.

That all interpretants are qualia seems a reasonable enough assumption—especially if we allow that some qualia are so lightly felt as not quite to reach full directed awareness. That all qualia are interpretants is a position that is likely to encounter more resistance. But even if we accept that *some* qualia are interpretants, the necessity that interpretants be collectively organized and wield regulatory force in order for civil society to be possible will obviously entail the necessity that at least some qualia as well be collectively organized and wield regulatory force. I will return to this thesis in §5.3 and §5.4.

4.6 Conclusion

Before we leave Peirce on qualia, tones, and interpretants, a Peircean anticipation of my argument in chapter 5: "But are we shut up in a box of flesh and blood? When I communicate my thoughts and my sentiments to a friend with whom I am in full sympathy, so that my feelings pass into him and I am conscious of what he feels, do I not live in his brain as well as in my own—most literally?" (1931–1958: 7.591). If feelings are both qualia and emotional interpretants, and "conscious[ness] of what he feels" is arguably both a quale and a logical interpretant, this passage picks out the transferability of far more than *signs*. (All that is missing from Peirce's rhetorical question is the *conative* quale as energetic interpretant—the subject of chapter 3.)

Along similar lines, Gilbert (1989: 17, 147, 152–155, 167–168, 186, 209, 216, 358, 415; based on Wittgenstein 1953, paragraph 172) writes of the collective "we-agent" of a walk two friends take, Searle (1990, 1995, 1999) writes of "collective intentionality" or "shared intentionality" as the glue of social construction,[15] and Tomasello (1999b, 2008, 2009) builds three decades of empirical research into joint attention and other forms of social nonverbal (gestural, tonal) communication as "recursive mindreading" (Tomasello 1988, 1991, 1992, 1994, 1995, 1998, 1999a, 2004, and several hundred co-authored research studies of small children and other primates[16]) into a comprehensive model of the cultural origins of human cognition, communication, and cooperation.

I submit, in fact, that the radical neo-Kantian idealism called social constructivism entails the shareability of qualia. If everything that we take to be reality is socially constructed—if the interpretants our brains bring to bear on sense data are similar not because God made us all in His image, as Kant argued, but because they have been collectivized by culture (see also the appendix)—then regulatory qualia/interpretants must be *reticulated* through the members of that culture. How this is possible, neurologically speaking, remains to be seen (§5.1).

Now, obviously we have alternatives to this radical view. We have Kant's own subjective universalism, premised on a uniform Creation in God's image. But if we reject both Kant's universalized subjectivism and direct and indirect realism, we need something like social constructivism to explain the commonality of most perception. And what is striking about that possibility, I suggest, is that it requires that qualia be understood more or less as Owen Flanagan argued: "Those who would quine qualia are bothered by the fact that they seem mysterious—essentially private, ineffable, and not subject to third-person evaluation. Qualia are none of these things." If qualia are transferrable from person to person, they are neither private nor ineffable; and, to cite a moment from Oscar Wilde's philosophical dialogue "The Decay of Lying" (1891/1982: 313), to which the appendix is devoted, while standing at the window with Mrs. Arundel Vivian does subject her qualia to third-person evaluation.

The problem, of course, is that this conception of qualia seems wildly counterintuitive—oddly so, from a modern naturalizing point of view, since in a sense it is implied by the folk-psychological theory that we all perceive more or less the same world. Folk psychology says both [a] that the world is more or less the same place to all of us and [b] that our fleeting inward impressions and experiences are ours alone, not shared with anyone else. What explains the apparent anomaly is that for folk psychology there is no contradiction between (a) and (b), as direct or "naive" realism doesn't attribute to qualia the power to represent the external world accurately (or indeed at all): they are fancies, daydreams, castles in the air. Perception is one thing; qualia are another. It is only with the modern scientific rejection of direct realism that a conflict emerges between the belief that we all perceive the same world and the belief that qualia are private and ineffable—and, with it, the need for shared qualia as extended (body-becoming-)mind.

Andy Clark's (2008: 180) tendency to refer to qualitative explanations of mind as "the qualia trap," I suggest, ill serves the EMT. Like many of his most determined critics, Clark tends to define cognition ontologically, in terms of *what mind is*, and to swathe in thick cotton the thorny epistemological question of *how we know* what mind is. We not only experience mind; to the extent that mind *is* anything at all, it *is*, or qualitatively seems to be, none other than the experience of mind experiencing the body-becoming-mind and the rest of the world. We can try to triangulate what we know experientially about mind, to impose empirical tests on our qualia (see the appendix); but of course our experience of the results of those tests are qualia too, as are our interpretations of those results. The Greek word *empeiria* means experience, and empirical science is an ever finer tuning of the experiential testing of beliefs and other dispositional states.

But to a materialist like Clark qualia seem to be the very opposite of empirical reality: the flickering of phantasmatic shadows on the mental wall. Because empirical *science* is historically materialist, empirical *reality* ought to be not our experience of matter, but matter itself. This is a *belief*, and one of the defining characteristics of what Kuhn (1962/1970) calls "normal scientists" is a deep-seated dispositional disinclination to test that belief empirically. Empirical testing, after all, might reveal the extent to which empirical science rests on the gossamer foundation of qualia. For Clark, therefore, as for many other "empirically" minded materialists, qualia are wispy temptations that must be resisted and renounced. I take it that what Clark means by "avoiding the qualia trap" is precisely that ascetic renunciation. The problem is that, since mind is not matter, avoiding the qualia trap leaves him only analogical approximations and comparisons to fall back on, like the man in Plato's allegory, chained to a wall deep in a cave, or like the three blind men in the Sufi parable about the elephant, who famously describe it as like a snake, a wall, and a tree trunk. The difference, of course, is that Clark has voluntarily blinded himself to qualia—or rather, since he occasionally springs the qualia trap himself, voluntarily *aspired to talking* as if he were blind to qualia. To the sighted person, an elephant patently *has parts* that are like a snake, a wall, and a tree trunk, but *is visibly* a pachyderm with a snake-like trunk, a wall-like torso, and four trunk-like legs; in the same way, to anyone other than a strict materialist (and indeed even to some strict materialists), mind may be compared to many things, but it *is*, or at least seems experientially or qualitatively to be, an experiential or qualitative construct. Clark knows as well as I do that nothing material extends when "mind" extends. It would be silly for him to argue otherwise. But calling the extended mind a *quale* might make it sound phantasmatic. So, caught between a materialist Scylla and a phenomenalist Charybdis, he analogizes: Otto's use of his notebook is *like* a normal person's use of her intracranial neural pathways. The undeniable absurdity of materialist explanations of the extended mind and the apparent absurdity of qualitative explanations leave him nothing positive to say about the extended mind; all he can say is optative speculation.

My brief in this chapter and the next (and in the appendix) is that there is nothing in the slightest absurd about qualitative explanations of mind, or of the extended body-becoming-mind. In fact, they are as natural and as inescapable an explanatory mode for talking about mind as visual explanations are for whole elephants. Once we have worked up the courage to admit that affect, conation, and cognition are fundamentally qualitative experiences, all we need in order to banish the fear of the absurd is the recognition I've offered here in chapter that qualia are not fleeting private will-o'-the-wisps but collectively reticulated interpretive representations and pressures that *organize* reality in coherent ways. As I began to hint in my discussion of speech acts as channels of affective-becoming-conative force in chapter 3, the "fantasies" or "seemings" as which strict materialists have dismissed qualia are in fact fantasies and seemings that *do work*. They press on bodies-becoming-minds, and those bodies-becoming-minds yield to their pressure.

In chapter 5, drawing on extensive research in social neuroscience, I will show that our bodies-becoming-minds are designed to convert qualia into collective behavioral pressure. The notion that mind-as-qualia is somehow too ethereal to guide or steer the body is sheer atavistic Cartesianism—and, as I suggested in the introduction, Andy Clark the self-declared anti-Cartesian is himself heavily infected with that atavism. Our various affective and cognitive mental systems show us home movies called qualia; our autonomic nervous systems display our qualitative states both proprioceptively, on the inner stages of our bodies, and kinesically, on our bodies' outer stages; and our mirror-neuron systems convert other people's qualitative-becoming-kinesic displays into conative pressure, which activates a behavioral response. If the body-becoming-mind is the emerging of cognitive representations out of kinesthetic, affective, and conative subsystems, those representations nevertheless remain interactively engaged with the less intellectually rarefied subsystems out of which they emerge, and can activate them in a myriad of powerful ways. What Clark dualistically derogates as "the qualia trap" is in fact primary evidence of the radical social situatedness and embodiment of mind.

5 Empathy, Face, and Ritual

Can I really read your mind? Does body-becoming-mind really extend in social interactions, so that you and are part of the same organism? In the terms I offered at the end of chapter 3, do we really have access to something like the indirect speech acts other people perform for and upon us? Are qualia actually shared, as I wanted to believe in chapter 4? Or is our sense that social interaction and communication constitute an extended body-becoming-mind just another seeming, just another quale, like the feeling I explored in chapter 1 that mind extends to epistemic artifacts?

To frame the answers I will be offering to those questions in this chapter, let us take another look at the propositions MacKinnon (1994: 15–40) offers that together define his emerging synthesis of symbolic interactionism and affect control theory (ACT). In particular, let us look at the three that deal with emotions:

[18] *The Emotion Principle*: An interactant's emotion after an event reflects the outcome of the event and the identity that the person is maintaining. Specifically, the emotion is a function of the transient impression of the interactant that was created by the event; and the discrepancy between this transient impression and the fundamental sentiment associated with the interactant's situated identity.
[19] People tend to maintain emotions that are characteristic of their salient identities.
[20] Emotion displays facilitate intersubjective sharing of definitions of situations and of the operative social structures that are implied by definitions of the situation. (ibid.: 39)

While accepting the "common understanding that emotions are episodic, situationally instigated, ephemeral affective experiences with physiological and cognitive components," MacKinnon (ibid.: 31) writes, affect control theory also takes emotions to be "cognitive signals, rich in affective meaning, that inform people how they are doing in establishing and validating situated identities in social interaction." Social actors do strive to "maintain emotions that are characteristic of their salient identities," but because that is not always possible situationally, they tend to use interactive emotions as indicators of their relative (and transient) success or failure at maintaining their situated identities. What is most useful for my purposes here is proposition (20): the notion that "intersubjective sharing of definitions of situations" is facilitated by displays of emotion. Reminding us that emotion is both experienced subjectively (inwardly, *in* the body) and displayed objectively (outwardly, *on* the body), ACT posits that the outward displays "reveal to others how a person is experiencing his or her identity" (ibid.: 33).

The questions I propose to address in the first two sections of this chapter arise out of inadequacies in the account of "affect control" offered by this approach. In §5.1, moving past the answer offered by ACT (that *verbal language* is the only extant channel of intersubjectivity, and thus that the only possible way emotion displays can be used in the sharing of "definitions of situations" is through verbal reports of those displays), I explore how "definitions of situations" are shared intersubjectively on the basis of emotion displays. In §5.2, I explore how inward subjective experiences of emotion and outward objective displays of emotion cycle through each individual body and through the bodies in a group, and in so doing reticulate (distribute) regulatory evaluations of situated identities through the group—again moving past the answer offered by ACT (that the only form of affect control worth talking about is that wielded by the individual on or over her-/himself, based on her or his cognitive and affective assessment of what is going on in and among the others present). As we've seen, ACT has a strong collectivist orientation toward social action, and has a sense that situated identities and activities are group constructs, and that it is neither fruitful nor ultimately even possible to reduce that kind of collective action to the perceptions and intentions of individuals; yet at crunch time, affect control theorists back away from their own best collectivist inclinations and insist that individuals use affect to control *only* themselves—not others. This may be simply because they lack the kind of model of affective communication that we will find (in §5.1) in the social neuroscience research on empathy—without such a model, obviously, there is no empirically credible explanation for how you can use affect to control me, or how I can work in a group to channel affect into the controlling of you.

This chapter is organized around ten propositions:

[1] Empathetic simulation of the affective and other body states of one person (P_1) by another (P_2) involves P_2's empathetic simulation of P_1's (Q_1) qualia—what it *feels like* to be in those states.
[2] Relative accuracy in the empathetic simulation of P_1's body states thus also involves relative accuracy in the empathetic simulation of Q_1.
[3] Relative accuracy in the simulation of Q_1 means their partial recreation (reiteration) as Q_2 in P_2.
[4] Q_2 as partial recreation or reiteration of Q_1 is part stable and accurate reproduction of Q_1 ($Q_2 = Q_1 - x$) and part new expressive content ($Q_2 = Q_1 + y$) provided by P_2.
[5] Empathetic communication in a group entails not just the unilinear circulation of qualia ($Q_1 > Q_2 > Q_3 \cdots Q_n$) but the semi-simultaneous *reticulation* (distribution, as through a network) of Q-simulations from all group members to all group members.
[6] Partial Q-sharing throughout a group enables the formation of a partial group organism (one collective body-becoming-mind).
[7] To the extent that qualia are interpretants that regulate interpretation, they wield a conatively regulatory influence on their hosts, constraining and channeling affective inclinations, action tendencies, and cognitive dispositions along collectively approved lines.
[8] The regulatory influence in (7) constitutes the collective organization of shared qualia.
[9] The fact that there is as much group Q-sharing as there is (what we might call the *x* factor) enables the creation, maintenance, and enforcement of group norms and values.
[10] The fact that group Q-sharing is never total (what we might call the *y* factor) means that the creation, maintenance, and enforcement of group norms and values is never total.[1]

I will argue propositions (1)–(4) in §5.1, in connection with social-neuroscientific empathy research; proposition (5) in §5.2, in connection with an exploration of a significant convergence between Aristotle's theorization of shame in the *Rhetoric* and Goffman's (1967) theorization of face-loss; propositions (6)–(8) in §5.3; and propositions (9) and (10) in §5.4, both in connection with a discussion of Connerton (1989) on ritual as social memory. In the concluding section (§5.5) I will ask whether and to what extent all this counts as extended body-becoming-mind.

5.1 Empathy as affective communication

The first question, how emotion displays help us share "definitions of situations" intersubjectively, will also return us to the issue raised at the end of §0.3 of whether, in Clark and Chalmers' (1998) terms, we rely cognitively on other people "automatically," transparently, without being aware of doing so, as we do on our own brains—and as Clark and Chalmers claimed Otto does on his notebook. In §0.3 I promised to show that we do indeed use other people epistemically in that automatic way; in this section I make good on that promise.

It has long been a part of folk psychology that emotions and behaviors—yawns, hilarity, depression, specific postures and gestures—are contagious. Not irresistibly contagious, however; with a sufficient expenditure of energy, one can resist the temptation to yawn even when everyone around one is yawning, or can keep on nursing a grudge even when surrounded by boisterous partiers. Not until the late nineteenth century, however, when William Carpenter (1874) published his findings on what came to be known as the Carpenter Effect—that in conversation we preconsciously ("automatically," "transparently") tend to mimic the body language of our conversational partners—did this tenet of folk psychology receive its first scientific confirmation and some fine-tuning. The Carpenter Effect is not irresistible either; in fact we only tend to mimic the body language of people we like and admire. When we feel antagonistic toward a conversational partner, we preconsciously tend to adopt facial expressions and body positions and movements that are in some way opposed to those the partner is displaying. (This is a powerful kinesic argument in favor of what Aristotle calls reasoning through *ēthos*: if our audiences like and respect us, their body language tends to align unconsciously with ours.)

Early in the twentieth century, sociologists began to discover other contexts in which behavioral contagion worked. Eidelberg (1929) found, for example, that when experimenters simultaneously gave subjects verbal instructions to raise their right hands and themselves *lowered* their right hands, almost every subject did as the experimenter did and not as the experimenter said. Unconscious or automatic behavioral contagion was more powerful than verbal instruction.

Howard Friedman and colleagues, studying nonverbal communication, picked up the Carpenter Effect as the channel for what they identified as the interpersonal transmission of emotional states (Friedman 1979; Friedman et al. 1980, 1981); their work was continued by Hatfield et al. (1994). William Ickes and colleagues (Ickes 1993; Ickes et al. 1990, 2000; Flury et al. 2008; Marangoni et al. 1995; Gesn and Ickes 1999; Simpson et al. 1995, 2003; Stinton and Ickes 1992; see also Ickes 1997 and Decety and Ickes 2009) began studying the accuracy of state inferences based on empathetic understanding, increasingly describing that understanding as "mindreading," and even "accurate mind-reading" (see also Tomasello 2008: 321, 335–337 on "recursive mindreading"), insisting that it didn't necessarily entail the formation and testing of analytical inferences.[2]

None of this work had a basis in neuroscience until the discovery, by Giacomo Rizzolatti and colleagues (Di Pellegrino et al. 1992; Rizzolatti et al. 1996; Gallese et al. 1996), of mirror neurons, which fire equally upon performing a certain action and upon seeing that same action performed by another. That discovery sparked a forest fire of research into the social neuroscience of empathy. One of the earliest studies of the Carpenter Effect in connection with the new work being published on mirror neurons was conducted by the Damasio team at the University of Iowa. Ralph Adolphs headed up a smaller group that began to investigate it, and in 1994 that subgroup began to publish papers that addressed subjects' ability to recognize somatic states in other people's faces (Adolphs et al. 1994, 1998, 2000). None of the subgroup's publications of the late 1990s, however, addressed the question of an actual transfer or transmission of evaluative/regulatory social feelings from one person to another. It was not until a medical paper published in 2002 that the subgroup offered a very sketchy neurophysiological model for the Carpenter Effect, suggesting in a scant eight lines that "knowledge of other people's emotions may rely on simulating the observed emotion" (Adolphs 2002: 171). The next year, in *Looking for Spinoza*, Damasio reported the group's findings in greater detail: "It also is apparent that the brain can simulate certain emotional body states internally, as happens in the process of turning the emotion sympathy into a feeling of empathy. Think, for example, of being told about a horrible accident in which someone was badly injured. For a moment you may feel a twinge of pain that mirrors in your mind the pain of the person in question. You feel as if you were the victim, and the feeling may be more or less intense depending on the dimension of the accident or on your knowledge of the person involved" (2003: 115). For a recent publication from this team showing that "cognitive empathy"—consciously imagining oneself in another's shoes—also triggers the mirror system, but only when the cognitive empathy exercise connects up in some way with the subject's own personal experience, see Preston et al. 2007.

More work on this vicarious activation of the mirror system at two removes—not just seeing someone being injured, say, but hearing the sounds of the crash, or hearing someone tell the story—has been done by Christian Keysers and colleagues (Kohler et al. 2002; Keysers and Gazzola 2009; Gazzola et al. 2009). Their work has also shown that birds as well as primates have mirror neurons. The Keysers team and the Rizzolatti team collaborated in a research study that showed a "common neural basis of seeing and feeling disgust" (Wicker et al. 2003).

Kenneth Leslie and colleagues (2003: 601) studied the activation of the mirror system through motor mimicry, and "found evidence for a common cortical imitation circuit for both face and hand imitation." Marianne Sonnby-Borgström (2002: 433) obtained very similar results through facial mimicry alone, comparing high-empathy and low-empathy subjects and finding that high-empathy subjects mimicked facial expressions at very short exposure times, which the researchers found to represent automatic reactions, and that low-empathy subjects tended to "show inverse zygomaticus muscle reactions, namely 'smiling' when exposed to an angry face." The subjects' verbal reports of their empathetic reactions showed no differences. "Thus," Sonnby-Borgström concludes, "the difference between the groups in emotional empathy appeared to be related to differences in automatic somatic reactions to facial stimuli rather than to differences in their cognitive interpretation of the emotional situation."

Tania Singer and colleagues (2004) have shown that the pain qualia experienced through activation of the mirror system are affective rather than sensory; Marco Loggia and colleagues found that "compassion for another increases *both* sensory and affective components of pain perception" (2008; emphasis added). In similar work, Michael Banissy and Jamie Ward (2007: 815) have shown that "watching another person being touched activates a similar neural circuit to actual touch and, for some people with 'mirror-touch' synesthesia, can produce a felt tactile sensation on their own body."

Jean Decety and colleagues (Decety and Batson 2007; Decety and Grezes 2006; Decety and Jackson 2004, 2006; Decety and Lamm 2006; Decety and Meyer 2008; Decety and Moriguchi 2007; Decety et al. 2008) have been among the most active researchers into the social neuroscience of empathy, with particular interest in the tension between "emotion sharing (bottom-up information processing) and executive control to regulate and modulate this experience (top-down information processing)" (Decety and Lamm 2006: 1146).

According to the great integrator of psychological, psychoanalytical, and psychobiological research on affect regulation in our time, Allan Schore (1994, 2003a, 2003b), the research model now being developed out of John

Bowlby's (1953, 1969, 1979, 1988) attachment theory, Heinz Kohut's (1971, 1977, 1985) self psychology, and Antonio Damasio's (1994, 1999, 2003) somatic-marker hypothesis portrays affect regulation and dysregulation as products of nonverbal and largely unconscious or preconscious right-brain-to-right-brain communication, and specifically the communicative synchronization of affect through the mirroring of body language. Beatrice Beebe and Frank Lachmann (1988), for example, studied films of mutual mother-infant gaze interactions made during the second and third quarters of the first year of life and found synchronous rapid changes in movements and affective expressions. The extreme rapidity of these changes—within 300 milliseconds—has been taken to indicate unconscious affective communication. Drawing on the Carpenter Effect, Schore (2003b) writes, "Beebe and Lachmann (1988) postulated that "as the mother and the infant match each other's temporal and affective patterns, each recreates an inner psychophysiological state similar to the partner's."

What this empirical research strongly suggests is that we don't necessarily *know* what others are feeling, but we do tend to *feel* what they are feeling. Qualia-simulations through activation of the mirror-neuron system are primary, automatic, and mostly unconscious; conscious cognitive representations of the resulting qualia as maps of another person's body states are secondary, and far rarer. Also, as Stephanie Preston and colleagues (2007) show, starting at the conscious end—inducing conscious cognitive empathy, or what cognitive scientists call "theory of mind" and "simulation" strategies (see note 2 in this chapter, pp. 220–221)—tends to trigger the mirror-neuron system as well, but only through the parallel activation of memory networks.

Now, according to Damasio's model each individual brain only *simulates* the body states of another human actor, so that, as Adams and Aizawa will be happy to insist, cognition technically remains intracranial. There are other models for this process (see Brennan 2004) that posit actual physiological (pheromonic) transfers of information from organism to organism; presumably Brennan's model would offer a stronger challenge to Adams and Aizawa's anti-transcranialist critique. But even if we stick to Damasio's model, as I am inclined to do, Adams and Aizawa's intracranialism remains problematic. The Adolphs team has determined empirically that it is specifically the body-sensing neural systems—proprioception and enteroception—that simulate the body states of another human actor, suggesting another soritic or scalar spectrum: those neural systems sense the states of both the central actor's own body and various peripheral actors' bodies, and in simulating the latter blur the distinction between other-awareness and self-awareness. This phenomenological blurring of the self-other or I-you distinction is what makes it possible for empathy to create what Schore (2003b: 8), following Stern (1983), calls "a mutual regulatory system of arousal," in which, as Schore (ibid.: 13) notes further, "the child is using the output of the mother's right cortex as a template for the imprinting—the hard wiring of circuits in his/her own right cortex that will come to mediate his/her expanding affective capacities. It has been said that in early infancy the mother is the child's 'auxiliary cortex' (Diamond, Krech, and Rosenzweig, 1963)."

This model, obviously, would explain the contagiousness of yawns, or of affective states like hilarity and depression, as well as more complex psychoanalytical phenomena like projection and introjection, transference and countertransference. Body-sensing consists of *qualia*: we have a qualitative feeling or sensation or experience of a body part or body state. The blurring of the distinction between other-awareness and self-awareness would entail the generation of locationally indeterminate qualia: we have a feeling of a body state but are unable to distinguish its precise source, whether it is my body or your body (or both). Introspection suggests that such locationally indeterminate qualia are in fact quite common; and the existence of technical terms for them (projection and introjection, transference and countertransference) suggests that such introspective or intuitive orientations are not solipsistic forms of derangement.

The question is, then: If we can't always *feel* or *experience* the difference between my affect and yours, how can we confidently state that affect doesn't extend?

Thinking back to the soritic series that I began back in §2.3 and continued in §3.0 and §3.4, we may note now that according to the neuroscience of empathy, the irritation or anger that I didn't "feel" in (a) was also an interactive affect that you could very well have felt before I did, had you been in the room, even though in the "individualized" terms cognitive internalists prefer it was "my" emotion *and not* yours. In other words, "my" affect in (a) was interactive not just in the sense that someone or something outside my head did something that I responded to intracranially with irritation, but also in the sense that it was communicatively "available" to you at the same time it was available to me. You and I could technically begin feeling it simultaneously; or, as I say, you could even feel it before I did. A group indirect speech act conatively *reticulates irritation through the group*, conditioning each group member's ability to feel it, to participate in it, and to define it as irritation.

5.2 Face as the reticulation of affect

What can we conclude, from the socioneuroscientific research on empathy, about the sharing and collective organization of affective qualia? Is it now possible to provide philosophically or scientifically adequate support for Flanagan's (1992) notion that qualia are not private, not ineffable, and (not not) subject to third-person evaluation? No. The rest of this chapter is pure speculation. The speculation does rest on the empathy research, however, which does seem to offer an empirically supported explanation for the enthymeme to which I reduced Flanagan's argument, namely that (a) we recognize other people's qualitative states because (b) we experience those states ourselves and as a result (c) recognize *classes* of qualia, like "beliefy feels" and "desirey feels." The mirror-neuron system would appear to allow us to move more or less reliably there from (b) to (a).

Proposition (5), the topic of this section, reads: "Empathetic communication in a group entails not just the unilinear circulation of qualia ($Q_1 > Q_2 > Q_3 \cdots Q_n$) but the semi-simultaneous *reticulation* (distribution, as through a network) of Q-simulations from all group members to all group members." We have seen brief anticipations or adumbrations of (5) in previous chapters. In §1.2.1, for example, *your* encouragement became *my* motivation (affect reticulated as conation), and in §3.3 Bourdieu's *habitus* was itself a kind of formative reticulation of Q-simulations through a group, so that your stand-up was reticulated not only as my laughter, and not only as *our* laughter, but as *our enhanced inclination to laugh at your stand-up in the future*; or, again, in my discussion of Aristotle's keyword *pistis*, so that your persuasive speech acts were reticulated as my/our inclination to believe you, now and henceforward.

Now let's look at another reticulatory Aristotelian term: the noun *doxa*, which has posed logical problems for scholars (see Havelock 1963: 250–251) because it is both something *you* own (your opinion of me) and something *I* own (my reputation). The noun's verb form *dokeō* is also problematic: in its personal forms it means "I think" and in its impersonal form means "it seems,"[3] so that *ta dokounta* are literally "the seemings"—or, obviously, qualia, the way things seem to be.

The interesting way *doxa* crosses or blurs the cranial boundary can be demonstrated by looking at the opposing solutions two different English translators have imposed on the term in a specific passage in Aristotle's *Rhetoric* (1.10.9–10, 1369a15–23). Kennedy (1991/2007: 85) gives us "for good reputations [*doxai*] and sentiments [*epithumiai*] in regard to his pleasures follow immediately and equally for the temperate person from his temperance, and to the intemperate person the opposites [follow] in regard to the same things." Roberts (1984: 2179) renders the passage "it is no doubt true that the temperate man, for instance, because he is temperate, *is* always and at once attended by healthy opinions [*doxai*] and appetites [*epithumiai*] in regard to pleasant things, and the intemperate man by unhealthy ones." Here, clearly, Kennedy has interpreted *doxai* and *epithumiai* as attitudes and orientations coming from *outside* the actor, as other people's reactions to the person's behavior, while Roberts takes them to be attitudes and orientations coming from *within* the actor. For Kennedy, the individual acts temperately or intemperately and others react with their opinions and sentiments, which become the person's reputation; for Roberts, a temperate or intemperate character or disposition will naturally lead to (be attended by) "healthy opinions and appetites."

Although Roberts seems to have the weight of tradition behind him, and Freese (1926) and Cooper (1932) also locate *doxai* inside the individual actor, our first observation about Aristotle's use of *doxa* is that [a] it is opinion that is already in the reticulatory process of *becoming* reputation; and our second observation must therefore be that [b] it is typically the kind of *group* opinion that does tend to become reputation. To the extent that *doxai* seem to be *my* opinions, therefore, they are only temporarily or transitionally mine: they are definitively the opinions of some group to which I belong, and as such only "occupy" me for a time. Entailed in (a/b) is an entelechial conception of *doxa*, members of Group X circulating opinions about Individual Y until they emerge teleologically as Individual Y's reputation: the entelechy of *doxa* is for group opinion to become reputation.

Our third observation, then, is that [c] *doxa* is not a propositional belief or belief system so much as it is an affective orientation in the reticulatory process of becoming not a philosophy but an inchoate sense of reality. To the extent that this makes *doxa* a feeling-becoming-thinking entelechy, in fact, the thinking that it is constantly becoming is an under-the-radar kind of thinking, a matter more of shared tacit assumptions about the way things are than of consciously and analytically held concepts or precepts. Another common translation of *doxa*, in fact, is "fame." What is the propositional content of fame? There isn't one. Fame emerges not so much out of propositional beliefs as out of admiration—and specifically out of *many people's* admiration, which can be translated into propositional beliefs but doesn't normally exist in that form.

Yet a fourth observation about Aristotle's use of *doxa* would be that [d] it is a social *value*. In fact it may in many cases be translated as *face*, which

Erving Goffman (1955/1967: 5) defines as "the positive social value a person effectively claims for himself by the line others assume he has taken during a particular contact." Goffman's sociological theories are, of course, part of the prehistory of affective control theory; "the line others assume he has taken during a particular contact" is a precursor of the concept of situated identity. Goffman's primary metaphor for face is economic: to "gain face" is to raise the value of the line or situated identity one has been projecting, so that one's "stock goes up"; to "lose face" is to experience a drop in the value of that line, so that one's "stock goes down."

"Loss of face," in fact, works as an approximate translation of Aristotle's *adoxia* "ill-repute, disgrace," which Kennedy translates as "loss of reputation." David Konstan (2007: 87) seems to translate *adoxia* precisely thus in the sentence "If anger was a response to a loss of face or *doxa* as the result of an affront, then *praotēs* ['satisfaction'] as an emotion was elicited by behaviour that enhanced public respect and esteem"—there "face" and "public respect and esteem" are both translations of *doxa*, and it is at least arguable that by "loss of face" Konstan means *adoxia*. The "line" by reference to which the social actor gains or loses face is for Goffman "a pattern of verbal and nonverbal acts by which he expresses his view of the situation and through this his evaluation of the participants, especially himself" (ibid.: 5). A line might be defined in redynamized Aristotelian terms as situational *ēthos* or character—a more or less stable, but only situationally or contextually stable, presentation of self that serves as a kind of baseline reference point for the group in assigning relative social value to the actor's performance. If the line or situated identity one is projecting in a given encounter is solemn, as at a funeral, it will be important not to let one's outward presentation of that identity shift even momentarily into mirth. A single mirthful gesture, facial expression, or phrase would break the character's "line" in that encounter—would be "out of character."

Thus, Goffman situates face-as-value in a kind of social exchange where all social actors, like economic agents in a currency exchange, are constantly both monitoring the value of their face and others' face *and* raising or lowering other actors' face-value with respect to their own. Face isn't something an individual can control; control is reticulated through the entire social economy. As Goffman puts it, "while [an actor's] social face can be his most personal possession and the center of his security and pleasure, it is only on loan to him from society; it will be withdrawn unless he conducts himself in a way that is worthy of it" (ibid.: 10). If the culture values altruism, for example, it becomes virtually impossible to gain face through the loss of another person's face; indeed, one gains face by "giving" others face.

As Goffman makes clear, our typical reaction to a loss of face is shame. The adjective we use for people who don't seem to feel shame at the loss of face and so in some sense don't seem to lose face at all—"shameless"—is strongly negative. We expect the social economy of face to regulate individuals' behavior, to bring it into line with group norms, and we react with strong disapproval whenever someone refuses to surrender to that regulation. Aristotle too speaks of people who are "shameless through contempt of public opinion [*ho d' anaiskhuntos di' oligōrian doxēs*]" (1.10.4, 1368b23, Kennedy ibid.: 88). Kennedy renders *doxa* there as "public opinion," and it should be clear by now that what is being belittled (*oligōria* there is a belittling, a refusal to treat a weighty thing like public opinion with the proper seriousness) in that phrase is not a single person's opinion but the opinion(s) of a group. (Belittling a single person's opinion would be arrogance—*hubris*—leading to anger in the victim, not shamelessness in the perpetrator.) What causes shame is the imagination of group disapproval; what causes shamelessness, clearly, is not just contempt for group disapproval but a contemptuous or dismissive refusal to yield to group pressures to conform to social norms. What causes shamelessness, to put it in terms of face, is a refusal to yield to the social economy that controls face, that assigns face-gain or face-loss to specific behaviors. That economy is so powerful because it works through the reticulation of affect-becoming-conation, the power of shared evaluative affect to inflict regulatory pain and pleasure; it requires a supreme effort to resist that pressure precisely because the felt rewards for compliance and felt punishments for noncompliance are sociosomatically intense. The shameless person is, in effect, mustering an individualistic regime, an affective reinterpretation or "reconatizing" of group disapproval for the individual as individual contempt for the group.

Aristotle comes closest to anticipating Goffman on face in this passage: "Since shame is imagination about a loss of reputation [*peri adoxias*] and for its own sake, not for its results, and since no one cares about reputation [*doxēs*] [in the abstract (insertion Kennedy's)] but on account of those who hold an opinion of him [*dia tous doxazontas*], necessarily a person feels shame toward those whose opinion he takes account of" (2.6.14., 1384a22–27, Kennedy ibid.: 134). And here is how Goffman (ibid.: 8) describes the genesis of shame:

> When a person is in wrong face or out of face, expressive events are being contributed to the encounter which cannot be readily woven into the expressive fabric of

the occasion. Should he sense that he is in wrong face or out of face, he is likely to feel ashamed and inferior because of what has happened to the activity on his account and because of what may happen to his reputation as a participant. Further, he may feel bad because he had relied upon the encounter to support an image of self to which he has become emotionally attached and which he now finds threatened. Felt lack of judgmental support from the encounter may take him aback, confuse him, and momentarily incapacitate him as an interactant. His manner and bearing may falter, collapse, and crumble. He may become embarrassed and chagrined; he may become shamefaced.

For both Aristotle and Goffman it is the social actor's *sense* (*phantasia*) that s/he is "in wrong face or out of face" (*peri adoxias*) that causes the affective-becoming-conative-becoming-cognitive reaction that we call shame. What Goffman adds to Aristotle—but entirely in the spirit of Aristotle's discussion, it seems to me—is the notion that the actor becomes "emotionally attached" to "an image of self" (a "line," a situated identity), so that the sense of being "in wrong face or out of face" is actually born out of a felt clash or conflict between the desired line and the line s/he fears others may assign her or him. Goffman puts it this way: "Further, he may feel bad because he had relied upon the encounter to support an image of self to which he has become emotionally attached and which he now finds threatened."

What Goffman also seems to be adding to his own and Aristotle's discussions here is a new conception of face-as-emotion, face as the outward motion of the body, or body language, or what ACT calls "emotion displays": "Felt lack of judgmental support from the encounter may take him aback, confuse him, and momentarily incapacitate him as an interactant. His manner and bearing may falter, collapse, and crumble. He may become embarrassed and chagrined; he may become shamefaced." Face-as-value may be felt, but it is also somewhat abstract, in the sense that it must be *mapped* mentally as real; face-as-emotion is corporeally immediate, both viscerally felt in one's own body and unmistakably visible or audible on or in someone else's.

Goffman specifically theorizes the loss of face in shame as a sequence, moving from the sense of loss of face-as-value to loss of face-as-emotion: the actor's perception of being "in wrong face or out of face" generates fears of a loss of face-as-value, which produce bad social feelings that cause the loss of face-as-emotion. Or, schematically:

[1] the actor deviates from the line s/he is attempting to maintain (s/he "is in wrong face or out of face");

[2] the activity in which s/he is participating is disrupted in some crucial way;
[3] s/he senses this;
[4] s/he imagines future damage to her or his reputation as a result (imagined loss of face-as-value);
[5] his or her emotionally invested sense of self is threatened (threatened loss of face-as-self-esteem);
[6] s/he feels a "lack of judgmental support," presumably from the other members of the group;
[7] s/he loses face-as-emotion.

But Goffman's account is incomplete. First, in (6), what *is* that "lack of judgmental support"? Is it an evaluative affective response from the other members of the group? If so, what sort of response is a "lack"? Is it really just a lack of support, or is it active disapproval, a corporeally legible negative judgment? And what is the relationship between that response and the disruption of the activity in (2)? Is it possible that the group's affective response to the actor's deviation from the line s/he is maintaining *is* the disruption? If we imagine the actor giggling at a funeral, say, or hooting sarcastically at a wedding, what else could the disruption be besides the somatic signals of disapproval from the others present? Those other bodies-becoming-minds involved in face-work—or what we might call here "shame-work"—are only shadowy, barely imagined presences in Goffman's account. But surely shame-work is always a *collective* action? Surely the actor always produces and experiences shame with or through the people who, as Aristotle says, "hold an opinion of him" (*dia tous doxazontas*, 1384a24)? A literal translation of that passage (*oudeis de tēs doxēs phrontizei all' ē dia tous doxazontas*) would be "no one cares about reputation other than on account of the reputers"—where are those "reputers" in Goffman's account? (Even if we imagine the social actor sitting alone in a room in the evening and feeling intense shame over something that happened during the day, or thirty years ago, isn't s/he still experiencing that shame in relationship with the people who observed and so perhaps helped socially engineer her or his loss of face?)

Second, as Aristotle reminds us with *peri adoxias phantasia*, what about cases where no one present notices the face-threatening event, and shame is generated not by actual social disapproval but the *imagination* of social disapproval? For example, while conversing in the present, the actor remembers a face-threatening event from the past, and the feeling of shame associated with that event (re)generates the shameful images and the emotions that go with them, and those emotions begin moving toward open display on the body's theatrical stage, putting the actor at least potentially "in wrong face" or "out of face." As this new threat arises from within, the actor begins not only to imagine future damage to his or her reputation (imagined loss of face-as-value) if s/he is unable to suppress the unruly emotions, but also to feel anxiety about her or his ability to accomplish that suppression—and that anxiety may make it even more difficult to suppress the emotions. Both feelings of shame and feelings of anxiety are marked somatically with emotional responses—constriction of the throat or chest, increased heart rate, increased flow of blood to the face—which in turn threaten to "go public" (display themselves on the body's stage as blushing, fidgeting, darting eyes, etc.) and thus to precipitate the very shameful discovery and resulting loss of face on which the anxiety is fixed. The fear that these emotional signals of anxiety and shame might lead to that discovery reinforces the anxiety response at the same time as the speaker is trying to clamp down on it and prevent its public display as body language. To lose control over the public display of emotion would be to lose face; fear of losing face intensifies the somatic response and makes it more likely that it will in fact surface as emotion and disrupt the management of "line," of the desired/projected situated identity, and face will be lost.

This would entail a radical expansion of moments (4)–(6), which might be represented schematically as follows:

[4a] the actor remembers or imagines a deviation from the line s/he was attempting to maintain in some past activity, or remembers a fact about his or her past that, if the people now present knew about it, would cause her or him to lose face-as-value;
[4b] s/he imagines the body language of disapproval that the others would display as an expression of that loss of face-as-value;
[5a] his or her emotionally invested sense of self is threatened (threatened loss of face-as-self-esteem);
[5b] s/he feels the uprising of shame-emotions;
[5c] s/he feels an anxiety that the loss of face-as-emotion will reveal his or her shame and cause the loss of face-as-value;
[5d] the anxiety s/he feels at the possibility that his or her body will reveal the rising shame makes it even more difficult to suppress the outward display of face-threatening body states.
[6a] s/he imagines a "lack of judgmental support" from the other members of the group;
[6b] s/he feels or senses (6a) proprioceptively in her or his own body.

In other words, it may well be—as Aristotle seems to suggest, as if "correcting" Goffman—that the imagination of *adoxia* is primary and the *adoxia* itself is secondary. Both the imagination of face-loss and the "pain and confusion" (*lupē tis ē tarachē*, 2.6.2, 1383b13) attending face-loss seem to be (inter)subjectively constitutive of *adoxia*, so that the objective existence of *adoxia* out in the world, in society, in the bodies-becoming-minds of the rest of the group—if such a thing could even be objectively established—is not absolutely essential to the painful or confusing imagination that is shame.

The interesting question for me there is: what does it mean for the imagination of disgrace or loss of face to be "(inter)subjectively constitutive of *adoxia*"? That parenthetical "(inter)" suggests that the subjective constitution of *doxa*-as-face (including both *eudoxia* or face-gain and *adoxia* or face-loss) tends to be collective—the *group* doxic imagination gives or withholds face—but that group imagination may be energetically at work on *doxa* in the embodied imagination of a single social actor as well. Even if no one saw the embarrassing incident, and even if no one may ever find out about it, in other words, we have to imagine the ashamed social actor as still *reticulating* the imagined loss of face as shame.

What is at work in this reticulation, I suggest, is the networked distribution of body states through a group, via the motor mimicry of body language that social neuroscientists study under the rubric of "empathy." For example:

(4a) The social actor remembering a past or imagining a future deviation from the line s/he was attempting to maintain in a past activity or is attempting to maintain now will not just rationally *know* that such a deviation might mean trouble; s/he will *feel* it. S/he has empathetically experienced and mimetically internalized other people's emotional displays of disapproval for hypocrisy and other social sins in the past, and so has now developed in his or her autonomic system a kind of collectivized stockpile of what Damasio (1994) calls negative somatic markers (transcranial qualia felt not only intracranially but intracorporeally, in localized regions throughout the body) ready to warn against hypocrisy, and those markers are activated now to mark her or his still-private hypocrisy as socially wrong. Her or his autonomic nervous system marks the imagined or remembered deviation from the current or past line inwardly as dangerous, as to be avoided. Those earlier displays of social disapproval were enactively provoked on the (public) stages of the other bodies by their (private) negative somatic marking of some of his or her own or someone else's behavior that failed to conform to social standards; as those feelings activated various facial muscles, tightening lips, narrowing eyes, s/he mimetically reiterated or transiterated those emotional responses in his own body, made them her own, so that increasingly his or her own social failings triggered the same emotional displays on the outside as well as negative somatic markers on the inside.

(4b) Now, under pressure from his or her own autonomic nervous system, the actor imagines the body language of disapproval that the others would display if they knew of this still-private (imagined or remembered) deviation. In (4a), other people's disapproving body language (in the past) is transferred inward, internalized as the actor's own somatic markers; now those somatic markers are transferred outward again (in the present), projected onto the imagined future faces of other people—whether those people are physically present or only imagined.

(5a) To the extent that the actor's sense of self or identity is a social entity, created and maintained in relationship with other people, any felt or imagined disruption in the smooth flow of group approval for that self or identity poses a threat to it. It's not just, as Goffman says, that the actor feels an "emotional attachment" to that sense of self; it is also that the self is an affectively supported group construct (situated identity), created and maintained by the social exchange, and therefore easily threatened by the social exchange. We also develop individualistic defenses against such collective threats—we whisper to ourselves "Who cares what they think? It's what I think that matters"—but even such individualisms are powerfully tinged with the felt collectivism against which they defend.

(5b) The autonomic nervous system, designed to warn us against dangers we've encountered before, now begins to flood us with such warnings, specifically with inward somatic markers that we feel throughout the body either proprioceptively (increased heart rate, a prickliness in our extremities, a constriction of the throat or chest, a rush of blood to the face, etc.) or enteroceptively ("butterflies" or an ominous rumbling in the stomach) but that also may be displayed outwardly as body language for others to see.

(5c) Again, we have developed individualistic defenses against such warnings—we have some degree of control over our mapping of body states as feelings (our inward felt awareness of uprising shame, say), and even more control over what body states will be displayed outwardly on the body's theater—but we know from painful past experience that our control of such things is never perfect. This knowledge comes to us as the body-becoming-mind movement of somatic markers being mapped as anxious feelings, and then (though not inevitably) as thoughts, leading to an increasingly conscious concern that an outward display of shameful body states will reveal the actor's out-of-face condition.

(5d) The somatic markers of anxiety in (5b) combine with the somatic markers of shame in (5c), and together make it all the more difficult to keep the inward body state private. Having internalized social disapproval in the past, and re-externalized it in the present in imagined form—projected it onto the imagined bodies of those present or absent—the actor now struggles not to externalize it visibly onto the theater of his or her own body; but the pressures of the somatic exchange are powerful, and visible externalization of internal body states is difficult to resist. The "natural" or "default" or "teleological" tendency of body states is to "spread" (be distributed or reticulated) through the group; blocking that reticulation is socially "abnormal" or "unnatural," opposed to the entelechy of the somatic exchange that has made us what we are, and therefore exceedingly hard to manage successfully.

(6ab) The actor now has a powerful qualitative experience of what Goffman calls the "lack of judgmental support" from the other members of the group; given the extended proprioception enabled by the mirror-neuron system, it is normatively difficult to distinguish between (6a) the purely phantasmatic *worry* that others will judge one (or are already judging one) negatively and (6b) the simulatory *feeling* that others are judging one negatively.

This juxtaposition of Aristotle on shame and Goffman on face-loss has enabled us to explore proposition (5), namely that empathetic communication in a group entails not just the unilinear circulation of qualia $(Q_1 > Q_2 > Q_3 \cdots)$ but the semi-simultaneous *reticulation* (distribution, as through a network) of Q-simulations from all group members to all group members. The sixth and seventh propositions—

(6) Partial Q-sharing throughout a group enables the formation of a partial group organism (one collective body-becoming-mind).

(7) To the extent that qualia are interpretants that regulate interpretation, they wield a regulatory influence on their hosts, constraining and channeling affective inclinations, action tendencies, and cognitive dispositions along collectively approved lines.

—are the topic for §5.3, specifically as modeled in ritualization.

5.3 Ritual as collective embodied memory

Let me again set up this new complication by returning one last time to the soritic series as we left it in §5.0:

[g] "Oh. I see" <raised eyebrows, crossed arms, postural withdrawal, clipped tone of voice, narrowed eyes, flat gaze, tight mouth>
[h] "What?" <look and tone of hurt innocence>
[i] "You know perfectly well what!" <same body language as in (g), except your eyes flash briefly>
[j] "I don't, I swear!" <same hurt innocent look and tone as in (h), buttressed with a tonal escalation designed to establish sincerity>
[k] After some deliberation, I realize that you're right, I should have figured out what was going on, and it was only my unfathomable obtuseness that kept me in the dark.

Now let's add one last wrinkle: the next time I don't understand something that to you is perfectly and indeed overwhelmingly obvious, you [l_1] mimic my (h) <hurt, innocent> body language and say "What?" In a sense in (l_1) you satirically *commemorate* my ignorance in (h). This annoys me a little, but I swallow my hurt pride; after all, I did (k) realize that you were right. Since I am often obtuse in this way, you unfortunately have frequent occasion to commemorate my failure to understand a situation, and slowly [$l_{2...n}$] *ritualize* (h/l_1); it becomes a regular part of your repertoire. And gradually, as you perform this satirical little ritual in a variety of moods and contexts, including humorous and tender ones, I relax a little and begin to participate in ($l_{2...n}$) myself, saying "What?" with a humorously stylized version of the (h/l_1) body language, perhaps with my own iterative twist on it, a slight rueful self-deprecation or self-irony.

As Paul Connerton (1989) notes, this commemorative ritualization of my protest has the effect of creating a "social memory" for us—that is, helping us *collectively remember* my inclination to be obtuse about relationship matters. If Connerton's right, Adams and Aizawa's claim that memory processes don't extend beyond the skull is wrong. Following Oakeshott (1962), Connerton distinguishes between morality as the conscious following of a rule and morality arising out of collective habit-memory, learned by "living with people who habitually behave in a certain manner" (quoted in Connerton 1989: 30). What you and I are collectively remembering is in fact not only my obtuseness but also my need to pay more attention, to notice things that I'm in the habit of missing, and to reflect more complexly on them. And ($l_{2...n}$) has the effect of collectively reorganizing and redirecting my behavior according to an emergent morality in Oakeshott's second sense—what I would call an affective-becoming-conative morality, the kind of morality that grows out of "living with people who habitually behave in a certain manner."

Connerton is particularly interested in the trained synchronization of bodily movement as a ritual channel of social memory—the kinds of kinesthetic communication one finds in religious and patriotic ceremonies, in which group repetition of simplified and organized gestures, postures, and movements (as well as words) serves to reenact and thus retain in collective memory events that are significant for group identity. These ritual commemorations often arise without conscious, analytical planning or codification; they emerge out of group interactions, "living with people who habitually behave in a certain manner." They can, at any stage, be codified, written down, pre-scribed (though a better term for this belated codification might be "post-scribed"), and often are; but their commemorative power never depends on such codifications, and indeed codification may be resisted or even rejected by the participants in such commemorations as entirely lacking in the kind of deep preconscious affective-becoming-conative communication that is the actual channel of commemorative power.

The empathy research reviewed in §5.1 suggests that the trained synchronization of bodily movement—not just in ritual performances but in dance and other expressive performances as well—is made possible by the mirror-neuron system, which not only allows but *encourages* us to model our movements closely on the movements of the people around us. It is possible to train hundreds and even thousands of performers to synchronize their bodily movements so perfectly that they appear to be cleverly programmed and centrally controlled robots—as some said, for example, about the opening ceremonies at the 2008 Beijing Summer Olympics. If this is not exactly the creation of a single extended body-becoming-mind, it *feels* as if it is, and *looks* as if it is—and the empirical evidence suggests that for the mirror-neuron system it actually is one: that what enables us to distinguish my movement from yours, the individual from the group, is in fact a secondary cognitive (meta)quale that is belatedly imposed on transcranial proprioception. My mirror-neuron system makes my *feeling* that I am one with the others primary; but then I look around, notice that my own body ends at my skin, and tell myself that I am separate, not one with the others.

The kind of cognitive science that proceeds as if affective and conative communication didn't exist—as if "cognition" as a description of the activity of "the mind" were purely computational—would thus appear to start the analytical "clock" quite late in the game. By the time we humans are engaged in the kinds of mental activities these traditional cognitive scientists call "cognitive," we have already been through numerous layers or levels of affective and conative communication that have transcranially prepared us to "think thoughts" or experience perceptions and memories that appear to us private and nonderived. It is only in this narrowly defined sense of "cognition" that thoughts, perceptions, memories, and the rest seem intracranial; in the larger context of human mental activity, they are affective-becoming-conative-becoming-cognitive, and saturated in transcraniality.

One of the salient points Connerton makes about ritual is that it restricts participants' actional options. Rites are "expressive acts only by virtue of their conspicuous regularity. They are formalized acts, and tend to be stylized, stereotyped and repetitive. Because they are deliberately stylized, they are not subject to spontaneous variation, or at least are susceptible of variation only within strict limits" (ibid.: 44). Or, as Connerton puts these limits in kinesthetic terms, "performatives are encoded also in set postures, gestures and movements" (ibid.: 59). In religious and political rituals, "the body is held braced and attentive in standing; the hands are folded and placed as though bound in praying; persons bow down and express their impotence by kneeling; or they may completely abandon the upright posture in the abasement of bodily prostration" (ibid.). But, as my extension of the soritic series at the beginning of this section indicates, such ritualized restrictions of our outward displays of emotion are also common in ordinary conversation: what makes $(l_{2...n})$ recognizable as a ritual is precisely the stylized and highly formalized body language with which either of us performs it, the very specific tone of voice, perhaps the slight humorous/ironic widening or rolling of the eyes and brief twitching of the corners of the mouth; specific gestures and/or postures may accompany the ritual, satirically commemorating my increasingly infamous body language in the original performance of (h). "The relative sparseness of such repertoires," Connerton notes, "is their source of strength. The resources of ordinary language, its semantic range and flexibility of tone and register, the possibility of producing statements that can be qualified, ironised and retracted, the conditional and subjunctive tense of verbs, language's capacity to lie, to conceal, and to give ideational expression to that which is not present—all these constitute, from one vantage point, a communicative defect" (ibid.).

As proposition (6) would have it, then, "Partial Q-sharing throughout a group enables the formation of a partial group organism (one collective body-becoming-mind)"; and, as proposition (7) reformulates that, "To the extent that qualia are interpretants that regulate interpretation, they wield a regulatory influence on their hosts, constraining and channeling affective inclinations, action tendencies, and cognitive dispositions along collectively approved lines." And, as proposition (8) has it, "The regulatory influence in (7) constitutes the collective organization of shared qualia."

5.4 Organized innovation

But note that in the ordinary conversational ritual ($l_{2...n}$), Connerton's description of verbal rituals seems just slightly off. Though it is true that ($l_{2...n}$) narrows and focuses the range of expressive options open to ordinary conversational encounters, the "one vantage point" from which the ability to inject new expressive content into the ritual is "a communicative defect" tends to be that of highly formulaic public rituals, not the sort of *ad hoc* conversational ritual schematized above as ($l_{2...n}$). As you and I ritualize (h) "What?" as ($l_{2...n}$) "What?," the infinite numbering of the subscripts 2 . . . n specifically represents the slight but situationally significant "alterations of the same" that Derrida theorizes as reperformative iterations: the ironic raised eyebrow is added in one iteration, and becomes a permanent part of the ritual, or is used by both of us temporarily and then fades (perhaps becomes an allusive kinesthetic memory of irony that colors our understanding of future iterations that outwardly lack the raised eyebrow), or is instantly felt to be excessive, inappropriate, not welcome, and is forcefully dropped from the ritualistic repertoire. Our ritualized performances of ($l_{2...n}$) "What?" *harness* "language's capacity to lie, to conceal, and to give ideational expression to that which is not present" without ever actually repressing or foreclosing that capacity. "The subtlety of ordinary language is such that it can suggest or imply finely-graded degrees of subordination, respect, disregard and contempt. Social interactions can be negotiated through a linguistic element of ambiguity, indeterminacy and uncertainty. But the limited resources of ritual posture, gesture and movement strip communication clean of many hermeneutic puzzles" (Connerton 1989: 59). What we see in ($l_{2...n}$) is a middle ground between "the subtlety of ordinary language" as Connerton describes it in those first two sentences and "the limited resources of ritual posture, gesture and movement" in the third: limited resources, yes, but not as limited as in, say, high-church rituals like kneeling to pray; ordinary language's ability to communicate gradations of great subtlety, uncertainty, and unpredictability, but that ability conatively *organized* by the ritual into a behavioral habit.

Indeed, as many of the sociologists and social psychologists who laid the groundwork for affect control theory—especially Mead (1934), Goffman (1959, 1967, 1974), and Collins (1975, 1981)—have insisted, much of our ordinary communicative behavior is organized in something like this middle ground between absolute expressive freedom and the rigid regimentation of ritual. Our social interactions are *guided* by the group, through very much the same kind of reticulatory organizations of behavior that we see in ($l_{2...n}$). Commonly used terms for this sort of collective conative guidance are "regulation" and "control"; those terms are accurate and appropriate, but only once they have been stripped of their conventional connotation of *coercion*. We are not typically forced to act as we know we are expected to act; we are *guided* to conform to group expectations below the radar of conscious awareness, through not-quite-verbal affective-becoming-conative pressures. As we have seen in ($l_{2...n}$), those pressures organize group behavior in ways that help individuals remember things that are important to the group—as Connerton puts it, they constitute a form of collective nonpropositional memory—but they do so in ways that allow innovation, reperformative iteration as idiosyncratic commentary, or even counterpressure on the collectively habitualized form.

This tension between the conative conformation or habitualization of group behavior and individual iterative resistance to that conformation is obviously the channel through which what Bakhtin calls the "project" of unifying language is conducted. Without group habits, without the affective-becoming-conative policing of group norms, verbal communication wouldn't be possible; because that policing is never perfect, because iterative impulses escape the dragnet in a thousand minuscule ways, language changes, slowly, incrementally, but inexorably. The iterative tension between habitualization and dehabitualization is precisely the process by which Bourdieu's *habitus* is created, maintained, disseminated through a population, and altered—the process by which it slowly, incrementally but inexorably, differentiates one group from another while sustaining and guiding group solidarity.

Though it would appear to be the case, then, as proposition (9) has it, that the fact that there is as much group Q-sharing as there is (what we might call the *x* factor) enables the creation, maintenance, and enforcement of group norms and values, the limitation on that organization of proposition (10) also holds: the fact that group Q-sharing is never total (what we might call the *y* factor) means that the creation, maintenance, and enforcement of group norms and values is never total.

5.5 Conclusion

If proposition (10) means that humans are not hive creatures, then—not perfectly conformed to group conation—does that mean that the body-becoming-mind doesn't extend? Is it all or nothing—either we are bees, mere instantiations of a single collective will-system, or, in Peirce's (1931–1958: 7.591) words, we are "shut up in a box of flesh and blood"? If the affective-becoming-conative forces or pressures or impulses that we have been examining in chapters 3–5 aren't actually *transferred* from body to body but only simulated, and if those simulations aren't perfect replicas but what Derrida calls *iterations*, reperformances that alter slightly what they reperform, must we forgo the EMT altogether? Or is there some middle ground in which the social phenomena we have been examining might still "count" as extended body-becoming-mind?

It should be clear by now that Peirce's follow-up question about extended mind is problematic: "When I communicate my thoughts and my sentiments to a friend with whom I am in full sympathy, so that my feelings pass into him and I am conscious of what he feels, do I not live in his brain as well as in my own—most literally?" (ibid.). As is true of Clark's (2008: xxvi) insistence that the "machinery of mind" extends literally, the most glaring problem there is the final adverb. Just what kind of literalism does Peirce mean? Given that the brain is a material organ, would living in it "most literally" mean living in it materially? Or, more likely, does "live in his brain as well as in my own" signal the kind of quale-consciousness that Peirce theorizes in his 1898 notes by that name, but with a material substrate? If so, then to "live in a brain" would mean to have a qualitative sense of living—which is to say, to have a *mind-as-self*—and would relegate the neural location of that sense or self to secondary (meta-) explanation: I don't *feel* myself living in a brain, but I feel myself living, and I *know* I have a brain, so I can *imagine* that the feeling of living I have is a feeling of living in a brain. And once I've imagined or projected that feeling, I can go ahead and extend the same (or a similar) feeling to my sense that I know what my friend is thinking and feeling, and say that I "live in his brain as well as in my own." This series of imaginative projections and similitudes and analogues is obviously quite far from what we usually mean by "most literally." (I submit that what Peirce and Clark—and many of us—mean by "literally" in such contexts is actually a certain qualitative intensity indicating a strong belief that the phenomenon being described is *really true*. "You think I'm just making this up; you think this is just some kind of airy metaphor; but I mean it—*most literally*.")

Still, the empathy research I reviewed in §5.1 would seem to confirm something like Peirce's fundamental insight, namely that the mirror-neuron system can make it quite difficult for us to distinguish between an intracranial feeling and a transcranial feeling—that, even if we don't live in other people's brains "most literally," there is an empirically falsifiable sense in which we proprioceptively map other people's brain/body states *as if* we were living in them. To a strict materialist, of course, the word "simulation" in "simulation of other people's body states" is the red flag that makes the whole thing seem unreal, phantasmatic; but then the simulation of body states is what proprioception *is*—a mental representation or mapping of body states, and specifically a mapping of those states so that we *feel* them, so that they *feel real*. Proprioception is a qualitative experience. All perceptions, in fact, are simulations. They are qualia—representations—with built-in interpretive filters that make them (as far as we can tell) distortions of their originals. Every memory image is a qualitative simulation, and memory simulations are not noticeably more accurate than empathetic simulations of other people's body states. If one accepts that intracranial proprioception or perception or memory is real enough to count as cognition, therefore, one must, in principle, accept that transcranial proprioception, perception, or memory is real enough to count as cognition as well.

Of course it is always possible for Adams and Aizawa to protest that "transcranial proprioception" only has an *extra*cranial *object*, and that, like any other perception of extracranial objects, it remains itself firmly intracranial. And if transcranial proprioception gives us the *feeling* of being connected to other people, of being inside their skin, even of "most literally" living inside their brains, well, that feeling too is intracranial.

But let us ask, perhaps somewhat impertinently, what Adams and Aizawa gain by clinging so desperately to this internalism, this intracranialism. I suspect that from their perspective what they gain is the *truth*: Clark and his fellow EMT proponents have perpetrated a Big Lie, and Adams and Aizawa are setting the record straight. And surely for philosophers, at least for philosophers of a certain stripe, that is enough: truth is a significant enough quarry that we don't really need to search further for justifications. However, the fact that in this case Adams and Aizawa aren't just *seeking* truth, but are seeking to defend a *traditional* truth against a radical new theory, and specifically defending an *individualistic* truth against what would appear to be a collectivistic new theory, makes me think that there is more at stake in their critique than just the Truth. The advocates of situated, enactive, embedded, and extended cognition would *connect* the individual to the world. For them, we don't live alone, work alone, think alone; each of us is part of a larger whole. By denying this connectivity, Adams and Aizawa ensure that human beings are individuals—that we are not bees. If we think all our thoughts and remember all our memories and perceive the world's extracranial objects (including other people's feelings) inside our heads, individualism still holds.

For the central thesis of this book, the most telling of the anti-connectivist or anti-collectivist sentiments that seem to fuel Adams and Aizawa's radical intracranialism is their argument that language is noncognitive because it is public, conventional, and non-original. That, I submit, is the utterly unconvincing claim that tips their hand: that *your* thought, spoken aloud or written in a language I can read, never shapes *my* thinking. If they are willing to go to such lengths to protect the sanctity and inviolability of intracranial thought, there is more to their critique of the EMT than a quest for truth. The scalar or soritic series that I began developing in §2.3 suggests strongly that your thoughts and feelings begin shaping my thoughts and feelings even before you say a word—that in fact the transcranial connectivity instigated by language even as cognitive labels (let alone language as conative force) is ultimately just an outgrowth of a deeper preverbal connectivity. Adams and Aizawa's determination to "quine" this communicative transcraniality—to reduce it to verbal labels, and verbal labels to conventionality, and conventionality to derivativity and thus to noncognition—suggests to me that intracraniality is for them more an ideological hobby horse than a skeptically tested truth.

On the other hand, I think Adams and Aizawa are right that Clark and Chalmers (1998) overstate their case. As we saw in §0.2, the notion that in order for Otto's cognition to extend to his notebook he has to "endorse" the notebook sinks the EMT in an epistemological quagmire. Clark and Chalmers' case is that Otto's use of his notebook is *like* the brain's use of specific neurons and neural pathways, and therefore not the mere employment of a memory aid but actual extended cognition—but it is only *like* intracranial cognition, Clark and Chalmers insist, if it is automatic and transparent, not based on a conscious decision, and automaticity and transparency are guaranteed, they think, by Otto's "endorsement." Thus, the sole criterion separating the EMT from the fallback position their critics (including Adams and Aizawa) champion, that the notebook is simply a memory aid, is an endorsement-quale—something to which, Clark himself seems to believe, the world of non-Ottos has no access.

Consider the options, then, without the theory of sociality as extended body-becoming-mind that I have been constructing in this book. On the

Empathy, Face, and Ritual 173

one hand, ironically, [a] for Clark and Chalmers mind only extends when it is in a state that doesn't extend, so that ultimately we can never know whether and when it does; on the other, [b] for Adams and Aizawa mind keeps banging futilely against the inside surface of the skull, unable to escape. In (a), cognition connects us to our epistemic artifacts, but only speculatively, analogically, in an as-if world; in (b), language connects us to other people, but only conventionally, as a second-order noncognitive representation of cognition, which is not only private but utterly non-situated, non-embedded, non-enactive, non-connective, a perfectly isolated predetermined computational monad forged in the imagination of God (or Plato, or Alan Turing). In (a), connectivity seems a desperate speculative hope; in (b), it seems a vague threat to be warded off with strict border controls. These are not particularly inviting alternatives.

What I have been arguing in place of that Hobson's choice is that, to rehearse my seven propositions in the introduction, (1) mind is qualia, and typically *shared* qualia, making it qualitative overkill to quine the qualia that tell us when and how mind extends; (2) intracraniality is internalized transcraniality, which (3) begins to be internalized in all social animals, including humans, in the form of preconative affect, eventually giving rise in humans to the cognitive connectivity of verbal labels; (4) the affective-becoming-cognitive entelechy of verbal labels is further enriched by the transcranial conativity of speech acts, both direct (autodeictically verbal) and (5) indirect (preverbal); and the affective-becoming-conative communication that makes indirect speech acts and (6) empathy, the conative negotiations of face, and the social memory of ritual possible also (7) make the extended mind an extended body-becoming-mind.

Propositions (1–7) seem to me a far more robust version of the EMT than Clark and Chalmers (1998) or Clark (2008)—far better protected against anti-EMT critiques based on a narrow label-based philosophy of language, which would tend to binarize "original" intracranial cognition and "conventional" transcranial communication.

For Adams and Aizawa, natural language is:	For Clark, natural language is:
[a] the only extant channel of communication between human individuals, and consists of a collection of	[a] the only extant channel of communication between human individuals, and consists of a collection of
[b] conventional, and thus derived or nonoriginal,	[b] conventional, and thus derived or nonoriginal,

[c] syntactically ordered semantic labels or representations of thought or cognition, which is	[c] syntactically ordered semantic labels or representations of thought or cognition, which is
[d] a nonsituated monad.	[d'] situated, embodied, embedded, and enactive, and so heavily influenced and shaped by language.

The shift there from (d) to (d'), I've been arguing, is important but inadequate. As this tabulation suggests, Clark doesn't challenge much in the Fodorian philosophy of language Adams and Aizawa bring to the study of cognition. In the view I have been developing in this book, natural language is

[a'] one of at least two channels of human communication, and emerging integrally out of the other, namely affective (or affective-becoming-conative) communication, which is the most powerful channel of social regulation;

[b'] iterative, so that conventions are constantly being incrementally altered by reperformances; and consists of both

[c'_1] affective-becoming-cognitive semantic labels (powerfully felt verbal representations of feelings and thoughts) as syntactically and pragmatically ordered, and

[c'_2] affective-becoming-conative speech acts, which put pressure on people to change their behavior;

[d"] the "thought" or "cognition" that is represented by (c'_1) is, as for Clark, situated, embodied, embedded, and enactive, and thus heavily influenced and shaped by language, and is therefore also—a fact that Clark does not recognize—highly conventionalized, an internalized form of public transcraniality; and, as Clark or his critics also fail to recognize, it is

[e] not the only qualitative entity communicated through language, the other being the conative force communicated through (c'_2).

Whether (body-becoming-)mind extends may ultimately be a matter of perspective. Those who are determined to defend the individuality of the individual will always be able to find some criterial neural activity that does not and cannot extend beyond the skull and offer it as incontrovertible evidence that cognition is intracranial; those for whom cognition is not a purely neural activity, and indeed is not purely cognitive but kinesthetic-becoming-affective-becoming-conative-becoming-cognitive, will always be able to show that situated social actions and identities arise out of, constitute, and maintain transcranial channels of experiencing and feeling and thinking that are qualitatively different from intracranial ones.

Whichever perspective we prefer, however, it is about time we moved beyond the tired old notions that (a) humans communicate only through language, (b) language is purely public and conventional, and (c) language consists entirely of verbal labels or representations of thoughts. Language is much more than conventional public labels; it is also the stabilizing/destabilizing iterability of conative force as channeled through speech acts. And communication is much more than language; it is also the reticulation of affective-becoming-conative pressures through any group, so that the members of that group seem, both to themselves and to outsiders, to be part of a single extended body-becoming-mind.

Appendix: Liar-Paradox Monism

It should not be news in philosophy departments that qualia pose a serious philosophical problem. A succession of philosophers of mind, beginning with Levine (1983), have suggested that "the explanatory gap between materialism and qualia" is uncrossable. According to Galen Strawson (1994: 93), "the existence of experience [qualia] is the only hard part of the mind-body problem for materialists." What makes it hard for them, Strawson suggests (ibid.: 47), is that experiential phenomena don't *seem* physical, and indeed seem thoroughly alien to physical or physicalist explanation, but *must* be physical. Indeed, the very attempt to assimilate qualia to physics, or generally to a materialist or physicalist explanatory model, as Nagel (1974: 176) notes, makes it seem as if we don't really understand physicality at all.

While noting that some philosophers have been tempted to solve this problem by giving up on the dream of shoehorning qualia into a materialist monism and plumping instead for dualism, Strawson resists that temptation, offering in place of dualism two versions of materialist monism that arguably smuggle dualism into it. He cites the historical option (championed by William James—see Cooper 1990 and Crane 2000) of believing that "there is a fundamental sense in which reality is neither mental nor physical, as we understand those terms"—neutral monism—and yet another option, which Strawson himself cautiously champions, according to which "reality is, in its essential single-substanced nature, both mental and physical, both experiential and physical" (ibid.: 46). Strawson dubs the last view "mental and physical (M&P) monism."

Given that both conventional monistic idealism and conventional monistic materialism seek asymmetrically to normalize one data set and to reduce another ("deviant") data set to the monistic norm, Strawson calls both of them asymmetry theories; neutral monism and M&P monism, by contrast, are "equal-status theories." This distinction would appear to implicate all standard materialists in the former, but things are not so simple: because the qualitative phenomena that standard materialists must somehow reduce to physicality are so utterly unphysical in every imaginable way, materialists keep finding asymmetrical reduction ultimately impossible, and end up incorporating qualia into materialism in a tentative form that is only *marked* for reduction—as a problem in search of a future solution, a qualitative conundrum in search of a materialist resolution. Some day, they believe, we will *discover* the true material nature of qualia, and so will be able to reduce them to materiality. Until then, Strawson argues, standard materialists are, in practice, M&P materialists. Of course, not all materialists fit this description: Allport (1988), Wilkes (1988), and Dennett (1988, 1991) deny the existence of experience of qualia altogether; and reductive representationalists like Dretske (1993) and Tye (2000) build radical asymmetry into their claims about the physical and the experiential, reducing the latter to the former. Even so, Strawson notes, it is not *eccentric* for philosophers who believe themselves to be standard materialists to ascribe equal status to claims in favor of the physicality and the experientiality of reality. It is perfectly normal. The mind-body problem from within this viewpoint is *not* that there is some significant difference between the mental/experiential/qualitative and the physical; the mental is by default a subordinate category of the physical. The problem is rather that we don't yet know what the physicality of the mental or the experiential or the qualitative *is*. As Strawson puts it, this problem has been around for a few centuries: "Perhaps it only came to seem acute in the sixteenth and seventeenth centuries, when the evolution of a scientific conception of the physical as nothing more than particles in motion made it unclear how experiential phenomena could be physical" (ibid.: 58n). And it's still unclear. M&P monism—Strawson's solution to the difficulty, and, he argues, the fullest statement of the standard materialist position on experience or qualia—doesn't solve it either.

A year after Strawson's 1994 book appeared, Chalmers published an article arguing a very similar case. There are, he suggested, many consciousness-related problems that seem difficult but are actually fairly easy to resolve:

- the ability to discriminate, categorize, and react to environmental stimuli;
- the integration of information by a cognitive system;
- the reportability of mental states;
- the ability of a system to access its own internal states;
- the focus of attention;

Liar-Paradox Monism

- the deliberate control of behavior;
- the difference between wakefulness and sleep. (Chalmers 1995/1997: 10)

There is, however, one Hard Problem of Consciousness: the problem not only of *how* but of *why* certain physical structures give rise to consciousness (or experience, or qualia). The problem as Chalmers articulates it is that "causal closure" in physicalism—trying to explain qualia from within the physical—does not work, and cannot work. That leaves two options: a naturalistic or interactive dualism that posits two realms, the physical and the mental, and builds bridges between them, and a panpsychic monism that explains the physical as proto-experiential. Chalmers (1995/1997) cautiously votes for dualism; after reading the 26 responses other philosophers of mind wrote to his article, especially the defenses of panpsychism offered by Hut and Shepard (1996/1997), Rosenberg (1996/1997), and Seager (1995/1997), Chalmers (1997) cautiously opts for panpsychism.

"Where does this leave us?" Strawson (1994/2010: 78) asks. Dishearteningly, his reply is still, in the 2010 second edition of his book, that it leaves us "with a better feeling for our ignorance." In other words, M&P monism doesn't solve the problem. Nor does all the ink spilled by Chalmers and his respondents on the Hard Problem of Consciousness. It is still the Hard Problem.

What I propose to argue in this appendix is that what makes it the Hard Problem is not so much the puzzlements of reality as it is the job description of philosophers and scientists as professional truth tellers. Determining the truth and explicating it as accurately and clearly as possible is what they do. Admirable as the results of adherence to this ethos normally are, I suggest, it can also create apparently insoluble difficulties—among them the Hard Problem of Consciousness—that could easily be solved if, say, modern philosophers were more willing to *lie*, like novelists or playwrights.

I don't mean that as flippantly as it sounds. My brief in this appendix is that there is, or we can identify, a mixed or complex monism along the lines of neutral monism or M&P monism that can (criss-)cross the explanatory gap and solve the Hard Problem of Consciousness. I call it *liar-paradox monism* (LP monism for short). Like the classic liar paradoxes, it wants to have things both ways—to have what it claims to be true be a lie and to have what it claims is a lie to be true. It is ostensibly radically asymmetrical, though its asymmetries are mutual, rendering it a kind of equal-status wannabe-asymmetry. Hence, obviously, the problems attendant on setting it up as a coherent and principled philosophical *position*. But it is nevertheless, I want to argue, a principled and coherent philosophical position—not mere escapism, no mere eristic mind game.

Taking as my exemplary text Oscar Wilde's (1891/1982) witty philosophical dialogue "The Decay of Lying," I offer a summary of the dialogue in §A.1 and an Idiot Questioner reading of it in §A.2, by way of setting it up as a model of LP monism in §A.3 and §A.4.

A.1 Wilde's "Decay of Lying"

As the dialogue begins, Vivian (the Wilde mouthpiece) is sitting in the library of a house in Nottinghamshire, reading proofs for an article he has written, when Cyril (the foil) steps in through an open window off the terrace and chides him for cooping himself up indoors on such a "perfectly lovely afternoon": "The air is exquisite. There is a mist upon the woods, like the purple bloom upon a plum. Let us go and lie on the grass and smoke cigarettes and enjoy Nature" (ibid.: 290). Vivian responds by saying that he has fortunately lost the ability to enjoy nature: "My own experience is that the more we study Art, the less we care for Nature. What Art really reveals to us is Nature's lack of design, her curious crudities, her extraordinary monotony, her absolutely unfinished condition. Nature has good intentions, of course, but, as Aristotle once said, she cannot carry them out" (ibid.: 291).

This association prompts Vivian to read to Cyril from the article he's proofreading, entitled "The Decay of Lying: A Protest," which supplies the main argument of Wilde's dialogue (itself entitled "The Decay of Lying: An Observation"). The essay begins: "One of the chief causes that can be assigned for the curiously commonplace character of most of the literature of our age is undoubtedly the decay of Lying as an art, a science, and a social pleasure" (ibid.: 293). I want to come back in a moment to lying as a science. "The ancient historians," Vivian/Wilde adds, "gave us delightful fiction in the form of fact; the modern novelist presents us with dull facts under the guise of fiction." Historians and scientists used to lie; now they tediously tell the truth. He doesn't include philosophers in his nostalgia for a lost heyday of lying, but, as we've just seen, he invokes Aristotle early on, and after several pages devoted to a round condemnation of contemporary realistic and naturalistic fiction he coyly invokes Kant as well: "The only beautiful things, as somebody once said, are the things that do not concern us. As long as a thing is useful or necessary to us, or affects us in any way, either for pain or for pleasure, or appeals strongly to our sympathies, or is a vital part of the environment in which we live, it is outside the proper sphere of art. To art's subject-matter we should be more or less indifferent" (ibid.: 299). Again, more on this in a moment.

Liar-Paradox Monism

Eventually he comes to his main thesis, namely that "Nature is always behind the age" (ibid.: 300), by which he says he means this:

"Art begins with abstract decoration, with purely imaginative and pleasurable work dealing with what is unreal and non-existent. This is the first stage. Then Life becomes fascinated with this new wonder, and asks to be admitted into the charmed circle. Art takes life as part of her rough material, recreates it, and refashions it in fresh forms, is absolutely indifferent to fact, invents, imagines, dreams, and keeps between herself and reality the impenetrable barrier of beautiful style, of decorative or ideal treatment. The third stage is when Life gets the upper hand, and drives Art out into the wilderness. This is the true decadence, and it is from this that we are now suffering." (ibid.: 301)

Or, more pithily, "Life imitates art far more than Art imitates life" (ibid.: 307). More specifically, "A great artist invents a type, and Life tries to copy it, to reproduce it in popular form, like an enterprising publisher" (ibid.). And in the most famous (though rather lengthy) passage in the dialogue, Wilde offers a series of examples and paraphrases of Vivian's central claim:

Where, if not from the Impressionists, do we get those wonderful brown fogs that come creeping down our streets, blurring the gas-lamps and changing the houses into monstrous shadows? To whom, if not to them and their master, do we owe the lovely silver mists that brood over our river, and turn to faint forms of fading grace curved bridge and swaying barge? The extraordinary change that has taken place in the climate of London during the last ten years is entirely due to a particular school of Art. You smile. Consider the matter from a scientific or a metaphysical point of view, and you will find that I am right. For what is Nature? Nature is no great mother who has borne us. She is our creation. It is in our brain that she quickens to life. Things are because we see them, and what we see, and how we see it, depends on the Arts that have influenced us. To look at a thing is very different from seeing a thing. One does not see anything until one sees its beauty. Then, and then only, does it come into existence. At present, people see fogs, not because there are fogs, but because poets and painters have taught them the mysterious loveliness of such effects. There may have been fogs for centuries in London. I dare say there were. But no one saw them, and so we do not know anything about them. They did not exist till Art had invented them. Now, it must be admitted, fogs are carried to excess. They have become the mere mannerism of a clique, and the exaggerated realism of their method gives dull people bronchitis. Where the cultured catch an effect, the uncultured catch cold. And so, let us be humane, and invite Art to turn her wonderful eyes elsewhere. She has done so already, indeed. That white quivering sunlight that one sees now in France, with its strange blotches of mauve, and its restless violet shadows, is her latest fancy, and, on the whole, Nature reproduces it quite admirably. Where she used to give us Corots and Daubignys, she gives us now exquisite Monets and entrancing Pissarros. Indeed there are moments, rare, it is true, but still to be observed from time to time, when Nature becomes absolutely modern. Of course she is not always to be relied upon. The fact is that she is in this unfortunate position. Art creates an incomparable and unique effect, and, having done so, passes on to other things. Nature, upon the other hand, forgetting that imitation can be made the sincerest form of insult, keeps on repeating this effect until we all become absolutely wearied of it. Nobody of any real culture, for instance, ever talks nowadays about the beauty of a sunset. Sunsets are quite old-fashioned. They belong to the time when Turner was the last note in art. To admire them is a distinct sign of provincialism of temperament. Upon the other hand they go on. Yesterday evening Mrs. Arundel insisted on my going to the window, and looking at the glorious sky, as she called it. Of course I had to look at it. She is one of those absurdly pretty Philistines to whom one can deny nothing. And what was it? It was simply a very second-rate Turner, a Turner of a bad period, with all the painter's worst faults exaggerated and over-emphasised. (ibid.: 312–313)

A.2 Idiot questions about "The Decay of Lying"

The Idiot Questioner's first question: Are Vivian's claims in this passage literally true? (That adverb is becoming something of an anti-hero in this book, from Wilde to Peirce to Clark.) Does Vivian mean literally that fogs "have become the mere mannerism of a clique, and the exaggerated realism of their method gives dull people bronchitis. Where the cultured catch an effect, the uncultured catch cold"? Does he mean literally that "Nature is no great mother who has borne us. She is our creation. It is in our brain that she quickens to life"? Does he mean literally that there are times when "Nature becomes absolutely modern," but can't be relied on for modernity, given her subordination in matters of creativity to Art? "Art creates an incomparable and unique effect, and, having done so, passes on to other things. Nature, upon the other hand, forgetting that imitation can be made the sincerest form of insult, keeps on repeating this effect until we all become absolutely wearied of it": Is this intended as a true statement?

Friendly amendment to the Idiot Questioner's first question: Yes, Vivian is a *character*, in a sense a narrator—albeit a very Wildean one. Does he speak for Wilde? Does Wilde intend for these statements that he puts into the mouth of his mouthpiece to be taken as accurate descriptions of reality? Or should we take Vivian's to be a characterized point of view that we should regard as possessing the veridicality of, say, that of Swift's eponymous first-person narrator in *Gulliver's Travels*? (The Idiot Questioner is not such an idiot as to believe that all narrators and characters speak as or for their authors.)

Answer to the first question, bracketing the friendly amendment: Surely "truth" is an odd attribute to assign to the words of Vivian, who is, after all, defending *lying* as "an art, a science, and a social pleasure." He's lying. He is, to paraphrase his own early remark on art, "inventing, imagining, dreaming, and keeping between himself and reality the impenetrable barrier of beautiful style."

The Idiot Questioner's second question: Why does Vivian lie in this particular way? What does he hope to gain from his lies?

Answer to the Idiot Questioner's second question: Vivian's own answer is that "the aim of the liar is simply to charm, to delight, to give pleasure" (305).

The Idiot Questioner's third question: Is he lying about that too? If so, see question 2.

Answer to the Idiot Questioner's third question: Hm.

The Idiot Questioner's fourth question: Or could he be lying on one level and telling the truth on another?

Answer to the Idiot Questioner's fourth question: All right. Let's get serious here. There are several possible scenarios:

[1] When I said, in my answer to the Idiot Questioner's first question, that Vivian is lying, I was lying. Vivian is telling the truth, and so is Wilde. Wilde may have created Vivian in order to embellish and exaggerate the truth a little, to make it more charming, delightful, pleasurable— but it's still the truth, and Wilde stands behind it.
[2] Vivian is lying and Wilde is telling the truth. Vivian is a version of the unreliable narrator, whose manifest unreliability leads the reader to posit authorial disagreement, and hence to *accept* the author's implied views precisely because they are taken to be the opposite of the unreliable narrator's obviously false or despicable or ludicrous views.
[3] Vivian is lying and Wilde is lying as well.
 [a] Both are lying for the same reason: "the aim of the liar is simply to charm, to delight, to give pleasure." This is obviously a version of the liar paradox: if Vivian (with Wilde behind him) is himself the liar whose aim is simply (exclusively) to charm, etc., then this propositional declaration of the liar's aim is itself a lie, and the liar's aim is *not* simply to charm, etc. But if Vivian (and Wilde behind him) is telling the truth about the liar's simple (exclusive) aim, then his utterance exceeds the exclusivity implied in "simply" and he is not the liar whose aim is simply to charm, etc.

[b] The answer to the Idiot Questioner's fourth question is a simple *yes*: Vivian (with Wilde behind him) is lying on one level and telling the truth on another.
[c] The liar paradox outlined in (3a) is itself a model of a different (more complex) kind of truth.

[4] The upshot of (3c) is that (1) and (3) are both true, and (2) is a lie.

Well. I'm not sure I'd go so far as to say that (2) is a lie, but (2) does seem to be the least likely scenario. Vivian is far too Wildean to be an unreliable character/narrator. The only kind of potential unreliable-narrator scenario I can imagine for the dialogue, in fact, is a campy or tongue-in-cheek (proto-queer) one, designed to poke fun at the unreliable-narrator convention in fiction. But that seems unnecessarily baroque for an already quite baroque epistemological structure.

I do believe, in fact, that (3c) and its conclusion (4) are the "true" answers to this multiple-choice test. But before we go there, let's take a moment to explore (3b), which is not, I think, entirely wrong either.

A.2.1 Vivian/Wilde is lying on one level and telling the truth on another (3b)

Vivian's central argument in the dialogue is a "lie" not as petty everyday mendacity, but as a metaphysical *conceit*, a literary device that clearly falls under the purview of that artistic creativity that Wilde identifies as the best and most important kind of lying. Specifically, what Vivian/Wilde offers us in the dialogue is a radical idealist conceit according to which "Art" and "Nature" are great (female) minds working together, though from positions of hierarchical inequality, to create and shape everything that is. Vivian mocks Nature as a bungler—"But Nature is so uncomfortable. Grass is hard and lumpy and damp, and full of dreadful black insects. Why, even Morris' poorest workman could make you a more comfortable seat than the whole of Nature can" (ibid.: 291)—but she is a creating mind nonetheless. Wilde makes Art the teacher and Nature the clumsy and literal-minded pupil who struggles, rather pathetically, to emulate her teacher, but between them they distribute Creative Mind throughout the known universe.

A metaphysical conceit is an extended hyperbole, or what Helen Gardner (1961: xxiii) famously described as "a comparison whose ingenuity is more striking than its justness." This description seems apt for Wilde's/Vivian's conceit about Art and Nature—its hyperbolic ingenuity is indeed striking—but that still leaves open the question of its "justness," its truth value. Conceits don't invariably point allegorically beyond themselves to some deeper metaphysical truth claim, but many do, and it is fairly easy to demonstrate that this one does. Vivian's casual (nameless) invocation of Kant on the purposelessness of beauty is one clue Wilde drops as to the unstated philosophical burden of his dialogue. There are others:

> If we take Nature to mean natural simple instinct as opposed to self-conscious culture, the work produced under this influence is always old-fashioned, antiquated, and out of date. One touch of Nature may make the whole world kin, but two touches of Nature will destroy any work of Art. If, on the other hand, we regard Nature as the collection of phenomena external to man, people only discover in her what they bring to her. She has no suggestions of her own. Wordsworth went to the lakes, but he was never a lake poet. He found in stones the sermons he had already hidden there. He went moralizing about the district, but his good work was produced when he returned, not to Nature but to poetry. (ibid.: 300–301)

It is clear from internal evidence alone, in other words, that Vivian at least—and probably Wilde too—is a Kantian-style idealist who believes that we have no access to the *Ding an sich*, and that what we take to be reality is therefore a mental construct, a phenomenology, an organized collection of qualia with no reliable "transparency" (Tye 2000: 45–51) to external empirical reality. Unlike Kant, however, whose subjective universalism attributed what he took to be the functional identity of all humans' subjective construction of reality to God's unified creation, Wilde was a post-Kantian aestheticist who attributed the power to create this reality construct to the imagination—and took each individual's imagination to be variably shaped by art. "Things are because we see them, and what we see, and how we see it, depends on the Arts that have influenced us"—this statement is arguably intended to be taken literally, as a serious metaphysical (idealist/phenomenalist) truth claim. "Consider the matter from a scientific or a metaphysical point of view, and you will find that I am right": if one accepts Kant's idealist metaphysics but recognizes that his universalism is wishful thinking, then it does indeed follow that Vivian is right. (We shall see about science.) "At present," Vivian quips, "people see fogs, not because there are fogs, but because poets and painters have taught them the mysterious loveliness of such effects. There may have been fogs for centuries in London. I dare say there were. But no one saw them, and so we do not know anything about them. They did not exist till Art had invented them." In other words, they didn't exist *as fogs*. They were not then a part of the reality construct that art later created for our imaginations.

The continuation of Vivian's remarks on fogs quoted in the Idiot Questioner's first question is especially interesting: "Now, it must be admitted, fogs are carried to excess. They have become the mere mannerism of a clique, and the exaggerated realism of their method gives dull people bronchitis. Where the cultured catch an effect, the uncultured catch cold." How shall we read this? How literally? The notion that fogs are an artistic effect that somehow have the power to give "dull people bronchitis" is the kind of witty exaggeration for which Wilde is best known; should we dismiss it as a clever witticism that is not intended to be taken seriously? Perhaps. But let's consider two other interpretive options:

[1] It is a mere witticism, not intended to be taken seriously.
[2] The effects of fog on the "uncultured" are psychosomatic. Fogs are mere artistic effects, mere art-influenced qualia, but dull people *think* they are sufficiently material or real to give them bronchitis, and their imagined susceptibility to such adverse health effects becomes a self-fulfilling prophecy.
[3] The actual meteorological conditions that artists have taught us to see as fogs exist in a material world to which we have no reliable access. Our sensory fog qualia aren't accurate simulacra of those meteorological conditions, but they are cobbled together out of bits and pieces of artistic images *and* variably distorted sense data; and although the meteorologists who have studied fogs scientifically can't reasonably claim to have discovered the absolute and final truth about them (because they too have direct access only to their qualia), still their claims about fogs include observations (the condensation of water vapor in the air) that might explain fogs' ability to congest lungs.

I take (2) there to be the radical idealist viewpoint; (3) is more complicated, obviously, as it implies the ultimate powerlessness of Mind (the idealizing artistic imagination) to create the reality constructs that would enable us to live in an idealist paradise. In the (3) reading, Wilde's dialogue is not about the power of Art so much as it is about the *struggle* between Art and Nature—which is to say behind the conceit, between Mind (qualia) and Matter, between the creative imagination and the inertial resistance material reality puts up to our imaginative attempts to organize our sensory qualia into a coherent world. Again, following Kant, Wilde insists that we can't know material reality directly, "in itself"; but we are constantly feeling the effects of its existence, in that it is forever thwarting our imaginative desires, our qualia-based predictions: "Sunsets are quite old-fashioned. They belong to the time when Turner was the last note in art. To admire them is a distinct sign of provincialism of temperament. *Upon the other hand they go on*" (emphasis added). Nature, Life, Matter, the External World, Wilde recognizes, has an independent existence that is not (entirely) amenable to our designs. Vivian's complaints about nature—"But Nature is so uncomfortable. Grass is hard and lumpy and damp, and full of dreadful black insects" (ibid.: 291)—reflect this recognition as well. We may not have reliable access to the truth about the material world, but we know that it's there, and we can hazard tentative descriptions of it, because it stubbornly resists perfect form-fitting assimilation into our qualitative constructs.

A.2.2 The liar paradox (3c)

As I say, I take the standard-asymmetrical or "allegorical" reading presented in §A.2.1 to be an accurate summary, as far as it goes, of Wilde's metaphysics. It only has one rather debilitating flaw: it doesn't take into account the (wannabe-asymmetrical) ontological truth claims Wilde/Vivian makes in the dialogue about the impossibility of making ontological truth claims. If "things are because we see them, and what we see, and how we see it, depends on the Arts that have influenced us," then people who have been influenced by different arts will construct reality in significantly different ways, and it will be impossible (or dishonest) to make claims about reality in general. But of course "things are because we see them, and what we see, and how we see it, depends on the Arts that have influenced us" is itself a claim about reality in general.

One might argue, of course, that "things are because we see them, and what we see, and how we see it, depends on the Arts that have influenced us" is not so much a truth claim as it is a theoretically derived *hypothesis* about reality, like the EMT and the LOTH in some readings. Wilde, after all, was a writer; he got his ideas from other writers, especially Walter Pater, who taught Kant at Brasenose (Oxford) and channeled Kantian idealism into his wildly influential *Studies in the History of the Renaissance* (1873). Pater-influenced Kantian idealism had been in the air in Britain for several decades when Wilde wrote "The Decay of Lying," in the Keats-inspired Pre-Raphaelite Brotherhood, founded by Dante Gabriel Rossetti in 1848, and in the French-Symbolist-inspired decadence of Algernon Swinburne, Arthur Symons, and others.

But then Wilde doesn't *present* his claim as a hypothesis; he presents it as a true statement. And in any case the radical mutability implied by the claim would preclude any empirical testing of hypotheses. Like the EMT and the LOTH, "things are because we see them, and what we see, and how we see it, depends on the Arts that have influenced us" would appear to be an empirical hypothesis in the rhetorical form of a truth that is logically inaccessible to empirical proof or disproof.

A queer-theoretical approach to the social practices and philosophies that normatively linked aestheticism, decadence, dandies, effeminacy, and homosexuality from Pater to Wilde (and therefore inspired poets like Baudelaire and Swinburne to *pretend* to be queer; see Sinfield 1994) might insist that the aestheticist doctrine of intensity and mutability—you are whatever intense artistic and sexual experience makes you—was a queering or camping of the "panicked heterosexuality" (Butler 1991) that objectified "nature" as something permanent and stable and God-created. In this reading, to put it in Austin's (1962/1975) terms (see chapter 3), Wilde's statement that "things are because we see them, and what we see, and how we see it, depends on the Arts that have influenced us" is not so much a constative description of reality as it is a performative utterance designed to *make it so*.

Again, however, even if we read Wilde's wildest claims in "The Decay of Lying" as performatives, they nevertheless remain *indirect* performatives in the explicit outward form of constatives: they pretend, at least, to tell the truth about reality.

The truth is that there is no truth: it is, of course, only fitting that a dialogue entitled "The Decay of Lying" should be built argumentatively around a version of the liar paradox, which classically invokes an implicit claim to undermine or reverse an explicit claim. If Vivian's/Wilde's (3b) explicit philosophical claims offer up an aestheticist post-Kantian version of idealism in the form of (3c) a conceit that celebrates lying and thus implicitly identifies (3b) as a lie, obviously (3b) is going to be woefully inadequate as a summary of Wilde's position in the dialogue. The liar paradox has the inevitable effect of transforming the standard asymmetry of symbolism or allegory (the exaggerations of the conceit pointing beyond themselves to some deeper truth) into a much more complex kind of claim, which I'm calling equal-status wannabe-asymmetry.

Indeed the tricky thing about the liar paradox is that once you've invoked it you can't really do a time-out and say "I've been playing the liar-paradox game up till this moment, and will go back to it after this sentence, but when I say 'Things are because we see them, and what we see, and how we see it, depends on the Arts that have influenced us' I *really mean it*." That won't work. The liar paradox gobbles up that kind of ostensible time-out. It automatically converts any truth claim into a potential or putative lie and any lie claim into a potential or putative truth.

In other words, it isn't just that a Wildean-style post-Kantian idealist—someone who believes that reality is variable depending on what art you have been viewing—has no business making ontological truth claims, or rather, that any ontological truth claims he makes will be subject to a certain quite reasonable epistemological suspicion. That is part of it. But the specific fact that Wilde's dialogue and Vivian's essay are *defenses* of lying escalates that epistemological suspicion alarmingly; and incidental claims like "the aim of the liar is simply to charm, to delight, to give pleasure," which as we saw in (3c) mire the purport of the piece in the liar paradox, confirm our suspicions. Why is Wilde (or Vivian) writing his piece? *Simply* to charm, etc.? Then he has nothing to say—no philosophical position, no post-Kantian ontology. The slightest hint that he does have something to say, then, undermines his claim: either he is not the liar he is defending (he's a truth teller like all the others he has been ridiculing throughout), or the liar's aim is not simply to charm, etc.

What is significant about this apparent impasse in Wilde, I suggest, is that it is a camped-up version of a salutary methodological tension in contemporary neuroscience—hence my hint earlier that there may be some truth to Vivian's apparently reckless (or campy) urging that the reader "consider the matter from a scientific or a metaphysical point of view, and you will find that I am right." Antonio Damasio (1994, 1999, 2003) has offered an entirely reasonable materialistic hypothesis as to how and why consciousness emerges evolutionarily out of the physical: for homeostatic reasons organisms need to monitor both the external world and their own internal states. If they don't know when they are hungry, for example, they will neglect to eat; if they don't notice a predator, they may neglect to take evasive action in its presence. Meta-level awareness of the body state aroused by the predator—noticing one's fear, which Damasio (2004) follows William James (1890/1950: 2.449ff) in calling "feeling the emotion"—may not serve useful evolutionary purposes in simpler organisms, but in complex social animals like birds and mammals it serves the important purpose of providing fodder for the organization of a behavioral regime devoted to avoiding the places where that fear is typically felt. Feeling the more complicated social emotions, like embarrassment or jealousy, serves similar homeostatic purposes in the social realm. Damasio doesn't consider Strawson's (1994) argument about our feeling that we are thinking, or understanding, or perceiving (the topic of chapter 4), but the same kind of homeostatic explanation may be applied to it as well. In order to monitor their internal states, living organisms need to know what is going on, on the inside and out, and need to be able to review what they know; to that end, their brains show them home movies, or qualia.

The problem with this materialist explanation of qualia, of course, is that neuroscientists also possess a professional recognition and understanding of the ways in which our nervous systems don't so much *register* the world objectively as *construct* it interpretively, by sorting through and organizing qualia. In this sense neuroscientists are by default idealists of a Kantian stripe—or rather, they would be if they were willing or institutionally able to foreground this understanding of the nervous system as an epistemological condition for their own work. Instead, of course, they typically recognize that *humans* are by default Kantian-style idealists, while still insisting that they themselves, as *scientists*, are standard materialists.

With this observation we are, it should be clear, somewhere in the neighborhood of Wilde's epistemological impasse in "The Decay of Lying" at once [a] accepting the Kantian idealism that denies us access to the *Ding an sich* and [b] rejecting Kant's belief that we all experience the world in functionally identical ways because God shaped our understanding so as to construct the world identically leaves us [c] unable to tell the simple truth about anything. In order to restore the impression or shaky conviction of epistemological reliability to our philosophizing, we must fiddle with one or the other side of the post-Kantian world view: either (contra a) we do have reliable access to the *Ding an sich* (our qualia are transparent to their material objects—the reductive representationalist view championed by Adams and Aizawa) or (contra b) God did create us capable of constructing the same world (our qualia may be superficially different but function in parallel ways—the functionalist view championed by Clark and Chalmers).

The third way to approach this problem is to have it both ways, which is to say (contra c) to tell the *complex* truth about everything. Neutral monism and M&P monism are versions of this complex truth, but, as Strawson ruefully concludes, they don't solve the problem either, because there is no single perspective on the reality both of qualia and of extracranial events that will tame them into a single coherent monistic explanation. I submit that LP monism solves the problem at a higher (or at least more rhetorically entangled) level: like the Cretan who as a Cretan is by his own admission a liar, the neuroscientist insists that all humans construct out of sensory, affective, and cognitive qualia a reality of their own interpretive making; also like the Cretan, who presents himself or herself as telling the truth about all Cretans always lying, the neuroscientist presents herself or himself as a scientist who has established objectively that all humans construct their own reality out of qualia, and therefore is in some obviously impossible sense *not* among those who construct their own reality out of qualia.

But how is this monism? And how does it solve the Hard Problem of Consciousness?

A.3 Rhetorical analysis of the liar paradox

The earliest instance of the liar paradox (then called a *pseudomenon*) we have is from ancient Greece, attributed to the fourth-century-BCE Greek philosopher Eubulides of Miletus, who reportedly asked whether, if a man says he's lying, his statement is true or false. Bertrand Russell (1908: 222) was apparently the first to assimilate the line from a sixth-century-BCE poem by Epimenides of Knossos to the liar paradox: "The oldest contradiction of the kind in question is the Epimenides. Epimenides the Cretan said that all Cretans were liars, and all other statements made by Cretans were certainly lies. Was this a lie?" This famous formulation is actually based on the Apostle Paul's quotation from and commentary on Epimenides' poem in the Epistle to Titus (1:12–13, *RSV*): "One of themselves, a prophet of their own, said: 'Cretans are always liars, evil beasts, lazy gluttons.' This testimony is true." Three steps: Epimenides says that all Cretans are liars; Paul notes not only that it was a Cretan who called all Cretans liars but that what he said was the truth; Russell restates Paul's quotation and commentary as a paradox.

I begin with this backstory, though it is familiar to many, because it offers an illustration of a point that is so obvious that it is often missed. The liar paradox begins logically with an assumed truth semantics—the assumption that any statement by X about Y is a statement of what X believes to be true about Y.[1] It should be quite evident that without this assumption the mere propositional *form* of the liar paradox could not reliably be taken as paradoxical, or even as apparently containing the kind of logical contradiction or tension that is traditionally read as paradoxical. If, for example, Epimenides is taken to be deliberately exaggerating—if "all Cretans are liars" is taken to be an exaggeration of "most Cretans are liars," or even of "all Cretans but me are liars"—the "Epimenides paradox" collapses. To stand as the famous paradox it has become since Russell, it has to be read as a self-referential and self-contradictory claim, or rather a contradiction between two claims: the explicit "all Cretans are liars" (with the sense that "I'm lying right now") and the implicit "I'm telling the truth." Deliberate exaggeration obviously entails an awareness that one is *not* telling the full literal truth.[2]

And indeed in actual language-use contexts we do regularly and knowingly say things we don't mean. We exaggerate. We imply things (such as "I am the only decent and honest Cretan"). We use irony, and other tropes—to trope, after all, is etymologically to *turn away* from the literal statement of truth. Paul Grice's (1975/1989) theory of conversational implicature was such a bombshell in the philosophy of language when it began circulating in mimeograph form after he offered it in the 1967 William James Lectures because Grice suggested outright that the meaning of a sentence may not be spelled out in it, but may instead have to be worked out by its hearers. The implicit claim "I'm telling the truth" is not an empirical fact about every utterance, obviously, but neither is it a conversational implicature, something that the hearers of any given instance of the liar paradox work out; it is an *axiom*, derived by abstraction (decontextualization) and idealization (normativization) from an assumed semantics according to which the right sort of people *usually* mean what they say, or else really ought to. Every statement implies an assertion of its own truth, in other words, not in actual conversation, but in the notorious "null context"—that logical sleight of mind designed to dress negation (*no* context) up as positivity (*the* null context).

Indeed, even Grice's radical rethinking of linguistic meaning rests on a kind of displaced null context: the Cooperative Principle and its maxims, which he claims govern all human communication. For Grice, it is by *assuming* that all human communicators seek to cooperate with their interlocutors (by hearing behind every utterance the implicit assertion "I am cooperating with you") and then running every puzzling utterance through an algorithm derived from one or more maxims that listeners work out what the speaker is implicating. But of course not everyone contributes cooperatively to conversation, and we often manage to work out uncooperative speakers' implicatures nonetheless. And although Clyne (1981), Thomson (1982), and Loveday (1982) have detailed the ways in which Grice's maxims are the maxims not of all speakers but of a certain sex, class, nationality, and age group (Grice's own), we do nonetheless often manage to work out the implicatures of speakers from other groups, who bring different conversational maxims to bear on communication.

One of our primary channels for the successful interpretation of implicatures, of course, is body language—tone of voice, facial expression, gestures, posture, proximity, and so on. But, as Kenneth Burke (1950/1969: 185) notes, literate people tend to forget that. For literate people, Burke writes, "the written word omits all telltale record of gesture and tonality; and not only may our 'literacy' keep us from missing the omissions, it may blunt us to the appreciation of tone and gesture, so that even when we witness the full expression, we note only those aspects of it that can be written down." It seems natural to Grice, for example, to posit that disambiguation of ambiguous utterances must be guided purely by the Cooperative Principle and its maxims—to "forget" the guidance given interpretation by body language. And for decades before Grice it seemed natural to philosophers of language and linguists to assume that uptake of utterances must be governed "mechanically" by rules "in the language"—in the disembodied written words, as it were, or in the combinatory interstices lurking just behind the written words.

Consider, then, the following series, which offers tonal (emotional) representations of attitude alone:

[1] "All Cretans are liars," Epimenides said slyly.
[2] "All Cretans are liars," Epimenides said sheepishly.
[3] "All Cretans are liars," Epimenides said musingly.
[4] "All Cretans are liars," Epimenides said sarcastically.
[5] "All Cretans are liars," Epimenides said bitterly.

Surely these iterations of "All Cretans are liars" are *not* all the "same sentence"? Surely each one *means* something very different from all the others? It is, of course, possible to reduce them all to the same locution, and then to insist that that reduction "is" the basic semantics of the sentence (and that the manifest semantic differences among them are secondary supplementations). But each would unquestionably have its own illocutionary force and intended perlocutionary effect, and each would also be performing its own indirect speech acts, including such indirect speech acts (or what Altieri 1981: 88 calls "expressive implicatures") as "I'm telling the truth" or "I'm exaggerating for effect"—and only by *suppressing* such differences (rather than simply assigning them supplementary status) would the logician be able to continue to assume that "the sentence" implies the speaker's belief in its truth.

I submit, for example, that (1) is the only tonalization of the five that would warrant even a tentative paradoxical reading of the utterance; it seems to hint that Epimenides is implying some clever reversal of the face value of his words. In (2), he has probably just been caught lying about something relatively minor, by someone who likes and respects him, and whom he too likes and respects; saying sheepishly that all Cretans are liars is an exaggeration that might be taken to work implicitly (illocutionarily) as an apology. The musing tone in (3) seems to imply something like "There is *some displaced sense* in which all Cretans are liars"—that is, not every Cretan utterance is 100 percent mendacious. The anger in (4) and (5) makes the utterance into an exaggerated condemnation of Epimenides' fellow Cretans, from a position (say) of jaded moral superiority in (4) and from a position of hurt vulnerability in (5).

Nor are we limited in print to direct adverbial representations of the tonal/emotional attitudes with which speech is invariably charged. We could represent other kinesic signals as well:

[1'] "All Cretans are *liars*," Epimenides said with a sidelong glance, suppressing a wicked smile.
[2'] "All Cretans *are* liars," Epimenides said, hanging his head and heaving a pathetic little sigh.
[3'] "All Cretans," Epimenides said, drawing on his pipe and looking off into the distance for a few beats, "are liars."
[4'] "*All* Cretans are liars," Epimenides said, rolling his eyes comically.
[5'] "*All Cretans* are *liars*," Epimenides said, his eyes flashing.

Each of these versions gives us a different prosodic enactment of the four spoken words, along with verbal descriptions of facial expressions (1'), (4'), (5'), posture (2'), (3'), timing (3'), and meaningful breathing (2'). In spoken conversation, of course, we interpret multiple kinesic signals at once—and certainly would have done so automatically, without noticing our complex processing of those multiple signals, had we been present at the conversation Eubulides of Miletus describes in asking whether, if a man *says* he's lying, his statement is true or false. Eubulides not only neglects to give us the kind of kinesic information we would conversationally need to make that determination; he (or the philosophical tradition that explains him) seems to believe that it would somehow skew the (logical) experiment to provide that information.

It is indicative of the extent to which the theoretical traditions in linguistics and the philosophy of language have suppressed tonality and other forms of body language as significant channels of utterer's intention and listener's interpretation, in fact, that Christopher Hutton, in his discussion of the uses that have been made of Peirce's terms *type* and *token* in linguistics and philosophy of language, notes that in Peirce it is actually a triad (tone as First, token as Second, type as Third—see §4.3 above), but that no one quite knows what to do with tone: "The tone or qualisign corresponds to the category of Firstness, but it is by no means clear how the notions of 'qualities' and 'feelings' can be transferred into a discussion of language"

(Hutton 1990: 19). In fact, isn't tonality—as Peirce hints (and Bakhtin 1934–35/1981 argues more strenuously; see §3.2 above)—the First constitutive indicator of linguistic meaning? Hutton (1990) offers a salutary critique of the twentieth-century tendency among linguists and philosophers of language to assume sameness—to assume that the various tokens of a given linguistic type (say, all the uses of the word "the" in this appendix) are all precontextually organized by that type, so that their contextual variants need not be taken into consideration—but even he doesn't have a clear idea of how tone might be rendered significant in linguistic communication.[3] Peirce's primary example of the difference between types and tokens is the word "the": "There will ordinarily be about twenty *the*'s on a page, and of course they will count as twenty words [tokens]. In another sense of the word 'word,' however, there is but one word [type] 'the' in the English language" (1931–1958: 4.537). But Peirce too neglected to theorize the different ways we tonalize the word "the." Remember that a few paragraphs ago I described "the null context" sarcastically as "that logical sleight of mind designed to dress negation (*no* context) up as positivity (*the* null context)," italicizing "the" at the end to signal my sarcastic tonalization and thus rhetorically to undermine the *the-ness* of "the null context." This sort of meaningful tonalization is endemic in speech, of course, and, as the form of both series of attitudinalized "Epimenides paradoxes" above reminds us, that fact is commonly represented in novels. It is far less common in philosophical discourse, though the closer academic discourse comes to a representation of speech (think of Wittgenstein 1953, or Austin 1962/1975, or philosophical dialogues from Plato and Mencius to Wilde) the more overtly tone is indicated, and relied on for meaning, there. (See Lang 1990.) It seems to me that Peirce is quite right to insist on (but might have worked a little harder to theorize) tone as the qualitative First that is then put into dynamic relationship in a token as Second and habitualized as a type as Third: the First step in abstracting linguistic types out of actual use contexts into "the null context" is precisely the suppression of tone as a meaning-bearing quality of speech, and only when that suppression is fully accomplished can the logician proceed to suppress the Secondary variability of tokens.

Now, obviously it is possible, as many have suggested, to *strengthen* the liar paradox by tightening "All Cretans are liars" into "This sentence is a lie," or, more legalistically, "This sentence is not true, that is, it is false or meaningless." This patently closes the loophole left by the vagueness of "liar" (does a liar lie invariably, or only typically?). It also hampers our ability to "stage" the sentence as a spoken (and so complexly embodied) utterance, and so to constrain and guide interpretation *out* of the liar paradox through tonalizations, gestures, facial expressions, and the like—though of course it doesn't prevent such stagings entirely. For instance, imagine someone saying to you "This sentence is not true, that is, it is false or meaningless" with a mischievous wink. You wouldn't necessarily know exactly what the wink signified vis-à-vis the self-undermining truth claim; but you would suspect that the speaker intended some sort of elaborate complication of the apparent truth-lie binary, and perhaps intended an escape from it.

What I want from the liar paradox, however, is neither to escape it nor to tighten it so as to preclude the possibility of escape, but precisely to invoke the opening to conversational complexity that rhetorical readings of the paradox can offer. My interest in the liar paradox, in other words, is not logical but social-psychological. It emerges from the perception that reality often frustrates and exceeds our attempts to reduce it to neat categories, especially to neat logical binaries, and that in responding to the frustration of those attempts we sometimes try to convey more complex understandings of a state of affairs than binary logic can handle. For example, we sometimes try to have things both ways: to claim one thing on one level and another (sometimes even apparently the opposite) on another level, or to invoke poetic figures or rhetorical tropes (especially irony) that will implicate our claims in tensile relationships among conflicting views.

What can we conclude about Wilde's dialogue's status as a liar paradox from its tonalizations? Vivian, like all of Wilde's most attractive heroes, and like Wilde himself, is a wit, for whom making witty remarks is a competitive sport—specifically, a competitive form of theatricality, with a heightened meta-awareness (campy self-consciousness) of the interaction between himself as an actor and his audience. His wit is everywhere designed to impress, to make an impression, and specifically to make Cyril and the future readers of his essay laugh admiringly at the outlandish, over-the-top cleverness of his formulations. Unlike Epimenides in (a) above, however, he doesn't utter his witticisms slyly; if anything, he affects an ingenuous sincerity, so that, when Cyril protests at his wilder remarks, he protests that he is *right*. He never says explicitly that he is lying; indeed, his (or Wilde's) strategy is typically to say apparently absurd things with every verbal and nonverbal assurance that he is speaking the honest-to-God truth:

[VIVIAN.] "The crude commercialism of America, its materialising spirit, its indifference to the poetical side of things, and its lack of imagination

Liar-Paradox Monism 197

and of high unattainable ideals, are entirely due to that country having adopted for its national hero a man, who according to his own confession, was incapable of telling a lie, and it is not too much to say that the story of George Washington and the cherry-tree has done more harm, and in a shorter space of time, than any other moral tale in the whole of literature."
CYRIL. My dear boy!
VIVIAN.   I assure you it is the case, and the amusing part of the whole thing is that the story of the cherry-tree is an absolute myth. (ibid.: 304–305)

[VIVIAN.]   "They will call upon Shakespeare—they always do—and will quote that hackneyed passage forgetting that this unfortunate aphorism about Art holding the mirror up to Nature, is deliberately said by Hamlet in order to convince the bystanders of his absolute insanity in all art-matters."
CYRIL.   Ahem! Another cigarette, please.
VIVIAN.   My dear fellow, whatever you may say, it is merely a dramatic utterance, and no more represents Shakespeare's real views upon art than the speeches of Iago represent his real views upon morals. (ibid.: 306)

"Absolute" in "absolute myth" and "real" in "real views" imply a reliable realist access to reality that Vivian's/Wilde's Kantianism in the piece elsewhere belies. The tensions in the dialogue that would appear to justify a liar-paradox reading of it, then, are somewhat different from the classic versions of the liar paradox, in which the speaker *claims* to be lying: Vivian claims to be telling the truth, but the truth that he claims to be telling is that lying is far more admirable and important than truth telling; and his arguments in favor of lying are expressly designed to fly in the face of common sense and common morality, and thus to curry condemnation as *bad* lies—"bad" in both the qualitative sense (so unconvincing that no one would ever believe them) and the moral sense (flouting every decent value society holds dear).[4] Like the classic liar paradox, in other words, Wilde's in "The Decay of Lying" rests on two claims, one explicit and one implicit; unlike the classic liar paradox, however, where the explicit claim is "I'm lying" and the implicit claim is "I'm telling the truth," in Wilde's dialogue the explicit claim is "I'm telling the truth" and the implicit claim is "I'm lying." Also like the classic liar paradox, Wilde's in "The Decay of Lying" rests very uneasily on the implicit claim; unlike the implicit claim in the classic liar paradox, however, which is normatively assumed or posited, Wilde's, like Gricean implicatures, has to be (and can be) "worked out" rhetorically.

Together, do Vivian's celebration of lying and the deliberate outlandishness of his truth claims—an attribute he specifically associates with lying in the highest (artistic creativity) sense[5]—warrant an interpretation in which he is implicitly claiming to be lying as well? Does his apparent determination to provoke Philistine censure as a doubly "bad" (unconvincing and immoral) liar enhance or detract from the plausibility of a reading in which he is implicitly saying "I'm lying"? The very fact that in "The Decay of Lying" we have a rhetorical situation that is sufficiently fleshed out for us to be able to ask such questions, and weigh the textual evidence for the various interpretive answers to them, significantly distinguishes Wilde's dialogue from the classic liar paradox, where rhetorical situation is either pared down to the bare minimum (a man says he is lying) or eliminated entirely, as the paradox is first reduced to pure logical structure and then restated using logical notation.

This does not, obviously, exhaust the possibilities for rhetorical analysis of the dialogue. In particular, the question "Does his apparent determination to provoke Philistine censure as a doubly 'bad' (unconvincing and immoral) liar enhance or detract from the plausibility of a reading in which he is implicitly saying 'I'm lying'?" seems to demand further rhetorical unpacking. How is Vivian's snobbish sneering at Philistines rhetorically significant to a liar-paradox reading? At work in the dialogue is a double-readership strategy akin to that posited in theories of irony: Vivian/Wilde motivates one audience to "get it," to figure out that his apparently absurd (though ostensibly "true") explicit argument conveys a seriously intended (though presumably "lying") implicit message as well, and ideally to agree with his implicatures, by contrasting them favorably with a scapegoat lower-class Philistine audience that doesn't get it—that, as he says, catches from fogs not an effect but a cold. That latter audience does empirically exist, but its importance to Vivian/Wilde is more rhetorical than empirical: it serves as an implicit *threat* or *goad* to the audience he wants to woo. Agree with me, "get it," and regard yourself as smart, witty, cultured like me; find me shocking, absurd, unfathomable, and regard yourself as dull, a Philistine like Mrs. Arundel.

In Aristotle's terms, this constitutes a strategic doubling of the *ēthos/pathos* relationship. For the audience Vivian courts, beginning with Cyril, his ethical appeal constructs a character for himself that is smart, aesthetically sophisticated, witty, and truth-telling, and his pathetic (emotionally charged) appeal urges members of his audience to enhance their self-esteem by joining him in that character. For the audience Vivian scapegoats, his ethical appeal is actually a disappeal, a blocking or thwarting of appeal, setting up a negative character for himself as a snob and a dandy (a "queer") who is only interested in shocking the bourgeoisie (this would be his pathetic disappeal) with idle and overblown lies and fantasies, without the slightest concern for morality or the truth. *Logos* in this doubling is doubled as well: the very fact that his Philistine readers would associate his logical appeal with lies as immoral mendacity is mobilized to encourage his cultured readers to associate his logical appeal with lies as a higher artistic creativity, and thus a higher aesthetic truth. The risk Vivian/Wilde runs, obviously, is that he will alienate actual readers who identify with the cast-off Philistine audience and respond negatively to his snobbish, dandyish, iconoclastic liar *ēthos*, dismissing the entire dialogue as the worst kind of lies; but that is obviously a rhetorical risk he considers worth running. If in fact he alienates *all* his readers, he can at least feel superior to them; but if, as has obviously proved the case, some readers are inclined to admire and agree with him, the threat of being lumped with the Lumpenproletariat adds a dash of *pathos* to that inclination.

But even if we do accept a liar-paradox reading of the dialogue, how is the LP metaphysics thereby associated with it a form of monism? And how does it solve the Hard Problem of Consciousness?

A.4 LP monism

The notion that Vivian's logical appeal to members of his cultured audience might encourage them to associate his outlandish truth claims with lies as a higher artistic creativity, and thus a higher aesthetic truth, begins to move the liar paradox beyond sheer iconoclastic illogic to the monistic philosophical position I promised to outline in §A.0.

Let's begin with the outlandishness of those truth claims—those "witty remarks." Vivian/Wilde's rhetorical strategy in making them is to reverse commonsensical assumptions about lying and telling the truth:

> Many a young man starts in life with a natural gift for exaggeration which, if nurtured in congenial and sympathetic surroundings, or by the imitation of the best models, might grow into something really great and wonderful. But, as a rule, he comes to nothing. . . . He either falls into careless habits of accuracy, or takes to frequenting the society of the aged and the well-informed. Both things are equally fatal to his imagination, as indeed they would be fatal to the imagination of anybody, and in a short time he develops a morbid and unhealthy faculty of truth-telling, begins to verify all statements made in his presence, has no hesitation in contradicting people who are much younger than himself, and often ends by writing

novels which are so lifelike that no one can possibly believe in their probability. (ibid.: 294)

Wilde calls this young man's habits of accuracy "careless," which might be taken to imply that such habits develop randomly; but the rest of the passage suggests that it is so easy to fall carelessly into habits of accuracy precisely because "decent" "moral" society everywhere encourages such habits—because accuracy is a cultural norm. Presumably the young man "begins to verify all statements made in his presence" by asking "the aged and the well-informed," or by reading books and journal articles, or even by becoming a scientist, probably by doing what Thomas Kuhn (1962/1970) calls "normal" science, working to discover empirical evidence in support of a widely accepted paradigm—in all these ways "verifying" (as Wilde would see it) that "truth" is indeed whatever conforms to group norms.

We might in fact allegorize this passage as a model for the debate between the two prevailing monist positions, idealism and materialism: The young man with the "natural gift for exaggeration" is a budding idealist, committed not to matter but to mind, and specifically to the hyperbolic enhancement of qualia as art (higher lying); the counterpressures to which he succumbs in the end are the pressures of materialism, which has dominated scientific thought for the last several centuries, and, as Wilde argues at length, has dominated English fiction for the several decades previous to his writing. The fact that the verification of "statements" tends to involve appeals to authorities suggests the extent to which even materialism involves the collective hierarchical organization and regulation of qualia (see §4.5), a different kind of enhancement from the one Art perpetrates, but then that regulatory organization of qualia succeeds no more perfectly than Art does. Not all empirical science is "normal," after all—some is "revolutionary"—and normal science itself, as Kuhn insists, tends to produce anomalies that eventually lead to the breakdown of the existing paradigm. And, of course, science inescapably channels its findings through the "human element," namely qualia. The touchstone for this materialist enhancement of qualia is matter, and countless methodological workarounds have been developed to escape the experiential (empirical) primacy of qualia, to make it seem as if science were a simple registering of material reality. But of course the awareness that these are workarounds (hedging against "the human factor"), an awareness that is everywhere present in the protocols of scientific method, reminds us that the primacy of qualia is inescapable.

What Kuhn offers, needless to say, is an idealist critique of materialism. His insistence that science is driven by paradigms, and by the revolutionary scientists who develop them, and not by the normal scientists who painstakingly verify them (and ultimately undo them, simply because no paradigm can ever encompass the complexity of the *Ding an sich*), is fundamentally an insistence that science is driven by mind, not matter. Matter is the Martian kept chained to the wall down in the basement, the alien being that no one can understand; the succession of paradigms revolutionary scientists invent to explain that Martian are more akin to Wilde's "natural gift for exaggeration," or hyperbolic enhancement of qualia.

Wilde and Kuhn both recognize, however, that matter exists, and that it has the inertial capacity to resist assimilation to idealist explanatory paradigms. And, unlike most monists, idealist or materialist, Wilde and Kuhn both offer *rhetorical* models of reality: it's not that reality *is* this way or that way, but that people work interactively with other people and with nonhuman objects to *negotiate* explanations of reality. For Kuhn, these negotiations involve the interactive tensions between the revolutionary scientists who invent the reigning paradigms and the normal scientists who seek to verify them and, in so doing, discover anomalies that erode and ultimately unseat them; for Wilde, they take the rhetorical form of the liar paradox.

As we saw in §A.3, Wilde's liar paradox is saturated in rhetorical situation, and thus in interactive *perceptions* of truths and lies. For Wilde, the liar paradox is not so much a logical conundrum as it is a philosophical attempt to negotiate these interactive perceptions. And the propositional form his liar paradox takes—(outlandish) truth claims = creative (higher) lying = (higher conflicted) truth—depends for its philosophical engagement with reality on the experiential reaction from his readers (modeled for them in the dialogue by Cyril) that his truth claims are outlandish.

As we also saw in §A.3, this rhetorical dependency is complexly hierarchized and emotionally mobilized. For example, Vivian's quip that "if a man is sufficiently unimaginative to produce evidence in support of a lie, he might just as well speak the truth at once" (292) overturns our culturally normative assumptions [a] that telling the truth is preferable to lying, [b] that producing evidence in support of the truth is preferable to making unsupported truth claims, and [c] that imagination in support of a truth is somewhat suspect, but imagination in support of a lie is to be condemned outright. Wilde shifts the high value we place on truth telling to lying, and downgrades or devalues the high value we place on providing evidence for our truth claims. Recognizing that some people try to disguise a lie as the truth by providing evidence for it, he treats lying-as-misrepresentation as just another form of truth telling. After all, both lying-with-evidence and truth-telling-with-evidence are designed to convince listeners that X is Y. Since we tend to associate our commonsensical assumptions with "the truth," these iconoclastic reversals of our commonsensical assumptions seem at first—and for some readers always—to be a perverse kind of game playing with the truth, a *dissoi logoi* for purposes of sheer entertainment. We would not initially associate it with lying, since, as Vivian points out, lying is commonsensically associated with prevarication for immoral purposes, like cheating, or with escaping punishment for bad deeds, and clearly Vivian isn't trying to get away with anything here. He's just having fun—but having fun, and spreading that fun around, is how he redefines lying in the passage quoted earlier: "For the aim of the liar is simply to charm, to delight, to give pleasure" (ibid.: 305). Once we've granted him this premise, he goes on to insist that true artistic lying doesn't merely charm, delight, give pleasure, but actually shapes reality. At each stage of Wilde's argument, in other words, the liar paradox works by setting up affective, conative, and cognitive dissonance in the reader, creating in us a tension between opposing views. (See table 6.1.)

I suggest that it is this multilayered interactive tension, this complexly recursive interpersonal affective-becoming-conative-becoming-cognitive dissonance, that makes Wilde's liar paradox an effective model for a monist metaphysics. That dissonance is, after all, at the sharp edges of our attempts to understand ourselves and our world. We [a] start with our qualia, inevitably, and [b] want to be able to trust them, to rely on them to model the world for us more or less accurately. But [c] that reliance is frustrated by two forces outside ourselves: [d] other people and [e] things. To minimize our frustration, we [f] seek to master (d) and (e). Our desire/need to master (d) other people leads to [g] group dynamics (speech acts in chapter 3, the shared qualia of empathy, face, and ritual in chapter 5); our desire or need to master (e) things leads to [h] empirical science (triangulating our qualia

Table 6.1

[1a] Lying is a good thing	conflicts with	[1b] our conditioned preference for the truth
[2a] (Higher) lying is motivated only by the desire to charm and delight	conflicts with	[2b] our conditioned assumption that lying is motivated by dissembling (pretend truth telling) for immoral purposes
[3a] (Higher) lying has the power to transform our perception of reality	conflicts with	[3b] our willingness to go along with (2a)

with other people's, and with the readings off various measuring instruments). But both (g) and (h) repeatedly fail to eliminate (c) our frustrations, generating [i] affective-becoming-conative-becoming-cognitive dissonance between (a, b) the qualia-based world inside our own heads, which we are inclined to take as a reliable representation of the world outside it, and (d, e) the signals coming to us from outside our heads.

Most forms of metaphysical monism (and, for that matter, dualism) attempt to sort these tensions and dissonances out into stable states: in idealism, into the belief that mind generates, conditions, and projects matter; in materialism, into the belief that matter generates and conditions mind; in dualism, into the belief that there are these two separate worlds, a world of mind and one of matter, each of which operates according to its own stable laws. Because stable states are the default destination of metaphysical modeling, any tensions or dissonances left churning up the stable states are taken to be flaws in the modeling process; and the fact that those tensions and dissonances *are never* purified out of the modeling process—they are endemic to it—leads to complaints about an "explanatory gap" and "the Hard Problem of Consciousness." What LP monism does, I suggest, is embrace the dissonances, embrace the complex phenomenality and rhetoricity of our engagement with the world, and so offer a truer account of the world as we experience it.

What is it about the "strange loops" and "tangled hierarchies" (Hofstadter 1979) of LP monism that makes it a *monistic* philosophical position? Quite simply, it is the fact that the primacy of qualia in our relationship with the world seems to condemn or confine us to those loops and tangles. Our qualia condition us both to certainty (we *know* we are right about something, and will cling to our feeling of rightness even in the face of overwhelming empirical evidence to the contrary—see Burton 2008) and to uncertainty (the awareness that our qualia often let us down and lead us astray). The loopy strangeness that results is not simply a product of consciousness, however—not merely an idealism, say. It is, rather, a product of the relationality between consciousness and the external world. We know that there is something wrong with our qualia of certainty when they produce unexpected and unfortunate outcomes. It is the *interaction* between qualia and world that is strangely loopy. And that interaction is one thing, one (kind of) stuff.

LP monism would thus be a highly principled response to the complexity of human consciousness—to our simultaneous awareness (a, b) that we rely on our qualia as guides to reality and (c–g) that they let us down often enough that we know we can't (entirely) rely on them as guides to reality.

Because of (c–g) we have to be a bit cautious about (a, b); but also because of (c–g) we can't be sure when caution about (a, b) is indicated. So we play it by ear, sometimes staking our reputations on a truth claim about reality and hoping for the best, other times playing it safe and hedging.[6]

Or, well . . . so it seems to me now.

A.5 The problem of stability

The great explanatory problem faced by any idealism, even a fractured or failed idealism like LP monism, is the remarkable persistence or stability of certain qualia. On the one hand, [a] I can entertain the thought that I can flap my arms and fly, or that I can breathe underwater, but when I try to act on that thought, I don't rise off the earth, or I swallow great mouthfuls of water. On the other hand, [b] I can think that the sky is blue and the grass is green, or—to use one of Wilde's examples—that shadows are black, and when I mention such qualia-based beliefs to other people they don't think I am crazy. Not only do they agree; they take my stated beliefs to be givens, so normal as to be unworthy of discussion.

What makes the b-qualia so stable as to seem like reality and the a-qualia seem like harmless passing fantasies? The reductive representationalist's answer—that the b-qualia are *transparent* to reality—is only a slightly modified direct realism, and even that modified form has long since been discredited by neuroscience and quantum physics. If the reductive representationalist is standardly someone who believes in scientific truth, scientific fact, scientific proof, what makes his or her adherence to an earlier (pre-twentieth-century) scientific model of reality stick so hard as to outflank a more complex scientific awareness? Wilde's point about the shadows is that at some point in the nineteenth century painters began painting shadows on snow as *blue*, and viewers were indignant: everyone knows that shadows are *black*! But then, taught by painters, people began to notice that shadows on snow *are* blue—as Wilde puts it, shadows on snow then *became* blue—and "nature" began to imitate "art." This would suggest, again, that color perception is to some extent a cultural construct—that we see the colors we are culturally conditioned to see. But what makes our cultural conditioning stick? Why is it so difficult to change our perceptions, even after we become conscious that what or how we are perceiving is just cultural conditioning and not "reality"?

LP monism channels both the idealist belief that these culturally conditioned qualia are mental constructs that by and large constitute what we take to be reality and the materialist belief that culturally conditioned qualia are subject to unexpected counterpressures and partial falsification from a mostly mysterious and inaccessible material *Ding an sich*. If every quale were subject to total and absolute falsification from the *Ding an sich*, there would be no need for an idealist component at all; materialism would reign supreme. If it were as easy to test our belief that grass is green as it is to test a belief that we can flap our arms and fly, we would all be complacent materialists. But it isn't, so we need idealism; and yet idealism can't explain the falsificatory counterpressures we sporadically feel from something outside our neatly organized qualia, so we need either dualism or a mixed monism, like neutral monism, M&P monism, or LP monism.

The question remains: what gives culturally conditioned mental constructs their persistence, their stability? It can't be a propositional stability—the mere fact, say, that everyone in our group professes belief in them. Propositional disproof rarely has the power to dislodge mental constructs; indeed even apparently undeniable empirical disproof often meets with tenacious resistance. We tend to have a deep and strong preverbal and preconscious need to believe that certain qualia accurately represent reality. Why?

One materialist explanation for this persistence is offered by Antonio Damasio in his famous somatic-marker hypothesis. According to Damasio, the ventral-medial prefrontal cortex (necessary for making feelings available to consciousness) channels what we have learned through experience into somatic reminders or "markers" that incline us one way or another in any decision-making process (1994) or the coherent organization of qualia (1999). We are typically not aware of these signals, but with practice we can usually bring them into awareness; they are what we might call prequalia on the cusp of affective-becoming-conative-becoming-cognitive action potentials. We have quite a few words for the action potentials that result: gut feelings, hunches, vague inclinations, sudden intuitions, and so on. The signals themselves are neuroelectrical packets that can be measured with a skin-conductance test—they are *material* entities, even though we experience them as *ideal* entities, mental nudges in this direction or that (yes or no, thumbs up or thumbs down, signaled physiologically as a subtle pleasure or pain in a certain area: constriction of the throat or chest, "butterflies" in the stomach, a tingling in the spine, sweaty palms, etc.). There is, in other words, a material (neurological) substrate that actively supports belief in the veridicality of certain qualia or qualitative clusters or systems and actively discourages belief in certain others—and the active somatic support marshaled for *shared* qualia is the neurological channel through which "collective mind" (or "culture") affectively-becoming-conatively regulates social action and belief systems. The belief that shadows are black, and that a painting of blue shadows on snow is therefore inaccurate (or "artistic license"), would tend to receive support from the autonomic nervous systems of people conditioned culturally to believe in the blackness of shadows, and probably would continue to receive such support even in the face of apparently undeniable empirical evidence to the contrary, at least for a while. These resistant individuals' somatic markers would also probably continue to signal strong disapproval or discouragement for blue shadows on snow, either in paintings or photographs or on actual physical snow, as well as for arguments designed to convince these individuals that they are simply empirically wrong about the color of shadows on snow—at least until they had a conversion experience and came to realize that shadows on snow really are blue.

Note, however, that Damasio calls this his somatic-marker *hypothesis*. He doesn't present it as a hard neurological fact. I tend to accept it, because it feels intuitively right; in terms of Damasio's model, recursively, my somatic markers support it. Some others, including some influential neuroscientists (see, e.g., Rolls 1999, 2005), reject it, for what they consider compelling reasons—but since they are so far just as powerless to prove it wrong as Damasio is to prove it right, those reasons ultimately come down to (what I take to be) the fact that for them it feels intuitively wrong. I accept Damasio's *materialist* somatic-marker hypothesis for *idealist* reasons—but with the LP-monist proviso that I am willing to be dissuaded by counterpressure from that mysterious realm outside what I know that all too often thwarts and undermines what I take to be true. Because I can imagine a qualitative experience that would fill me with misgivings about the accuracy of the somatic-marker hypothesis, even when I present it as *the way things are*, as a kind of neuroontology, there is a voice in my head that says "but I could be lying to myself." And sometimes, as in this paragraph, I let that voice out.

Notes

Introduction

1. On AI and robotics see Agre and Chapman 1987; Brooks 1991; Beer 1995. On perception studies see Warren 1984; Solomon and Turvey 1988. On developmental psychology see Thelen and Smith 1995. On mathematical modeling see Kugler and Turvey 1987; Kelso 1995; Port and van Gelder 1995. See also the pre-1998 work in enactive cognition (Varela, Thompson, and Rosch 1991), existential cognition (McClamrock 1995), situated cognition (Vera and Simon 1993; Hutchins 1995; Clancey 1997), and embodied cognition (Clark 1997).

2. For example, Clark (2008: 172) praises Alva Noë (2004) for his "emphasis on skills rather than on qualia as traditionally conceived," adding on the next page that "what is at issue is not the presence or absence of mysterious, ineffable qualia but simply the presence or absence of distinctive loops linking real-world objects and properties to changing patterns of sensory stimulation." Or again: "According to this account, differently embodied beings will not be able to directly experience our perceptual world not because it is populated by its own mysterious qualia but because they lack the requisite 'sensorimotor tuning'" (ibid.: 176).

3. "What is really at stake in the play—the real conflict—is, in fact, the opposition between two views of language, one that is cognitive, or constative, and another that is performative" (Felman 1980/2003: 13).

Chapter 1

1. Unless we are realtors, in which case that putative or anticipatory affective incorporation becomes a way of *marketing* a house or an apartment as the client's next home.

2. Cf. Strawson (1994: 195): "Some, indeed, may think that philosophers who insist on the richness of the purely experiential content of episodes of conscious thought are subject to illusion, an illusion that arises because they surreptitiously and

illegitimately smuggle the richness of the external world into their conception of such purely experiential content. To combat this, one needs to make suitably vivid the fact that the richness of experiential content is something that it has just as 'purely experiential content.'"

3. It would be possible, of course, to reduce this passage to Cartesian mind-body dualism, but only if one had read no more of Hegel than this. The phrase "the spiritual tone diffused over the whole, which at once announces the physical body as the externality of a higher nature" might then be read to imply that the body *just is* the *res extensa* of the "spiritual tone" or the "higher nature" as the *res cogitans*. But in the very next paragraph (412) Hegel theorizes Cartesian mind-body dualism like this: "*In itself* matter has no truth within the soul; the soul, since it is for itself, cuts itself off from its immediate being, and places this being over against itself as bodiliness, which can offer no resistance to the soul's incorporation into it."

4. Here Crisafi and Gallagher quote from the Remark to Hegel (1830/2007, paragraph 411); the paragraph itself begins as follows: "The soul, when its bodiliness has been thoroughly trained and made its own, becomes an *individual* subject for itself; and bodiliness is thus the *externality* as a predicate, in which the subject is related only to itself."

5. As we'll see in §4.3, tone is the feeling-based First of Peirce's Hegelian tone-token-type triad.

6. Ikäheimo (2007) draws on Hegel's theory of *Anerkennung* (recognition) in order to distinguish three "layers of personhood"—"layers and dimensions of what it is to be a person in the full-fledged sense of the word." He takes these to be "features that are defining of personhood." This seems backward to me, both in terms of what Ikäheimo takes to be the spirit of Hegel's account of spirit and in terms of Ikäheimo's own itemization of the layers. The spirit of spirit, as Ikäheimo notes, is specifically *rhetorical*:

> According to this thesis, the essentially distinguishing features of the realm that Hegel called *Geist*—that is, of personhood and of the basic structures characteristic of the life-world of persons—are, on the one hand, not reducible to natural facts or processes, nor, on the other hand, do they flow from any extraterrestrial source or authority called 'God'. On this view, in important senses we persons bootstrap ourselves into personhood and maintain personhood simply by taking each other as persons—that is, through interpersonal recognition.

In other words, personhood is not a state or a condition that has certain stable "features" or "layers" or "dimensions"; it is a social construct, which presumably may be generated and maintained in significantly different ways in different groups and cultures. Rather than itemizing the "layers and dimensions of what it is to *be* a person in the full-fledged sense of the word," therefore, it seems to me Ikäheimo should be itemizing the rhetorical practices by which personhood is recognitively constructed and maintained. And indeed the three "layers or dimensions of what it is to be a person in the full-fledged sense of the word" that he adduces are "person-making psychological capacities, person-making interpersonal significances, and person-making institutional or deontic powers": not only are the second and third items "layers or dimensions" not of personhood but of the recognitive rhetoricity of "person-making," but even the first, which does seem to reflect some sort of stable ontological category ("psychological capacities"), is still framed as person-*making*.

I should note, in fact, that in the article itself Ikäheimo is mostly concerned with how we *take* someone to be a person. The reservations I have expressed so far are aimed at the objectifying language of his abstract, which he concludes as follows: "The multiplicity of ways to understand what 'personhood' means is only apparently chaotic and reveals, on a closer look, a well-ordered and dynamic internal structure." A concern with the "well-ordered and dynamic internal structure" of personhood is emphatically not the same thing as a concern with the rhetorical interactivity of taking someone to be a person.

Even in his most careful attempts to separate these two constructions of his topic out, however, Ikäheimo fudges a little:

> The first point to make in this regard is that 'taking' is *not* meant here in the sense of the epistemic act or attitude of (A.c.) *identifying* something as a person generically—this is clearly not what respect or love are. Both of these, in the relevant senses, are rather some kind of a practical attitude toward something/-one. (Preliminarily, think of Wittgenstein's "attitude towards a soul"; Wittgenstein 1953, part II, paragraph IV). The second point relates to a question raised in the recent discussions on recognition: this is whether recognitive attitudes should be understood as responses to something pre-existing or rather as bringing about something. As I see it, they clearly have to be understood in both ways, and the question is only how, exactly. As regards personhood, recognition seems to be both responsive to and constitutive of it. To grasp this responsive-constitutive relation of recognition to personhood we need to distinguish, however, between different senses of 'personhood'.

His first point would seem to be that "taking" is a rhetorical act rather than an act of objective classification based on stable pre-existing criteria. But then his second point seems to take that back, suggesting that it is *both* a constitutive rhetorical act and an act of objective classification; and the last sentence of that quotation seems to suggest that the best way to understand how the second point works is to itemize the classificatory criteria, which would appear to phase rhetoricity out of the equation entirely. (In fact those criteria of "personhood" turn out to be the three "layers and dimensions of what it is to be a person in the full-fledged sense of the word," which, as we saw above, are more about the rhetoricity of *person-making* than about personhood as a stable category.)

Surely, if personhood is constructed socially, rhetorically, through recognition or "taking someone as a person," that will be done locally, in each group (ranging in size from dyads to linguistic, religious, and national groups numbering in the hundreds of millions), with a history of collective regulation—and thus will *not* be something that will yield to universal description? In Hegel's terms, after all, the "psychological capacities" or "note of mentality" to which others respond by recognizing someone as a person are understood specifically as "*announc[ing]* the body as the externality of a higher nature"—the recognitive response is specifically not to "capacities" but to a rhetorical act.

7. I wrote the first draft of this chapter while teaching at the University of Mississippi, where I swam in the 25-yard lap-swim segment of a much larger pool; since then I have moved to Hong Kong, where I swim in an outdoor Olympic-sized pool. Though I find it easier to keep a running count of the laps I have swum in a 50-meter pool than it was when I was swimming 25-yard lengths, there are new environmental factors that negatively affect my mental math—especially the excessive heat of the water (around 32 degrees Celsius, roughly the air temperature) and the sun in my eyes when I breathe.

8. I have never seen encouragement, cheerleading, or other forms of strong emotional support for a performance categorized as emotions, and so think that they must be traditionally categorized as attitudes; but they seem so similar to other categorized emotions that I suggest a good case might be made for including them as emotions.

The Inclusion-of-Other-in-Self (IOS) scale (Aron et al. 1992) measures closeness "as the degree to which cognitive representations of the self overlap with those of the partner," and includes "feeling close" and "behaving close" as subdimensions of (cognitive) closeness (Berscheid and Reis 1998: 200; see also Aron and Aron 1986, 1996; Aron et al. 1991). Since the IOS is a sliding scale, presumably "behaving close" would include encouragement at various degrees of closeness, from an intimate relationship to cheering on a teammate at a swim meet.

9. *Sicheinbilden* usually means "imagining," but in his commentary M. J. Inwood (Hegel ibid.: 396n2) notes that "Hegel often stresses its derivation from *bilden*, 'to form, mould, etc.' and gives it the sense of "building or moulding oneself [*sich*] into [*ein*]'."

10. This distinction, between "first-language learning" and "second-language acquisition," is the established vocabulary in the field, predicated on precisely the kinds of distinctions Krashen articulates. Though I recognize that such differences exist, I resist using those terms; I prefer to describe all language learning as language *learning*, whether of one or two or three "first" languages, from birth till death (not just the first five years), or of later languages. I don't believe there is a difference *in kind* between learning a language from birth and learning it later in life. Whatever radical differences seem to warrant a binary semantics are by and large an artifact of the foreign-language classroom—and, as we'll see below, anyone who actually transcends the deleterious effects of that pedagogical artifact well enough to speak and write a language fluently ends up drawing powerfully on very much the same affective channels of language learning as an infant.

11. A personal example, from a Spanish 201 class I audited in the early 1990s: The instructor was teaching the subjunctive in terms of four verb types and five sentence types, plus a long list of verbs that took the subjunctive in certain narrowly specified structural contexts. Every time you wanted to use a verb in one of those contexts, you had to decide between the indicative and the subjunctive, which required that you review all the verb types and sentence types for the subjunctive in your head; and they were so complicated that you really needed to look at the tables in your textbook to process them properly. I found this so frustrating that I spent an hour one day working through all the cases in the book and came up with a single rule that was at least as much affective as cognitive: If the thing you're saying *feels* real, use the indicative; if it feels unreal, use the subjunctive. I proposed this simplified rule to the instructor, and she was stern: "No," she said, looking pointedly around the class to caution the other students against putting any credence in my suggestion, "No, that won't work. That doesn't cover all the possible cases!"

My fellow students disregarded her warning, however, and immediately began using my rule, and guessing right almost every time. Their success with my rule made the instructor very nervous, and she insisted on checking to make sure that the students were guessing right for the right reasons: "Is it *espero que viene* or *espero que venga*?" ("I hope s/he comes" in the indicative and subjunctive, respectively.) A student would say, correctly, "*Espero que venga*," and the instructor would ask why. "Because, um . . . s/he hasn't come yet?" the student would venture. "No!" the instructor would pounce. "Because *esperar* is a verb of emotion!" This is the "narrow-cognitive" computational ideal with a vengeance.

12. A similar extended proprioceptive phenomenon occurs even when we aren't driving a car. Once my (now former) wife stormed out of a fight, got in our car—which was in the garage immediately underneath our bedroom—and went to drive off. I stood at the window over the garage door and watched her back out, too fast, incautiously, no doubt still as upset by the fight as I was, and cut the wheel too hard to the right, crunching the car's left front fender on the jamb of the garage door. At what felt like the exact same instant—but was probably 200–300 milliseconds later—I felt a stabbing pain in my left shoulder. My nervous system, mapping my body onto the car's, lying prone with my wife "steering" me, simulated in my body the "pain" "felt" by the car's body. Antonio Damasio (1999: 80) calls the neuronal system that makes this simulation possible the "as-if body loop," but mainly means by it our bodies' tendency to mimic the body states of other *people*. The possibility that we also simulate the "body states" of inanimate objects would be a materialist explanation of the pathetic fallacy. More on the as-if body loop in §3.3 and §5.1.

Chapter 2

1. Sterelny (2012: xi–xii) seems to be seconding this notion that sociality is the most important (and indeed ubiquitous) form of extended mind when he writes: "One message of this book is that human cognitive competence is a collective achievement and a collective legacy; at any one moment of time, we depend on each other, and over time, we stand on the shoulders not of a few giants but of myriads of ordinary agents who have made and passed on intact the informational resources on which human lives depend." He adds: "Another is that human cognitive competence often depends on epistemic engineering: on organizing our physical environment in ways that enhance our information-processing capacities." This could be read as resistance to my notion that sociality *rather than* epistemic engineering is the primary channel of extended mind, but in that second point Sterelny is actually making the less controversial claim that epistemic engineering *improves* cognition, not that it *is* cognition.

2. Clark (2008: 91) writes:

The force of Adams and Aizawa's worry does not lie in any simple (and surely naive) identification of the neural and the cognitive. Rather, the real worry is that the inscriptions in Otto's notebook (unlike, say, the hybrid neural and silicon-based activity that now underlies control of the oscillatory rhythms in the stomatogastric ganglion in the California spiny lobster) are out-and-out conventional. They are passive representations that are parasitic, for their meaning, on public practices of coordinated use.

Let us agree that there is something quite compelling about the idea that the notebook encodings are all conventional and derivative. Let us agree also, at least for the sake of argument, that some parts of any genuinely cognitive system have to trade in representations that are not thus conventional and derivative.

3. I have always wondered what people mean by "the materiality of language." Surely language has no material existence. A spoken utterance has an acoustic aspect, as a written word has a visual one, but neither the acoustics of speech nor the visual appearance of letters is *language*; both are sense data that competent language users *interpret* as language. And both that interpretation and the "text" that the interpretation produces are intersubjective constructs; they have no materiality. Indeed, people who speak of the materiality of language typically don't seem to mean acoustics or visual representations; they appear to mean something else, which they almost never define. For Clark, for example, the materiality of language seems to entail "linguistic forms and structures"—and if there is some aspect of language that is *less* material than forms and structures, which stand at least three levels of abstraction away from anything literally material, I don't know what it is.

4. The examples Adams and Aizawa (2008) do discuss involve either linguistic conversation (e.g. in their discussion of Gibbs on pages 96–98) or the observation of bodies and logical inference: "How could one understand why a person's eyes dilate

at a given time, if one does not know that she is playing Texas Hold 'Em and has just drawn the top full house? How could one understand why a person is thinking about a bandage without knowing that the person cut her finger with a knife?" (ibid.: 111).

I find that first example puzzling. If I am in a game of Texas Hold 'Em with you, and therefore in a position to notice the dilation of your eyes, the only way I can *know* you have just drawn the top full house is by cheating, in which case noticing and being able to analyze the dilation of your eyes is for me supererogatory; and if I am not playing but sitting behind you and watching you play—looking at your cards, so that I do know you have just drawn the top full house—the only way I can see your eyes dilate is with an elaborately rigged mirror. What Adams and Aizawa presumably mean is either that I am a cardsharp who has learned to make affective communication conscious (and therefore "cognitive" in the strict sense) and take the dilation of your eyes to be an affective signal or "tell" that you have a strong hand, which I only later discover was the top full house, or else that this is one of those great hypothetical examples in which I know everything in the hands, pupils, and minds of everyone present.

5. Should we assume that this specification that "*natural* language has merely derived content" constitutes an *a priori* exclusion of symbolic language, which would thus be either completely nonderived or less derived than natural language? Or do Adams and Aizawa mark the form of language that "has merely derived content" inclusively rather than exclusively? Surely, after all, symbolic language was carefully *developed* by logicians and mathematicians to perform certain specific operations? Surely it is explicitly and consciously *taught* by teachers to students?

6. One rather extreme line of reasoning that Adams and Aizawa don't pursue here, but that seems implicit in the binary opposition between cognitive private thoughts and noncognitive public utterances, would be the skeptical argument (see Avramides 2001) that only the central actor demonstrably generates nonderived content, and the peripheral actor is functionally no better than an automaton. Since no human actor can occupy more than a single body at a time, anyone participating in this thought experiment will mentally occupy the central actor's body and become by default incapable of proving that the peripheral actor is able to generate nonderived content (have original thoughts). After all, from the central actor's point of view the peripheral actor emits utterances such as "Yes, I can hear you" and "No, you're breaking up," which as natural language have "merely derived content" and thus cannot serve as evidence of cognition. And even if the subject participating in this thought experiment then mentally jumps to the peripheral actor's body and mentally (hypothetically) occupies it in turn, that body thereby becomes the central actor's body and so is capable of generating nonderived representations, and the body that was previously the central actor's is thereby automatically reduced to automaton status. It doesn't matter how rapidly one flips between the two bodies

in mental simulation; only one body at a time can be the central actor's and thus capable of cognition.

7. Adams and Aizawa (2008: 31, 55) make passing mention of the origin of the distinction between derived and nonderived representations in the field of naturalized semantics. As Adams and Aizawa (2010) trace the development of this field, it was first formulated by Stampe (1977), greatly expanded by Dretske (1981), and most fully developed in the 1980s by Jerry Fodor, especially in his 1984 discussion of Stampe and Dretske in "Semantics, Wisconsin style" (reprinted in Fodor 1990) and in his two-part 1987 article "A theory of content" (ibid.: 53–136). (Also see Dretske 1988, 1999; Fodor 1994.) Fred Adams did his PhD work at the University of Wisconsin with Stampe and Dretske, and Fodor's naturalized semantics was one of the first fields in which Adams and Aizawa (1992, 1993, 1994a, 1994b) began collaborating in the early 1990s.

8. These attitudes have changed dramatically since the 1980s, but Sterelny (2012: xi) still sounds somewhat radical in presenting his argument about the social enrichment of human learning environments as "a plausible, first-approximation model of a striking natural phenomenon: the evolution of the distinctive features of human cognition and human social life."

9. Damasio (2003, pp. 30–31) writes:

All living organisms from the humble amoeba to the human are born with devices designed to solve *automatically*, no proper reasoning required, the basic problems of life. Those problems are: finding sources of energy; incorporating and transforming energy; maintaining a chemical balance of the interior compatible with the life process; maintaining the organism's structure by repairing its wear and tear; and fending off external agents of disease and physical injury. The single word homeostasis is convenient shorthand for the ensemble of regulations and the resulting state of regulated life.

In the course of evolution the innate and automated equipment of life governance—the homeostasis machine—became quite sophisticated. At the bottom of the organization of homeostasis we find simple responses such as *approaching* or *withdrawing* of an entire organism relative to some object; or increases in activity (*arousal*) *or* decreases in activity (*calm* or *quiescence*). Higher up in the organization we find *competitive* or *cooperative* responses.

"No proper reasoning required," obviously, signals what Adams and Aizawa would want to call noncognitive processes. The iterative nature of the evolutionary development of this "homeostasis machine," however, means that higher levels tend to incorporate the functioning of lower levels, so that, for example, our conscious (uncontestedly cognitive) decisions to approach or withdraw from some object, or to excite ourselves or calm ourselves down, or to compete or cooperate, still partake of the automated nature of lower-level "noncognitive" reflexes. The conscious/cognitive decision, in other words, is often accompanied by a lower-level automated reflex, even preceded and conditioned by it. Human cognition is soritic in the sense that it never entirely separates from the noncognitive or precognitive ("derived") processes that give rise to it.

10. Nor, naturally, does animal cognition. Although both nonhuman mammalian cognition and human cognition are affective-becoming-cognitive, human cognition is affective-becoming-*more*-cognitive.

11. This is far too complex a matter to discuss in detail here. Perhaps it will suffice as a stopgap measure to note that I am drawing on the metalinguistics of Mikhail Bakhtin (1934–1935/1981), who insists that every uttered word is saturated with the attitudinalizations of every speaker or writer who has ever used it—that, in other words, some affective charge to the "thought" "behind" the word makes the jump across the airspace between me and you and becomes yours as well. See §3.2 for further discussion.

Chapter 3

1. Felman (1980/2003: 55–56) notably and perhaps notoriously disagrees with Derrida here. "If the capacity for misfire is an inherent capacity of the performative," she writes, "it is because the act as such is defined, for Austin, as the capacity to *miss its goal* and to *fail to be achieved,* to remain *unconsummated.*" In other words, in Felman's view Austin anticipates and incorporates Derrida's critique.

2. Michael Holquist (1990: 428) glosses heteroglossia as follows: "The base condition governing the operation of meaning in any utterance. It is that which insures the primacy of context over text. At any given time, in any given place, there will be a set of conditions—social, historical, meteorological, physiological—that will insure that a word uttered in that place and at that time will have a meaning different than it would have under any other conditions; all utterances are heteroglot in that they are functions of a matrix of forces practically impossible to recoup, and therefore impossible to resolve. Heteroglossia is as close a conceptualization as possible of that locus where centripetal and centrifugal forces collide; as such, it is that which a systematic linguistics must suppress."

3. For Bakhtin's Russian originals, see Bakhtin 1934–1935/1975.

4. Unlike Derrida's graphematics, Bakhtin's metalinguistics is normatively oriented toward the spoken word, the voiced word, the accented or tonalized word, the word as shaped by the body. (This tonalization of voice can be reorganized in writing. All the passages I've cited are from "Discourse in the *Novel,*" an extended discussion of the power of these vocal dialogisms in prose fiction, but their theoretical force is derived from embodied face-to-face dialogue.)

5. Here I begin to move past Bourdieu's model. Bourdieu insists that the intimidator doesn't intimidate, nor does the speech act of intimidation intimidate, rather state power intimidates, and the intimidator and his or her speech act are only the authorized or delegated or "vested" channels of that power: "The power of words is nothing other than the *delegated power* of the spokesperson, and his speech—that is, the substance of his discourse and, inseparably, his way of speaking—is no more

than a testimony, and one among others, of the *guarantee of delegation* which is vested in him" (ibid.: 107). "Nothing other than," "no more than"—here, as everywhere, Bourdieu is determined to clear and police wide vacant DMZs between binary poles, in this case between the power of words and the power of the state. The "spokesperson" or dominant/powerful speaker mediates between those poles, but *purely* in the delegated service of the state power. Whatever that normatively male speaker says points "testimonially" past his own agency to the power of the state.

What this model misses, however, is the extent to which speakers don't merely *channel* power but *condition* it, and are conditioned by it. Bourdieu (ibid.: 51) himself seems to hint in this direction when he remembers the diffuse complexity of the *habitus* as he himself has repeatedly theorized it: "Thus the modalities of practices, the ways of looking, sitting, standing, keeping silent, or even of speaking ('reproachful looks' or 'tones,' 'disapproving glances' and so on) are full of injunctions that are powerful and hard to resist because they are silent and insidious, insistent and insinuating." But even such formulations stop short of theorizing this saturation of speech acts with "injunctions that are powerful and hard to resist" as the primary channel of habitualization, of social conditioning.

Part of Bourdieu's problem may be that he binarizes word and act, so that words are effectively disembodied, disenacted, returned to their idealized Saussurean status as abstract code, and then merely *situated* in an embodied social context that carries them. And indeed as long as we think of speech acts as *words*—as discrete lexical units separated analytically by blank spaces on the page, and sometimes, in careful enunciation (often conditioned by the reading and writing of spatially separated words), by a slight pause in speech—it will seem counterintuitive to study the embodiment of language. An affective charge in this binarized view is not *in* words, *of* words; it is *added to* words.

6. In describing laugh tracks as "data compression" I'm thinking of Sandy Stone's (1995: 396) remarks on data compression in phone sex:

> The more I observed phone sex the more I realized I was observing very practical applications of data compression. Usually sex involves as many of the senses as possible: taste, touch, smell, sight, hearing—and, for all I know, short-range psychic interactions—all work together to heighten the erotic sense. Consciously or unconsciously, phone sex workers translate all the modalities of experience into audible form. . . . The sex workers took an extremely complex, highly detailed set of behaviors, translated them into a single sense modality, then further boiled them down to a series of highly compressed tokens. They then squirted those tokens down a voice-grade phone line. At the other end of the line the recipient of all this effort added boiling water, so to speak, and reconstituted the tokens into a fully detailed set of images and interactions in multiple sensory modes.
>
> Further, what was being sent back and forth over the wires wasn't just information, it was *bodies*.

Note here, too, that the phenomenon Stone half-whimsically imagines as "short-range psychic interactions" is precisely the affective or "empathetic" communication that I will be theorizing in §5.1. In other words, it isn't that lovers communicate telepathically, but that they develop extremely rapid and intertwined as-if body loops that enable them to experience each other's body states vicariously but with a high degree of mimetic accuracy and somatic intensity.

7. For Felman's (1980/2003: 13) distinction between "performative" and "constative" linguistics, see note 3 above. For book-length explorations of this distinction, see Robinson 2003 and 2006.

Chapter 4

1. In a footnote to "Quale-consciousness" (Peirce 1931–1958: 6.150n), the editors identify it as "'Notes for Eight Lectures,' which Peirce specifically says are to follow the preceding." It is only when we turn to "the preceding" (ibid.: 6.147n) that we find the series of lecture notes that we now know includes "Quale-consciousness" dated to 1898.

2. Neither historian of qualia, however, mentions that in 1920, when Lewis was given his first office at Harvard, it happened to come with an odd stack of papers in one corner that turned out to be the Peirce papers. Lewis was the first to sit and read through them.

3. Note that James, having argued that "the emotional reaction usually terminates in the subject's own body" (1890: 2.442), also goes on to discuss the ways in which, "as emotions are described in novels, they interest us, for we are made to *share* them" (ibid.: 2.448, emphasis added). His explanation of this sharing seems to anticipate the cognitive "simulation" theory of empathy (Ravenscroft 1998): "We have grown acquainted with the concrete objects and emergencies which call them forth, and any knowing touch of introspection which may grace the page meets with a quick and feeling response" (James ibid.).

4. See also the appendix to the present book—though Peirce (1931–1958: 5.340) himself labored, in an 1868 article in the *Journal of Speculative Philosophy*, to resolve the liar paradox logically in terms of a single consciousness.

5. Note that this account of qualia is utterly congruent with the contention-scheduling or "pandemonium" model of consciousness offered in Dennett 1991—despite the fact that Dennett later in that book so flamboyantly "quines" the existence of qualia. The problem is almost certainly semantic, specifically Dennett's aversion to the semantics of qualia. He recognizes the phenomena that philosophers call qualia, but thinks the term too fuzzy for scientific inquiry.

6. James specifically selects the term "feeling" as a "general term by which to designate all states of consciousness as such, and apart from their particular quality or cognitive function" (1890/1950: 1.185), worrying only that the term "has specific meanings as well as its generic one, sometimes standing for pleasure and pain, and

being sometimes a synonym of *'sensation'* as opposed to *thought*; whereas we wish a term to cover sensation and thought indifferently" (ibid.: 1.185–186).

7. As Hutton (1990: 12) notes, in Peirce's triadic thinking "Fi[rs]tness is a 'suchness', a quality, a feeling." "By a feeling," Peirce (1931–1958: 1.303) writes of Firstness, "I mean an instance of that kind of consciousness which involves no analysis, comparison nor any process whatsoever, nor consists in whole or in part of any act by which one stretch of consciousness is distinguished from another." This account of feeling as Firstness is virtually identical to his 1898 account of quale-consciousness. It is not, however, until 1907 that Peirce begins to apply the Firstness of feeling to his theory of the interpretant. For a useful tracing of the history of Peirce's thinking on the interpretant, see Short 2004.

8. Note here the equation of feeling with quale-consiousness: "to feel" for Peirce *is* "to be immediately conscious."

9. Here is how Peirce expresses the ideas in this paragraph and the next two:

> It is not to be supposed that upon every presentation of a sign capable of producing a logical interpretant, such interpretant is actually produced. The occasion may either be too early or too late. If it is too early, the semiosis will not be carried so far, the other interpretants sufficing for the rude functions for which the sign is used. On the other hand, the occasion will come too late if the interpreter be already familiar with the logical interpretant, since then it will be recalled to his mind by a process which affords no hint of how it was originally produced. (1931–1958: 5.489)

The occasion that is too early for a logical interpretant would be the interpretive work done by the inexperienced listener, who, say, only gets the "series of feelings" (the emotional interpretant sufficing), or who gets a general feeling and is happy to tap his or her foot or fingers to the beat, or whistle the melody later (the energetic interpretant sufficing). The occasion that is too late for a logical interpretant is one in which the sophisticated listener has so often done the interpretive work on this piece or pieces like it that it has become automatic, subliminal, unconscious. My suggestion that it will then only be *registered* by the emotional interpretant is an extrapolation from "it will be recalled to his mind by a process which affords no hint of how it was originally produced" and the "sense of comprehending the meaning of the sign."

Note that Jackendoff is a Chomskyan cognitivist (Lerdahl is the composer and music theorist) who needs the telic idealization of "the final state of his understanding" to supplant the full teleology in order to justify theorizing a TG-grammar of music as "competence." Peirce, like his precursors Aristotle and Hegel, is far more interested than the authors of this book in the full entelechy/dialectic/triad—even when the "fullness" of his triad means that a given individual doesn't actually complete it.

10. It is also significant that Peirce begins by theorizing the type, the Third, then moves to the token, the Second, and, after briefly theorizing the tone, the First, returns to a discussion of type and token: "In order that a Type may be used, it has

to be embodied in a Token which shall be a sign of the Type, and thereby of the object the Type signifies. I propose to call such a Token of a Type an *Instance* of the Type" (1931–1958: 4.537). It is possible that he had not worked out the full triadic implications of this formulation, and never quite got around to theorizing the tone properly; and it does seem as if he were far more interested in tokens as instances of types than in the full triad.

Accordingly, Hutton typically refers to the full triad not as "the tone-token-type triad" but as "the type-token-tone relation" (1990: 17, 21), "the type-token-tone distinction" (ibid.: 20), or "the type-token(-tone) distinction" (ibid.: 11). And in his first chapter, an exposition of Peirce's use of the terms, after complaining that "Most expositions of the type-token distinction fail to mention the category of tone" (ibid.: 21), he too most often refers to "the type-token relation" (ibid.: 8, 9, 10, 16, 19, 28, 30; this collocation also appears in the subtitle of his book) or "type-token distinction" (ibid.: 3, 21), dropping tone from the triad, reversing the order of token and type, and converting Peirce's triad into a "relation." (Champagne 2009 refers to it as "the type-token-tone trichotomy.") A Google search turned up ten times as many hits for "tone-token-type" as for "type-token-tone," but there were more than 200 hits for the latter.

Though this nomenclature does seem to reflect the unfinished state in which Peirce left the triad, a full thinking of the triad's entelechy would certainly need to reframe the token not as an *instance* of the type but as a dynamic interactive object that eventually (but not inevitably) *gives rise* to mediatory conceptions of the type as an habitualization of tone and token. Note also that "The category of Secondness is essentially one of relation" (Hutton 1990: 13), and a token is a Second—but Secondness in this particular triad would involve not a "type-token relation" but a "tone-token relation." Peirce's Third will by definition bring the First and the Second into relation—but while Peirce can imagine a triad that falls short of Thirdness, leaving in this case tone and token in dynamic interaction without moving into the finality of type, there is no triad without Firstness.

11. As the rough synonymy between "tone" and "qualisign" indicates, Peirce doesn't mean by "tone" only tonalities; he means qualities in general, *for example* tone of voice. Tonality is the primary exemplar after which qualities/qualia/qualisigns are named—which is to say that in the conceptualization of qualities "tone" (and specifically "tone of voice") is the leading token of the type "quality" (or "qualisign").

12. Speaking of sensations that are ostensibly "not about anything," is the quale that is the motion illusion not a sensation of motion?

13. For example, is an orgasm an interpretant? It has its emotional and energetic aspects, obviously, but toward what logical interpretation does it guide us? If stand-up comedians and movies are to be believed, some partners ask "Was it good for you?" after sex; would answering that question entail using the orgasm as one interpretant (along with foreplay, etc.) regulating the interpretation of the overall

experience of sex? Or would it entail summoning up a new interpretant to aid in the interpretation of the quality of the noninterpretive quale that was the orgasm? Another question, obviously, is whether an orgasm is a single quale or a whole slew of qualia, and whether, if they are legion, they are all equally interpretive.

14. And thus come to be thought of as "memes." For the debate on Dawkins' (1976) coinage of "meme," see Brodie 1996; Lynch 1998; Blackmore 1999; Gabora 1999; Miller 2000. Significantly, one of Gabora's complaints is that "memeticists" don't tackle the difficult question of *how* memes are transmitted from head to head, body to body—a criticism that is not unlike the one intracranialists aim at Clark. Again, I offer a research-based model for that transmission in §5.1.

15. "Most philosophers," Searle writes, "would agree that collective behavior is a genuine phenomenon; the disagreement comes in how to analyze it. One tradition is willing to talk about group minds, the collective unconscious, and so on. I find this talk at best mysterious and at worst incoherent" (1990: 404). Since the tradition that Searle dismisses is the tradition in which I am working, I suggest that it seems mysterious and incoherent to him largely because he doesn't know of an empirical model that would explain it to his satisfaction; it is my project here to provide one.

16. For a complete listing see http://email.eva.mpg.de/~tomas/pdf/cv_2012-05-09.pdf. For the papers most relevant to our present purposes, see Call and Tomasello 1995, 2003; Carpenter and Tomasello 2000; Carpenter, Call, and Tomasello 2002; Carpenter, Nagell, and Tomasello 1998; Carpenter, Tomasello, and Savage-Rumbaugh 1995; Graefenhein, Behne, Carpenter, and Tomasello 2009; Kirschner and Tomasello 2009; Liebal, Behne, Carpenter, and Tomasello 2009; Tomasello and Haberl 2003; Tomasello and Rakoczy 2003; Tomasello and Farrar 1986; Tomasello and Todd 1983; Tomasello, Carpenter, Call, Behne, and Moll 2005.

Chapter 5

1. It may be totalitarian, of course; but totalitarian regimes arise precisely because total regulation of human groups is, by default, impossible. Total regulation would mean no possibility of resistance or recalcitrance or inadvertent deviation was possible—as in the so-called hive mentality.

2. Adams has also published on empathy. His 2001 article considers two possible explanations of empathetic identification, neither of which draws on affective communication: a "theory of mind theory," according to which "we use a theory of mind to make attributions of intentional states to others (Churchland, 1998, 3–15; Gopnik, 1995; Stich and Ravenscroft, 1994)," and a simulation theory (which Adams considers mostly in terms of Ravenscroft 1998), according to which "we use our cognitive capacities to simulate and pretend to be in the situation of others" (Adams 2001: 368). Unsurprisingly in view of his narrow-cognitivist/representationalist assumptions, Adams leans in that article toward the former theory; but both of the

options Adams weighs are "cognitive" in the strict sense, excluding affective communication. (Adams almost certainly means not Gopnik 1995 but Gopnik and Wellman 1995.).

For philosophical and cognitivist studies of empathy, see Adams 2001; Deigh 1995; Deonna 2007; Kögler and Stueber 2000; Malle and Hodges 2005; Nichols 2001; Ravenscroft 1998; and Thompson 2001. For psychotherapeutic studies of empathy, see Bohart and Greenberg 1997; Clark 2006. For social-psychological studies of empathy, see Chlopan et al. 1985; Cialdini et al. 1997; Davis 1996; Zaki et al. 2008. For neuroscience studies of empathy, see Decety and Ickes 2009; Lamm et al. 2007; Loggia et al. 2008; Preston et al. 2007; Ruby and Decety 2004. Of these, Loggia et al. 2008 offers the most overwhelming empirical evidence that empathy is not merely a "theory" or a mental "simulation" but actually increases sensory and affective pain—something that Aristotle first observed, in fact, in the emotion chapters (2–11) of book 2 of the *Rhetoric*.

3. Like *doxa*, *dokeō* cycles through both opinion and reputation—that is, from "I think" to "I seem." What I think of you fades imperceptibly into what you seem to me to be, and perhaps even into what you seem to yourself to be. These two apparently opposed usages resemble the results of what in other Greek verbs would be the active and passive voice—"I think" as active, "I seem" as passive—but in *dokeō* both are, rather unusually, active in form, so that they are morphologically indistinguishable from each other. In fact, it's even more complicated than that. Not only can what you think of me become what I seem to be without giving grammatical notice; I can even surreptitiously *shape* what you think of me, and thus what I seem to be, without changing verbs or verb forms: *dokeō* can mean "I think," "I seem," or "I pretend or feign." If "I think" is the obvious and presumably original "active" meaning of the verb, and "I seem" is the secondary or displaced "passive" meaning, "I pretend" would involve a double displacement, so that I wield a concealed active influence over my apparently passive seeming. For Aristotle's original Greek, see Aristotle 4th century BCE/1959.

Appendix

1. A. N. Prior (1976: 139) notes approvingly that John Buridan (ca. 1300–ca. 1360) built an argument *against* the paradoxicality of the liar paradox on the assumption that "every proposition, whatever else it may signify or assert, signifies or asserts, by its very form as a proposition, that it is itself true. Any proposition, therefore, which asserts or implies its own falsehood asserts both its falsehood and its truth, and is bound to be in fact false, since at least *something* that it asserts to be the case is not so." If the liar paradox is false, it is not paradoxical. Prior goes on to discuss Buridan's later objection that "propositions do *not* in general signify in virtue of their very form that they are themselves true" because there is a difference between signifying something "formally" (linguistically) and signifying something "virtually" (metalinguistically). Prior (ibid.: 141) rebuts this later theory and, citing Peirce's

discussion of the liar paradox (*"every proposition asserts its own truth"* (1931–1958: 5.340, emphasis in original)) in support of his view, reinstates Buridan's earlier theory: "In other words, a language *can* contain its own semantics, that is to say its own theory of meaning, provided that this semantics contains the law that for any sentence *x*, *x* means that *x* is true."

It should be noted, of course, that these implicit self-referential truth claims do apply to all propositions, which are artificial logical reductions of spoken or written utterances that have whatever characteristics logicians assign to them. The confusion arises through logicians' assumption that actual spoken or written utterances are propositions too—propositions in the rough, so to speak—and that once they have been pruned of all their contextual/communicative/interactive complexity they can be treated as propositions. When Eubulides of Miletus asks whether a man *saying* "I'm lying" is lying or telling the truth, the hypothetical man's utterance is obviously not a proposition until logicians agree to treat it (and purify it) as one; but this is a nicety that is almost always forgotten by logicians.

2. Or consider Eubulides of Miletus asking whether, if a man says he's lying, his statement is true or false: presumably the man *tells someone* that he's lying, in a specific speech context. The conversational context of the question would lead the unsuspecting non-logician to expect a full answer to depend heavily on rhetorical situation: who the man is talking to, and where, and when, and why, and what the history of their relationship is, and what he's feeling about the situation, and what impression he's trying to make on the other(s), etc. Certainly the non-logician would expect to be able to draw inferences from the man's tone of voice, and more generally from what is collectively known about the man's personal tonalization habits: if he says "Yeah, I'm lying" *cheerfully*, does that really indicate, as it seems to, that he is light-heartedly insouciant about it all, or do we in fact know that he often uses a cheerful tone to mask bitter irony? If the non-logician in question were an ethnographer of speech, s/he would want to analyze not only the vocal tonalities but the full body language (facial expressions, gestures, postures, proximity, eye contact, timing, etc.) of everyone present, preferably for the entire conversation, ideally for every conversation everyone present has ever been in. Eubulides of Miletus—like the philosophers who have weighed in on the liar paradox ever since— seems to be asking us to suppress all that information that we rely on so heavily in ordinary linguistic communication, and *just answer the question*, in the abstract, in the null context: quick, true or false? To the non-logician interested more in the complexity of communication than in abstract intellectual puzzles, that seems like a mug's game—like being asked to admire great paintings through a welder's helmet, or to run a marathon with both legs splinted at the knee.

3. Hutton tells me in private correspondence that what he meant by that was that linguistics in its late-1980s incarnation was unable to deal with tone—which is to say that "it is by no means clear how the notions of 'qualities' and 'feelings' can be transferred into a discussion of language" should be read as a kind of indirect-speech

semi-quotation from late-1980s linguists: "it is by no means clear [*to linguists*] how the notions of 'qualities' and 'feelings' can be transferred into a discussion of language."

4. Consider, for example, remarks made by G. R. Carpenter (1891: 572) in the same year in which Wilde's dialogue was originally published. Quoting the passage from Vivian's first monologue to the effect that "what Art reveals to us is Nature's lack of design, her curious crudities, her extraordinary monotony, her absolutely unfinished condition," Carpenter notes that "a statement at first thought so astonishing and almost revolting as this is shortly followed by others scarcely less surprising." Quoting Wilde's line to the effect that action is "the last resource of those who do not know how to dream," he opines that "statements like these, seemingly so flippant, prejudice the casual reader against Mr. Wilde."

5. "Who he was who first, without ever having gone out to the rude chase, told the wondering cavemen at sunset how he had dragged the Megatherium from the purple darkness of its jasper cave, or slain the Mammoth in single combat and brought back its gilded tusks, we cannot tell, and not one of our modern anthropologists, for all their much-boasted science, has had the ordinary courage to tell us. Whatever was his name or race, he certainly was the true founder of social intercourse" (Wilde, 1891/1982: 305).

6. I say "we," implying that this is folk psychology, though of course there are people who believe they are always right, and have no sense of (c–g) whatsoever; but I submit that even always-righters must know, lying in bed at night, that they aren't always right, that reality doesn't quite conform to their views of it, that their predictions about reality don't always come true, and so on. In Freudian terms, their belief that they are always right is a *defense* against their preconscious pre-awareness that they are not.

References

Adams, Frederick. 2001. Empathy, neural imaging and the theory versus simulation debate. *Mind & Language* 16: 368–392.

Adams, Frederick, and Kenneth Aizawa. 1992. "X" means X: Semantics Fodor-style. *Minds and Machines* 2: 175–183.

Adams, Frederick, and Kenneth Aizawa. 1993. Fodorian semantics, pathologies, and Block's problem. *Minds and Machines* 3: 97–104.

Adams, Frederick, and Kenneth Aizawa. 1994a. Fodorian semantics. In *Mental Representation: A Reader*, ed. S. Stich and T. Warfield. Blackwell.

Adams, Frederick, and Kenneth Aizawa. 1994b. "X" means X: Fodor/Warfield semantics. *Minds and Machines* 4: 215–231.

Adams, Frederick, and Kenneth Aizawa. 2001. The bounds of cognition. *Philosophical Psychology* 14: 43–65.

Adams, Frederick, and Kenneth Aizawa. 2008. *The Bounds of Cognition*. Wiley-Blackwell.

Adams, Frederick, and Kenneth Aizawa. 2009. Why the mind is still in the head. In *Cambridge Handbook of Situated Cognition*, ed. P. Robbins and M. Aydede. Cambridge University Press.

Adams, Frederick, and Kenneth Aizawa. 2010. Causal theories of mental content. *Stanford Encyclopedia of Philosophy* (http: //plato. stanford. edu/entries/content-causal/).

Adolphs, Ralph. 2002. Neural mechanisms for recognizing emotion. *Current Opinion in Neurobiology* 12: 169–178.

Adolphs, Ralph, Daniel Tranel, and Antonio R. Damasio. 1994. Impaired recognition of emotion in facial expressions following bilateral damage to the human amygdala. *Nature* 372: 669–672.

Adolphs, Ralph, Daniel Tranel, and Antonio R. Damasio. 1998. The human in social judgment. *Nature* 393: 470–474.

Adolphs, Ralph, Hannah Damasio, Daniel Tranel, Gregory Cooper, and Antonio R. Damasio. 2000. A role for somatosensory cortices in the visual recognition of emotion as revealed by 3-d lesion mapping. *Journal of Neuroscience* 20: 2683–2690.

Agre, Philip E., and David Chapman. 1987. PENGI: An implementation of a theory of activity. In *Proceedings of the Sixth National Conference on Artificial Intelligence (AAAI-87)*, 268–272. American Association for Artificial Intelligence.

Aizawa, Kenneth, and Frederick Adams. 2005. Defending non-derived content. *Philosophical Psychology* 104: 5–25.

Alexander, C. Norman, Jr., and Mary Glenn Wiley. 1981. Situated activity and identity formation. In *Social Psychology: Sociological Perspectives*, ed. M. Rosenberg and R. Turner. Basic Books.

Allport, Alan. 1988. What concept of consciousness? In *Consciousness in Contemporary Science*, ed. A. Marcel and E. Bisiach. Oxford University Press.

Aristotle. Fourth century BCE/1959. *tekhnē rhetorikē*. Clarendon.

Aron, Arthur, and Elaine N. Aron. 1986. *Love as the Expansion of Self: Understanding Attraction and Satisfaction*. Hemisphere.

Aron, Arthur, and Elaine N. Aron. 1996. Self and self expansion in relationships. In *Knowledge Structures in Close Relationships: A Social Psychological Approach*, ed. G. Fletcher and J. Fitness. Erlbaum.

Aron, Arthur, Elaine N. Aron, and Daniel Smollan. 1992. Inclusion of Other in the Self Scale and the structure of interpersonal closeness. *Journal of Personality and Social Psychology* 63: 596–612.

Aron, Arthur, Elaine N. Aron, Michael Tudor, and Greg Nelson. 1991. Close relationships as including other in self. *Journal of Personality and Social Psychology* 60: 241–253.

Austin, J. L. 1961. Pretending. In Austin, *Philosophical Papers*, ed. J. Urmson and G. Warnock. Oxford University Press.

Austin, J. L. 1962/1975. *How to Do Things with Words*, ed. M. Sbisa and J. Urmson. Harvard University Press.

Averett, Christine, and David R. Heise. 1988. Modified social identities: Amalgamations, attributions, and emotions. In *Analyzing Social Interaction: Advances in Affect Control Theory*, ed. L. Smith-Lovin and D. Heise. Gordon and Breach.

Avramides, Anita. 2001. *Other Minds*. Routledge.

Bagozzi, Richard P. 1992. The self-regulation of attitudes, intentions, and behavior. *Social Psychology Quarterly* 55: 178–204.

References

Bakhtin, Mikhail. 1934–35/1975. *Slovo v romane*. In Bakhtin, *Voprosy literatury i estetiki: Issledovaniia raznykh let*. Khudozhestvennaia literatura.

Bakhtin, Mikhail. 1934–35/1981. Discourse in the novel. In *The Dialogic Imagination: Four Essays*, ed. M. Holquist. University of Texas Press.

Banissy, Michael J., and Jamie Ward. 2007. Mirror-touch synesthesia is linked with empathy. *Nature Neuroscience* 10 (7): 815–816.

Baron, Robert A. 1987. Affect and organizational behavior: When and why feeling good (or bad) matters. In *Social Psychology in Organizations: Advances in Theory and Research*, ed. J. Murnighan. Prentice-Hall.

Barsalou, Lawrence W. 1999. Perceptual symbol systems. *Behavioral and Brain Sciences* 22: 577–609.

Bartlett, James C., and John W. Santrock. 1979. Affect-dependent episodic memory in young children. *Child Development* 50: 513–518.

Beebe, Beatrice, and Frank M. Lachmann. 1988. The contribution of mother-infant mutual influence to the origins of self- and object-representations. *Psychoanalytic Psychology* 5: 305–337.

Beer, Randy D. 1995. A dynamical systems perspective on autonomous agents. *Artificial Intelligence* 72: 173–215.

Benveniste, Emile. 1966/1973. *Problems in General Linguistics*, volume 1. University of Miami Press.

Berscheid, Ellen, and Harry T. Reis. 1998. Attraction and close relationships. In *The Handbook of Social Psychology*, fourth edition, ed. D. Gilbert. Oxford University Press.

Blackburn, Susan. 1984. *Spreading the Word*. Oxford University Press.

Blackmore, Susan. 1999. *The Meme Machine*. Oxford University Press.

Block, Ned. 2005. Review of Alva Noë, *Action in Perception. Journal of Philosophy* 102: 259–272.

Boghossian, Paul A. 1995. Content. In *A Companion to Metaphysics*, ed. J. Kim, E Sosa, and G. Rosenkrantz. Blackwell.

Bohart, Arthur C., and Leslie S. Greenberg. 1997. *Empathy Reconsidered: New Directions in Psychotherapy*. American Psychological Association.

Bohm, David. 1992. *Thought as a System*. Routledge.

Bourdieu, Pierre. 1982/1991. *Language and Symbolic Power*, ed. J. Thompson. Harvard University Press.

Bower, G. H. 1981. Mood and memory. *American Psychologist* 36: 129–148.

Bower, G. H. 1985. Review of research on mood and memory. Paper presented at Symposium on Affect and Cognition, British Psychological Society, Oxford.

Bowlby, John. 1953. *Child Care and the Growth of Love*. Penguin Books.

Bowlby, John. 1969. *Attachment and Loss*, volume 1. Hogarth.

Bowlby, John. 1979. *The Making and Breaking of Affectional Bonds*. Tavistock.

Bowlby, John. 1988. *A Secure Base: Clinical Applications of Attachment Theory*. Routledge.

Brennan, Teresa. 2004. *The Transmission of Affect*. Cornell University Press.

Brodie, Richard. 1996. *Virus of the Mind: The New Science of the Meme*. Integral.

Brooks, Rodney A. 1991. Intelligence without representation. *Artificial Intelligence* 47 (1.3): 139–159.

Burke, Kenneth. 1950/1969. *A Rhetoric of Motives*. University of California Press.

Burton, Robert. 2008. *On Being Certain: Believing You Are Right Even When You're Not*. St. Martin's.

Butler, Judith. 1991. Imitation and gender insubordination. In *Inside/Out: Lesbian Theories, Gay Theories*, ed. D. Fuss. Routledge.

Butler, Judith. 2003. Afterword. In Shoshana Felman, *The Scandal of the Speaking Body: Don Juan with J. L. Austin, or Seduction in Two Languages*, revised edition. Stanford University Press.

Call, Josep, and Michael Tomasello. 1995. The use of social information in the problem-solving of orangutans and human children. *Journal of Comparative Psychology* 109: 308–320.

Call, Josep, and Michael Tomasello. 2003. Social cognition. In *Primate Psychology: The Mind and Behavior of Human and Nonhuman Primates*, ed. D. Maestripieri. Harvard University Press.

Carpenter, G. R. 1891. Three critics: Mr. Howells, Mr. Moore, and Mr. Wilde. *Andover Review* 16: 568–576.

Carpenter, Malinda, and Michael Tomasello. 2000. Joint attention, cultural learning, and language acquisition: Implications for autism. In *Autistic Spectrum Disorders: A Transactional Developmental Perspective*, ed. A. Wetherby and B. Prizant. Brookes.

Carpenter, Malinda, Josep Call, and Michael Tomasello. 2002. Understanding others' prior intentions enables 2-year-olds to imitatively learn a complex task. *Child Development* 73: 1431–1442.

Carpenter, Malinda, Katherine Nagell, and Michael Tomasello. 1998. Social cognition, joint attention, and communicative competence from 9 to 15 months of age. *Monographs of the Society for Research in Child Development* 63 (4): 1–174.

Carpenter, Malinda, Michael Tomasello, and Sue Savage-Rumbaugh. 1995. Joint attention and imitative learning in children, chimpanzees, and enculturated chimpanzees. *Social Development* 4: 18–37.

Carpenter, William B. 1874. *Principles of Mental Physiology, with Their Applications to the Training and Discipline of the Mind, and the Study of Its Morbid Conditions*. Appleton.

Cavell, Stanley. 1995. What did Derrida want of Austin? In Cavell, *Philosophical Passages: Wittgenstein, Emerson, Austin, Derrida*. Blackwell.

Cavell, Stanley. 2003. Foreword. In Shoshana Felman, *The Scandal of the Speaking Body: Don Juan with J. L. Austin, or Seduction in Two Languages*, revised edition. Stanford University Press.

Chalmers, David J. 1995/1997. Facing up to the problem of consciousness. *Journal of Consciousness Studies* 2 (3): 200–219. Reprinted in *Explaining Consciousness: The Hard Problem*, ed. J. Shear. MIT Press.

Chalmers, David J. 1997. Moving forward on the problem of consciousness. In *Explaining Consciousness: The Hard Problem*, ed. J. Shear. MIT Press.

Chalmers, David J. 2005. The matrix as metaphysics. In *Philosophers Explore* The Matrix, ed. C. Grau. Oxford University Press.

Champagne, Marc. 2009. Explaining the qualitative dimension of consciousness: Prescission instead of reification. *Dialogue* 48: 145–183.

Chemero, Anthony. 2009. *Radical Embodied Cognitive Science*. MIT Press.

Chlopan, Bruce E., Marianne L. McCain, Joyce L. Carbonell, and Richard L. Hagen. 1985. Empathy: Review of available measures. *Journal of Personality and Social Psychology* 48: 635–653.

Churchland, Paul M. 1995. *The Engine of Reason, the Seat of the Soul*. MIT Press.

Churchland, Paul M. 1998. Knowing qualia: A reply to Jackson. In *On the Contrary: Critical Essays, 1987–1997*, ed. P. M. Churchland and P. S. Churchland. MIT Press.

Cialdini, Robert B., Stephanie L. Brown, Brian P. Lewis, Carol Luce, and Steven L. Neuberg. 1997. Reinterpreting the empathy-altruism relationship: When one into one equals oneness. *Journal of Personality and Social Psychology* 73: 481–494.

Clancey, William J. 1997. *Situated Cognition: On Human Knowledge and Computer Representations*. Cambridge University Press.

Clark, Andy. 1996. Connectionism, moral cognition and collaborative problem solving. In *Mind and Morals*, ed. L. May, M. Friedman, and A. Clark. MIT Press.

Clark, Andy. 1998. Magic words: How language augments human computation. In *Language and Thought: Interdisciplinary Themes*, ed. P. Carruthers and J. Boucher. Cambridge University Press.

Clark, Andy. 2000a. A case where access implies qualia? *Analysis* 60 (265): 30–38.

Clark, Andy. 2000b. Word and action: Reconciling rules and know-how in moral cognition. In *Moral Epistemology Naturalized*, ed. R. Campbell and B. Hunter. University of Calgary Press.

Clark, Andy. 2003. *Natural-Born Cyborgs: Minds, Technologies, and the Future of Human Intelligence*. Oxford University Press.

Clark, Andy. 2004. Is language special? Some thoughts on control, coding, and coordination. *Language Sciences* 26: 717–726.

Clark, Andy. 2005. The twisted matrix: Dream, stimulation, or hybrid? In *Philosophers Explore* The Matrix, ed. C. Grau. Oxford University Press.

Clark, Andy. 2006. Material symbols. *Philosophical Psychology* 19: 1–17.

Clark, Andy. 2008. *Supersizing the Mind: Embodiment, Action, and Cognitive Extension*. Oxford University Press.

Clark, Andy, and David J. Chalmers. 1998. The extended mind. *Analysis* 58: 7–19.

Clark, Arthur J. 2006. *Empathy in Counseling and Psychotherapy: Perspectives and Practices*. Erlbaum.

Clark, Margaret S. 2002. We should focus on interpersonal as well as intrapersonal processes in our search for how affect influences judgments and behavior. *Psychological Inquiry* 13: 32–37.

Clark, Margaret S., and Alice M. Isen. 1982. Towards understanding the relationship between feeling states and social behavior. In *Cognitive Social Psychology*, ed. A. Hastorf and A. Isen. Elsevier.

Clore, Gerald L., and Maya Tamir. 2002. Affect as embodied information. *Psychological Inquiry* 13: 37–45.

Clyne, Michael. 1981. Culture and discourse structure. *Journal of Pragmatics* 5: 61–66.

Clynes, Manfred E., and Nathan S. Kline. 1960/1995. Cyborgs and space. *Astronautics* 5, no. 9: 26–27, 74–76. Reprinted in *The Cyborg Handbook*, ed. C. Grey. Routledge.

Collins, Randall. 1975. *Conflict Sociology: Toward an Explanatory Science*. Academic Press.

Collins, Randall. 1981. On the microfoundations of macrosociology. *American Journal of Sociology* 86: 984–1014.

Connerton, Paul. 1989. *How Societies Remember*. Cambridge University Press.

Cooper, Lane, translator. 1932. *The Rhetoric of Aristotle*. Appleton-Century-Crofts.

References

Cooper, W. E. 1990. William James's theory of mind. *Journal of the History of Philosophy* 28: 571–593.

Crane, Tim. 2000. The origins of qualia. In *The History of the Mind-Body Problem*, ed. T. Crane and S. Patterson. Routledge.

Crisafi, Anthony, and Shaun Gallagher. 2010. Hegel and the extended mind. *AI & Society* 25 (1): 123–129.

Damasio, Antonio R. 1999. *The Feeling of What Happens: Body and Emotion in the Making of Consciousness*. Harcourt.

Damasio, Antonio R. 2003. *Looking for Spinoza: Joy, Sorrow, and the Feeling Brain*. Harcourt.

Damasio, Antonio R. 2004. William James and the modern neurobiology of emotion. In *Emotion, Evolution, and Rationality*, ed. D. Evans and P. Cruse. Oxford University Press.

Davies, Martin. 1989. Connectionism, modularity, and tacit knowledge. *British Journal for the Philosophy of Science* 40: 541–555.

Davies, Martin. 1991. Concepts, connectionism, and the language of thought. In *Philosophy and Connectionist Theory*, ed. W. Ramsey, S. Stich and D. Rumelhart. Erlbaum.

Davis, Mark H. 1996. *Empathy: A Social Psychological Approach*. Westview.

Dawkins, Richard. 1976. *The Selfish Gene*. Oxford University Press.

Decety, Jean, and William Ickes. 2009. *The Social Neuroscience of Empathy*. MIT Press.

Deigh, John. 1995. Empathy and universalizability. *Ethics* 105: 743–763.

Dennett, Daniel C. 1981. *Brainstorms: Philosophical Essays on Mind and Psychology*. MIT Press.

Dennett, Daniel C. 1988. Quining qualia. In *Consciousness in Modern Science*, ed. A. Marcel and E. Bisiach. Oxford University Press.

Dennett, Daniel C. 1991. *Consciousness Explained*. Little, Brown.

Dennett, Daniel C. 1996. *Kinds of Minds*. Basic Books.

Denzin, Norman K. 1980. A phenomenology of emotion and deviance. *Zeitschrift für Soziologie* 9 (July): 252–261.

Denzin, Norman K. 1984. *On Understanding Emotion*. Jossey-Bass.

Denzin, Norman K. 1985. On the phenomenology of sexuality, desire, and violence. *Current Perspectives in Social Theory* 6: 39–56.

Deonna, Julian A. 2007. The structure of empathy. *Journal of Moral Philosophy* 4: 99–116.

Derrida, Jacques. 1972/1988. Signature event context. In Derrida, *Limited Inc*, ed. G. Graff. Northwestern University Press.

Derrida, Jacques. 1977/1988. Limited Inc a b c. . . . In Derrida, *Limited Inc*, ed. G. Graff. Northwestern University Press.

Derrida, Jacques. 1988. Afterword: Toward an ethic of discussion. In Derrida, *Limited Inc*, ed. G. Graff. Northwestern University Press.

Dewey, John. 1897. The psychology of effort. *Philosophical Review* 6: 43–56.

Di Pellegrino, Giuseppe, Luciano Fadiga, Leonardo Fogassi, Vittorio Gallese, and Giacomo Rizzolatti. 1992. Understanding motor events: A neurophysiological study. *Experimental Brain Research* 91: 176–180.

Dretske, Fred. 1981. *Knowledge and the Flow of Information*. MIT Press.

Dretske, Fred. 1988. *Explaining Behavior: Reasons in a World of Causes*. MIT Press.

Dretske, Fred. 1993. Conscious experience. *Mind* 102 (406): 263–283.

Dretske, Fred. 1999. *Naturalizing the Mind*. MIT Press.

Eich, Eric. 1986. Epilepsy and state specific memory. *Acta Neurologica Scandinavica* 74: 15–21.

Eich, Eric. 1989. Theoretical issues in state dependent learning. In *Varieties of Memory and Consciousness: Essays in Honour of Endel Tulving*, ed. H. Roediger and F. Craik. Psychology Press.

Eich, Eric. 1995. Mood as a mediator of place dependent memory. *Journal of Experimental Psychology. General* 124: 293–308.

Eich, Eric. 2007a. Mood and memory at 25: Revisiting the idea of mood mediation in drug-dependent and place-dependent memory. In *Memory and Mind: A Festschrift for Gordon H. Bower*, ed. M. Gluck, J. Anderson, and S. Kosslyn. Psychology Press.

Eich, Eric. 2007b. Mood, memory, and the concept of context. In *Science of Memory: Concepts*, ed. H. Roediger, Y. Dudai, and S. Fitzpatrick. Oxford University Press.

Eich, Eric, and Dawn Macaulay. 2000. Are real moods required to reveal mood-congruent and mood-dependent memory? *Psychological Science* 11: 244–248.

Eich, Eric, and Dawn Macaulay. 2006. Cognitive and clinical perspectives on mood dependent memory. In *Affect in Social Thinking and Behavior*, ed. J. Forgas. Psychology Press.

Eich, Eric, John L. Reeves, Bernadette Jaeger, and Stephen B. Graff-Radford. 1985. Memory for pain: Relation between past and present pain intensity. *Pain* 23: 375–379.

Eidelberg, L. 1929. Experimenteller Beitrag zum Mechanismus der Imitationsbewegung. *Jahresbücher für Psychiatrie und Neurologie* 45: 170–173.

Esterhammer, Angela. 2001. *The Romantic Performative: Language and Action in British and German Romanticism*. Stanford University Press.

Felman, Shoshana. 1980/2003. *The Scandal of the Speaking Body: Don Juan with J. L. Austin, or Seduction in Two Languages*, revised edition. Stanford University Press.

Fernandez, A., and A. M. Glenberg. 1985. Changing environmental context does not reliably affect memory. *Memory & Cognition* 13: 333–345.

Ferrari, Pier Francesco, Elisabetta Visalberghi, Annika Paukner, Leonardo Fogassi, Angela Ruggiero, and Stephen J. Suomi. 2006. Neonatal imitation in rhesus macaques. *PLOS Biology* 4: 1501–1508.

Flanagan, Owen. 1992. *Consciousness Reconsidered*. MIT Press.

Flury, Judith M., William Ickes, and William Schweinle. 2008. The borderline empathy effect: Do high BPD individuals have greater empathetic ability? or are they just more difficult to "read?" *Journal of Research in Personality* 42: 312–332.

Fodor, Jerry A. 1975. *The Language of Thought*. Harvard University Press.

Fodor, Jerry A. 1987. *Psychosemantics: The Problem of Meaning in the Philosophy of Mind*. MIT Press.

Fodor, Jerry A. 1990. *A Theory of Content and Other Essays*. MIT Press.

Fogassi, Leonardo, Pier Francesco Ferrari, Benno Gesierich, Stefano Rozzi, Fabian Chersi, and Giacomo Rizzolatti, G. 2005. Parietal lobe: From action organization to intention understanding. *Science* 308: 662–667.

Forgas, Joseph P. 1995. Mood and judgment: The affect infusion model (AIM). *Psychological Bulletin* 117: 39–66.

Forgas, Joseph P. 2002. Feeling and doing: Affective influences on interpersonal behavior. *Psychological Inquiry* 13: 1–28.

Forgas, Joseph P. 2007. Affect, cognition, and social behavior: The effects of mood on memory, social judgments, and social interaction. In *Memory and Mind: A Festschrift for Gordon H. Bower*, ed. M. Gluck, J. Anderson, and S. Kosslyn. Psychology Press.

Forgas, Joseph P., and Gordon H. Bower. 1987. Mood effects on person perception judgements. *Journal of Personality and Social Psychology* 53: 53–60.

Forgas, Joseph P., and Stephanie J. Moylan. 1987. After the movies: The effects of transient mood states on social judgments. *Personality and Social Psychology Bulletin* 13: 478–489.

Freese, J. H., translator. 1926. Aristotle, *The "Art" of Rhetoric*. Heinemann.

Friedman, Howard S. 1979. The interactive effects of facial expressions of emotion and verbal messages on perceptions of affective meaning. *Journal of Experimental Social Psychology* 15: 453–469.

Friedman, Howard S., and Ronald E. Riggio. 1981. Effect of individual differences in nonverbal expressiveness on transmission of emotion. *Journal of Nonverbal Behavior* 6: 96–104.

Friedman, Howard S., Louise M. Prince, Ronald E. Riggio, and M. Robin DiMatteo. 1980. Understanding and assessing nonverbal expressiveness: The Affective Communication Test. *Journal of Personality and Social Psychology* 39: 333–351.

Gabora, Liane. 1999. To imitate is human: A review of *The Meme Machine* by Susan Blackmorn. *Journal of Consciousness Studies* 6, no. 5: 77–81.

Gallagher, Shaun. 2009. Two problems of intersubjectivity. *Journal of Consciousness Studies* 16 (6.8): 289–308.

Gallese, Vittorio, Luciano Fadiga, Leonardo Fogassi, and Giacomo Rizzolatti. 1996. Action recognition in the premotor cortex. *Brain* 119: 593–609.

Gardner, Helen. 1961. *The Metaphysical Poets*. Oxford University Press.

Garfinkel, Harold. 1967. *Studies in Ethnomethodology*. Prentice-Hall.

Gazzola, Valeria, and Christian Keysers. 2009. The observation and execution of actions share motor and somatosensory voxels in all tested subjects: single-subject analyses of unsmoothed fMRI data. *Cerebral Cortex* 19: 1239–1255.

Gazzola, Valeria, Lisa Aziz-Zadeh, and Christian Keysers. 2006. Empathy and the somatotopic auditory mirror system in humans. *Current Biology* 16: 1824–1829.

Gesn, Paul R., and William Ickes. 1999. The development of meaning contexts for empathetic accuracy: Channel and sequence effects. *Journal of Personality and Social Psychology* 77: 746–761.

Gilbert, Margaret. 1989. *On Social Facts*. Princeton University Press.

Goffman, Erving. 1955/1967. On face-work: An analysis of ritual elements in social interaction. In Goffman, *Interaction Ritual*. Doubleday.

Goffman, Erving. 1959. *The Presentation of Self in Everyday Life*. DoubledayAnchor.

Goffman, Erving. 1974. *Frame Analysis*. Harper and Row.

Gopnik, Alison, and H. M. Wellman. 1995. Why the child's theory of mind really is a theory. In *Folk Psychology*, ed. M. Davies and T. Stone. Blackwell.

Gräfenhain, Maria, Tanya Behne, Malinda Carpenter, and Michael Tomasello. 2009. One-year-olds' understanding of nonverbal gestures directed to a third person. *Cognitive Development* 24: 23–33.

References

Grey, Chris Hables, ed. 1995. *The Cyborg Handbook*. Routledge.

Grice, H. Paul. 1975/1989. Logic and conversation. In Grice, *Studies in the Way of Words*. Harvard University Press.

Griffiths, Paul, and Andrea Scarantino. 2009. Emotions in the wild: The situated perspective on emotion. In *The Cambridge Handbook of Situated Cognition*, ed. P. Robbins and M. Aydede. Cambridge University Press.

Grush, Rick. 2004. The emulation theory of representation: Motor control, imagery, and perception. *Behavioral and Brain Sciences* 27: 377–442.

Haraway, Donna. 1986/1991. A cyborg manifesto: Science, technology, and socialist-feminism in the late twentieth century. In Haraway, *Simians, Cyborgs and Women: The Reinvention of Nature*. Routledge.

Harman, Gilbert. 1990. The intrinsic quality of experience. *Philosophical Perspectives* 4: 31–52.

Hatfield, Elaine, John T. Cacioppo, and Richard L. Rapson. 1994. *Emotional contagion*. Cambridge University Press.

Havelock, Eric A. 1963. *Preface to Plato*. Belknap.

Hegel, G. W. F. 1802–03/1979. *System of Ethical Life*, ed. H. Harris and T. Knox. State University of New York Press.

Hegel, G. W. F. 1821/1991. *Elements of the Philosophy of Right*, ed. A. Wood. Cambridge University Press.

Hegel, G. W. F. 1830/2007. *Hegel's Philosophy of Mind*. In *From The Encyclopaedia of the Philosophical Sciences*. Clarendon.

Heider, Fritz. 1958. *The Psychology of Interpersonal Relations*. Wiley.

Heise, David R. 1969. Affective dynamics in simple sentences. *Journal of Personality and Social Psychology* 11: 204–213.

Heise, David R. 1970. Potency dynamics in simple sentences. *Journal of Personality and Social Psychology* 16: 48–54.

Heise, David R. 1977. Social action as the control of affect. *Behavioral Science* 22: 163–177.

Heise, David R. 1978. *Computer-Assisted Analysis of Social Action: Use of Program INTERACT and Survey UNC75*. Institute for Research in Social Science, University of North Carolina.

Heise, David R. 1979. *Understanding Events: Affect and the Construction of Social Action*. Cambridge University Press.

Heise, David R. 1985. Affect Control Theory: Respecification, estimation, and tests of the formal model. *Journal of Mathematical Sociology* 11: 191–222.

Heise, David R. 1987. Affect Control Theory: Concepts and model. *Journal of Mathematical Sociology* 13: 1–33.

Heise, David R. 1999. Controlling affective experience interpersonally. *Social Psychology Quarterly* 62: 4–16.

Heise, David R. 2002. Understanding social interaction with Affect Control Theory. In *New directions in contemporary sociological theory*, ed. J. Berger and M. Zelditch. Rowman and Littlefield.

Heise, David R. 2007. *Expressive Order: Confirming Sentiments in Social Actions*. Springer.

Heise, David R., and Stephen J. Lerner. 2006. Affect control in international interactions. *Social Forces* 85: 993–1010.

Hess, David. 1995. On low-tech cyborgs. In *The Cyborg Handbook*, ed. C. Gray. Routledge.

Hochschild, Arlie R. 1975. The sociology of feeling and emotion: Selected possibilities. In *Another Voice*, ed. Marcia Millman and Rosabeth Kanter, 280–307. Anchor.

Hochschild, Arlie R. 1979. Emotion work, feeling rules, and social structure. *American Journal of Sociology* 85: 551–575.

Hochschild, Arlie R. 1983. *The Managed Heart: The Commercialization of Human Feeling*. University of California Press.

Hofstadter, Douglas R. 1979. *Gödel, Escher, Bach: An Eternal Golden Braid*. Basic Books.

Holquist, Michael. 1990. *Dialogism: Bakhtin and His World*. Routledge.

Hut, Piet, and Roger N. Shepard. 1996/1997. Turning "the hard problem" upside down and sideways. *Journal of Consciousness Studies* 3: 313–329. Reprinted in *Explaining Consciousness: The Hard Problem*, ed. J. Shear. MIT Press.

Hutchins, Edwin. 1995. *Cognition in the Wild*. MIT Press.

Hutton, Christopher. 1990. *Abstraction and Instance: The Type-Token Relation in Linguistic Theory*. Pergamon.

Ickes, William. 1997. *Empathetic Accuracy*. Guilford.

Ickes, William, and Elliot Aronson. 2003. *Everyday Mind Reading: Understanding What Other People Think and Feel*. Prometheus Books.

Ikäheimo, Heikki. 2007. Recognizing persons. In *Dimensions of Personhood*, ed. Heikki Ikäheimo and Arto Laitinen, 224–247. Imprint Academic.

Irons, D. 1897a. The nature of emotion, part 1. *Philosophical Review* 6: 242–256.

Irons, D. 1897b. The nature of emotion, part 2. *Philosophical Review* 6: 471–496.

Isen, Alice M. 1984. Towards understanding the role of affect in cognition. In *Handbook of Social Cognition*, volume 3, ed. R. Wyer and T. Srull. Erlbaum.

Isen, Alice M. 1987. Positive affect, cognitive processes and social behavior. *Advances in Experimental Social Psychology* 20: 203–253.

Isen, Alice M. 2002. Missing in action in the AIM: Positive affect's facilitation of cognitive flexibility, innovation, and problem solving. *Psychological Inquiry* 13: 57–65.

Jackendoff, Ray S. 1987. *Consciousness and the Computational Mind*. MIT Press.

Jacob, Pierre. 1997. *What Minds Can Do: Intentionality in a Non-Intentional World*. Cambridge University Press.

James, William. 1879a. The sentiment of rationality. *Mind* o. s. 4: 317–346.

James, William. 1879b. The spatial quale. *Journal of Speculative Philosophy* 13: 127–136.

James, William. 1890/1950. *Principles of Psychology*. Holt.

Keeley, B. 2009. Early history of the quale. In *The Routledge Companion to Philosophy of Psychology*, ed. J. Symons and P. Calvo. Routledge.

Kelso, J. A. Scott. 1995. *Dynamic Patterns: The Self-Organization of Brain and Behavior*. MIT Press.

Kemper, Theodore D. 1978. *A Social Interactional Theory of Emotions*. Wiley.

Kennedy, George, translator. 1991/2007. *Aristotle, On Rhetoric: A Theory of Civic Discourse*, second edition. Oxford University Press.

Kirschner, Sebastian, and Michael Tomasello. 2009. Joint drumming: Social context facilitates synchronization in pre-school children. *Journal of Experimental Child Psychology* 102: 299–314.

Kirsh, David. 2005. Metacognition, distributed cognition, and visual design. In *Cognition, Education, and Communication Technology*, ed. P. Gärdenfors and P. Johansson. Erlbaum.

Kögler, Hans Herbert, and Karsten Stueber, eds. 2000. *Empathy and Agency: The Problem of Understanding in the Human Sciences*. Westview.

Kohler, Evelyne, Christian Keysers, M. Alessandra Umiltà, Leonardo Fogassi, Vittorio Gallese, and Giacomo Rizzolatti. 2002. Hearing sounds, understanding actions: Action representation in mirror neurons. *Science* 297: 846–848.

Kohut, Heinz. 1971. *The Analysis of the Self*. International Universities Press.

Kohut, Heinz. 1977. *The Restoration of the Self*. International Universities Press.

Kohut, Heinz. 1985. *Self Psychology and the Humanities*. Norton.

Konstan, David. 2007. *The Emotions of the Ancient Greeks: Studies in Aristotle and Classical Literature*. University of Toronto Press.

Krashen, Stephen D., and Tracy D. Terrell. 1983. *The Natural Approach: Language Acquisition in the Classroom*. Pergamon.

Kugler, Peter Noble, and Michael T. Turvey. 1987. *Information, Natural Laws, and Self-Assembly of Rhythmic Movement*. Erlbaum.

Kuhn, Thomas. 1962/1970. *The Structure of Scientific Revolutions*, second edition. University of Chicago Press.

Lamm, Claus, C. Daniel Batson, and Jean Decety. 2007. The neural basis of human empathy: Effects of perspective-taking and cognitive appraisal. *Journal of Cognitive Neuroscience* 19: 42–58.

Lang, Berel. 1990. *The Anatomy of Philosophical Style: Literary Philosophy and the Philosophy of Literature*. Blackwell.

Leeds, Stephen. 1993. Qualia, awareness, Sellars. *Noûs* 27: 303–330.

Lerdahl, Fred, and Ray S. Jackendoff. 1996. *A Generative Theory of Tonal Music*. MIT Press.

Leslie, Kenneth R., Scott H. Johnson-Frey, and Scott T. Grafton. 2004. Functional imagining of face and hand imitation: Towards a motor theory of empathy. *NeuroImage* 21: 601–607.

Levine, Joseph. 1983. Materialism and qualia: The explanatory gap. *Pacific Philosophical Quarterly* 64: 354–361.

Lewis, C. I. 1929/1956. *Mind and the World Order: Outline of a Theory of Knowledge*. Dover.

Liebal, Katja, Tanya Behne, Malinda Carpenter, and Michael Tomasello. 2009. Infants use shared experience to interpret pointing gestures. *Developmental Science* 12: 264–271.

Loggia, Marco L., Jeffrey S. Mogil, and M. Catherine Bushnell. 2008. Empathy hurts: Compassion for another increases both sensory and affective components of pain perception. *Pain* 236: 168–176.

Loveday, Leo J. 1982. Communicative interference: A framework for contrastingly analyzing L2 communicative competence exemplified with the linguistic behavior of Japanese performing in English. *International Review of Applied Linguistics* 20: 1–16.

Ludwig, Arnold M., Jeffrey M. Brandsma, Cornelia B. Wilbur, Fernando Bendfeldt, and Douglas H. Jameson. 1972. The objective study of a multiple personality. *Archives of General Psychiatry* 26: 298–310.

Lycan, William G. 1993. A deductive argument for the representational theory of thinking. *Mind & Language* 8: 404–422.

Lycan, William G. 1996. *Consciousness and Experience*. MIT Press.

Lynch, Aaron. 1998. *Thought Contagion*. Basic Books.

Macaulay, Dawn, and Eric Eich. 2002. Implications of the Affect Infusion Model: Conjectures and conflict. *Psychological Inquiry* 13: 68–70.

MacKinnon, Neil J. 1985. *Affective Dynamics and Role Analysis*. Department of Sociology and Anthropology, University of Guelph.

MacKinnon, Neil J. 1988. *The Attribution of Traits, Status Characteristics and Emotions in Social Interaction*. Department of Sociology and Anthropology, University of Guelph.

MacKinnon, Neil J. 1994. *Symbolic Interactionism as Affect Control*. State University of New York Press.

MacKinnon, Neil J., and David R. Heise. 1993. Affect Control Theory: Delineation and history. In *Theoretical Research Programs: Studies in the Growth of Theory*, ed. J. Berger and M. Zelditch Jr. Stanford University Press.

Malle, Bertrand F., and Sara D. Hodges, eds. 2005. *Other Minds: How Humans Bridge the Divide Between Self and Others*. Guilford.

Manstead, Antony S. R., and Joop van der Pligt. 2002. The what, when, and how of affective influences on interpersonal behavior. *Psychological Inquiry* 13: 71–73.

Marangoni, Carol, Stella Garcia, William Ickes, and Gary Teng. 1995. Empathetic accuracy in a clinically relevant setting. *Journal of Personality and Social Psychology* 68: 854–869.

Marcus, Gary. 2008. *Kluge: The Haphazard Construction of the Human Mind*. Houghton Mifflin.

Martin, Leonard L., Jeremy Shelton, and Ilan Shrira. 2002. The role of context in determining mood effects. *Psychological Inquiry* 13: 74–76.

McCall, George J., and Jerry L. Simmons. 1966. *Identities and Interactions*. Free Press.

McClamrock, Ron. 1995. *Existential Cognition: Computational Minds in the World*. University of Chicago Press.

McDougall, William. 1908. *An Introduction to Social Psychology*. Methuen.

McDowell, John. 1994. *Mind and World*. Harvard University Press.

Mead, George Herbert. 1934. *Mind, Self, and Society*. University of Chicago Press.

Menary, Richard. 2006. Attacking the bounds of cognition. *Philosophical Psychology* 19 (3):329–344.

Menary, Richard. 2007. *Cognitive Integration: Mind and Cognition Unbounded*. Palgrave/Macmillan.

Menary, Richard, ed. 2010. *The Extended Mind*. MIT Press.

Metzger, Richard L., Pamela F. Boschee, Terry Haugen, and Barbara L. Schnobrich. 1979. The classroom as learning context: Changing rooms affects performance. *Journal of Educational Psychology* 71: 440–442.

Miller, Geoffrey F. 2000. Memetic evolution and human culture. *Quarterly Review of Biology* 75: 434–436.

Miller, Susan. 2008. *Trust in Texts: A Different History of Rhetoric*. Southern Illinois University Press.

Mook, Douglas G. 1987. *Motivation: The Organization of Action*. Norton.

Nagel, Thomas. 1974. What is it like to be a bat? *Philosophical Review* 83: 435–450.

Nichols, H. 1892. The origin of pleasure and pain, part 1. *Philosophical Review* 1: 403–432.

Nichols, Shaun. 2001. Mindreading and the cognitive architecture underlying altruistic motivation. *Mind & Language* 16: 425–455.

Noë, Alva. 2004. *Action in Perception*. MIT Press.

Noë, Alva, and J. Kevin O'Regan. 2002. On the brain basis of perceptual consciousness. In *Vision and Mind: Selected Readings in the Philosophy of Perception*, ed. A. Noë and E. Thompson. MIT Press.

Oakeshott, Michael. 1962. *Rationalism in Politics and Other Essays*. Methuen.

O'Regan, J. Kevin, and Alva Noë. 2001. A sensorimotor approach to vision and visual consciousness. *Behavioral and Brain Sciences* 24: 939–973.

Osgood, Charles E. 1969. On the whys and wherefores of E, P, and A. *Journal of Personality and Social Psychology* 12: 194–199.

Osgood, Charles E., George C. Suci, and Perry H. Tannenbaum. 1957. *The Measurement of Meaning*. University of Illinois Press.

Osgood, Charles E., William H. May, and Murray S. Miron. 1975. *Cross-Cultural Universals of Affective Meaning*. University of Illinois Press.

Parkinson, Brian, Agneta H. Fischer, and Antony S. R. Manstead. 2005. *Emotions in Social Relations: Cultural, Group, and Interpersonal Processes*. Psychology Press.

Peirce, Charles Sanders. 1931–1958. *Collected Papers of Charles Sanders Peirce*. Harvard University Press.

Peirce, Charles Sanders. 1998. *The Essential Peirce: Selected Philosophical Writings*, volume 2. Indiana University Press.

Peltz, Benjamin. 2007. The moment of meaning: Apperception in the philosophy of Josiah Royce. *Cognitio-estudos* 4: 25–36.

Perrott, David A., and Galen V. Bodenhausen. 2002. The way you make me feel: Integral affective influences on interpersonal behavior. *Psychological Inquiry* 13: 84–86.

Piccinini, Gualtiero. 2004. The first computational theory of mind and brain: A close look at McCulloch and Pitts's "Logical calculus of ideas immanent in nervous activity." *Synthese* 141 (2): 175–215.

Port, Robert Frederick, and Timothy van Gelder. 1995. *Mind as Motion: Explorations in the Dynamics of Cognition*. MIT Press.

Postman, Neil. 1985. *Amusing Ourselves to Death*. Viking/Penguin.

Preston, Stephanie D., Antoine Bechara, Hanna Damasio, Thomas J. Grabowski, R. Brent Stansfield, Sonya Mehta, and Antonio R. Damasio. 2007. The neural substrates of cognitive empathy. *Social Neuroscience* 2: 254–275.

Prigogine, Ilya. 1973. Can thermodynamics explain biological order? *Impact of Science on Society* 23: 159–179.

Prinz, Jesse J. 2006. Putting the brakes on enactive perception. *Psyche* 12 (1): 1–19.

Prinz, Jesse J. 2009. Is consciousness embodied? In *The Cambridge Handbook of Situated Cognition*, ed. P. Robbins and M. Aydede. Cambridge University Press.

Prior, A. N. 1962/1976. Some problems of self-reference in John Buridan. In Prior, *Papers in Logic and Ethics*. University of Massachusetts Press.

Ravenscroft, Ian. 1998. What is it like to be someone else? Simulation and empathy. *Ratio* 11: 170–185.

Reus, Victor I., Herbert Weingartner, and Robert M. Post. 1979. Clinical implications of state-dependent learning. *American Journal of Psychiatry* 136 (7): 927–931.

Rey, Georges. 1991. Sensations in a language of thought. In *Philosophical issues 1: Consciousness*, ed. E. Villanueva. Ridgeview.

Rey, Georges. 1992. Sensational sentences switched. *Philosophical Studies* 67: 73–103.

Rey, Georges. 1993. Sensational sentences. In *Consciousness*, ed. M. Davies and G. Humphrey. Blackwell.

Rey, Georges. 1995. A not "merely empirical" argument for a language of thought. In *Philosophical Perspectives* 9: 201–222.

Rey, Georges. 1997. *Contemporary Philosophy of Mind: A Contentiously Classical Approach*. Blackwell.

Rey, Georges. 1998. A narrow representationalist account of qualitative experience. In *Philosophical Perspectives 12: Language, Mind, and Ontology*, ed. J. Tomberlin. Ridgeview.

Rizzolatti, Giacomo, and Michael A. Arbib. 1998. Language within our grasp. *Trends in Neurosciences* 21 (5): 188–194.

Rizzolatti, Giacomo, and Maddalena Fabbri-Destro. 2010. Mirror neurons: From discovery to autism. *Experimental Brain Research* 200: 223–237.

Rizzolatti, Giacomo, Luciano Fadiga, Vittorio Gallese, and Leonardo Fogassi. 1996. Premotor cortex and the recognition of motor actions. *Cognitive Brain Research* 3: 131–141.

Roberts, W. Rhys, translator. 1984. Aristotle, *Rhetoric*. In *The Complete Works of Aristotle*, ed. J. Barnes. Princeton University Press.

Robinson, Douglas. 2001. *Who Translates? Translator Subjectivities Beyond Reason*. State University of New York Press.

Robinson, Douglas. 2003. *Performative Linguistics: Speaking and Translating as Doing Things with Words*. Routledge.

Robinson, Douglas. 2006. *Introducing Performative Pragmatics*. Routledge.

Robinson, Douglas. 2008. *Estrangement and the Somatics of Literature: Tolstoy, Shklovsky, Brecht*. Johns Hopkins University Press.

Rogers, A. K. 1904. Rationality and belief. *Philosophical Review* 13: 30–50.

Rolls, Edmund T. 1999. *The Brain and Emotion*. Oxford University Press.

Rolls, Edmund T. 2005. *Emotion Explained*. Oxford University Press.

Rosenberg, Gregg H. 1996/1997. Rethinking nature: A hard problem within the hard problem. In *Explaining Consciousness: The Hard Problem*, ed. J. Shear. MIT Press.

Royce, Josiah. 1898/2005. Self-consciousness, social consciousness and nature. In *The Basic Writings of Josiah Royce*, ed. J. McDermott. Fordham University Press.

Ruby, Perrine, and Jean Decety. 2004. How would you feel versus how do you think she would feel? A neuroimaging study of perspective taking with social emotions. *Journal of Cognitive Neuroscience* 16: 988–999.

Rupert, Robert D. 1999. The best test theory of extension: First principle(s). *Mind & Language* 14 (September): 321–355.

Rupert, Robert D. 2004. Challenges to the hypothesis of extended cognition. *Journal of Philosophy* 101 (August): 389–428.

Rupert, Robert D. 2008. Causal theories of mental content. *Philosophy Compass* 3 (2): 353–380.

Rupert, Robert D. 2009. *Cognitive Systems and the Extended Mind*. Oxford University Press.

Rupert, Robert D. 2010a. Extended cognition and the priority of cognitive systems. *Cognitive Systems Research* 11: 343–356.

Rupert, Robert D. 2010b. Representation in extended cognitive systems: Does the scaffolding of language extend the mind? In *The Extended Mind*, ed. R. Menary. MIT Press.

Rupert, Robert D. 2010c. Systems, functions, and intrinsic natures: On Adams and Aizawa's *The Bounds of Cognition*. *Philosophical Psychology* 23 (1): 113–123.

Rupert, Robert D. 2011a. Cognitive systems and the supersized mind. *Philosophical Studies* 152: 427–436.

Rupert, Robert D. 2011b. Empirical arguments for group minds: A critical appraisal. *Philosophy Compass* 6 (9): 630–639.

Rupert, Robert D. Forthcoming. Against group cognitive states. In *From Individual to Collective Intentionality*, ed. S. Chant, F. Hindriks, and G. Preyer. Oxford University Press.

Ruskin, John. 1856/1891. Of the pathetic fallacy. In Ruskin, *Modern Painters*, fourth edition, volume 3. Allen.

Russell, Bertrand. 1908. Mathematical logic as based on the theory of types. *American Journal of Mathematics* 30: 222–262.

Saufley, William H., Sandra R. Otaka, and Joseph L. Bavaresco. 1985. Context effects: Classroom tests and context independence. *Memory & Cognition* 13: 522–528.

Scheff, Thomas J. 1984. *Being Mentally Ill: A Sociological Theory*. Aldine.

Schore, Allan N. 1994. *Affect Regulation and the Origin of the Self: The Neurobiology of Emotional Development*. Erlbaum.

Schore, Allan N. 2003a. *Affect Dysregulation and Disorders of the Self*. Norton.

Schore, Allan N. 2003b. *Affect Regulation and the Repair of the Self*. Norton.

Schwarz, Norbert. 1990. Feelings as information: Information and motivational functions of affective states. In *Handbook of Motivation and Cognition: Foundations of Social Behavior*, ed. E. Higgins and R. Sorrentino. Guilford.

Schwarz, Norbert, and Gerald L. Clore. 1983. Mood, misattribution and judgments of well-being: Informative and directive functions of affective states. *Journal of Personality and Social Psychology* 45: 513–523.

Seager, William E. 1995/1997. Consciousness, information and panpsychism. In *Explaining Consciousness: The Hard Problem*, ed. J. Shear. MIT Press.

Searle, John R. 1969. *Speech Acts*. Cambridge University Press.

Searle, John R. 1975. Indirect Speech Acts. In *Syntax and Semantics 3: Speech Acts*, ed. P. Cole and J. Morgan. Academic Press.

Searle, John R. 1977. Reiterating the differences: A reply to Jacques Derrida. In *Glyph: Johns Hopkins Textual Studies*, volume 1.

Searle, John R. 1990. Collective intentions and actions. In *Intentions in Communication*, ed. P. Cohen, J. Morgan, and M. Pollack. MIT Press.

Searle, John R. 1995. *The Construction of Social Reality*. Free Press.

Searle, John R. 1999. *Mind, Language, and Society: Philosophy in the Real World*. Basic Books.

Sedgwick, Eve Kosovsky. 2003. *Touching Feeling: Affect, Pedagogy, Performativity*. Duke University Press.

Short, T. L. 2004. The development of Peirce's theory of signs. In *The Cambridge Companion to Peirce*, ed. C. Misak. Cambridge University Press.

Shott, Sue. 1979. Emotion and social life: A symbolic interactionist analysis. *American Journal of Sociology* 84: 1317–1334.

Simpson, Jeffry A., M. Minda Orina, and William Ickes. 2003. When accuracy hurts, and when it helps: A test of the empathetic accuracy model in marital interactions. *Journal of Personality and Social Psychology* 85: 881–893.

Simpson, Jeffry A., William Ickes, and Tami Blackstone. 1995. When the head protects the heart: Empathetic accuracy in dating relationships. *Journal of Personality and Social Psychology* 69: 629–641.

Sinfield, Alan. 1994. *The Wilde Century: Effeminacy, Oscar Wilde and the Queer Moment*. Columbia University Press.

Singer, Tania, Ben Seymour, John O'Doherty, Holger Kaube, Raymond J. Dolan, and Chris D. Frith. 2004. Empathy for pain involves the affective but not sensory components of pain. *Science* 303 (20 February): 1157–1162.

Smith-Lovin, Lynn. 1990. Emotion as the confirmation and disconfirmation of identity: An affect control model. In *Research Agendas in the Sociology of Emotions*, ed. T. Kemper. State University of New York Press.

Smith-Lovin, Lynn, and David R. Heise, eds. 1988. *Analyzing Social Interaction: Advances in Affect Control Theory*. Gordon and Breach.

Snider, James G., and Charles E. Osgood, eds. 1969. *Semantic Differential Technique: A Sourcebook*. Aldine.

References

Solomon, H. Yosef, and Michael T. Turvey. 1988. Haptically perceiving the distances reachable with hand-held objects. *Journal of Experimental Psychology. Human Perception and Performance* 14: 404–427.

Sonnby-Borgström, Marianne. 2002. Automatic mimicry reactions as related to differences in emotional empathy. *Scandinavian Journal of Psychology* 43 (5): 433–443.

Stampe, Dennis. 1977. Toward a causal theory of linguistic representation. *Midwest Studies in Philosophy* 2, no. 1: 42–63.

Stanley, H. M. 1892. On primitive consciousness. *Philosophical Review* 1: 433–442.

Sterelny, Kim. 2004. Externalism, epistemic artifacts, and the extended mind. In *The Externalist Challenge*, ed. R. Schantz. De Gruyter.

Sterelny, Kim. 2012. *The Evolved Apprentice: How Evolution Made Humans Unique*. MIT Press.

Stich, Stephen, and Ian Ravenscroft. 1994. What is folk psychology? *Cognition* 50: 447–468.

Stinson, Linda, and William Ickes. 1992. Empathetic accuracy in the interactions of male friends versus male strangers. *Journal of Personality and Social Psychology* 62: 787–797.

Stone, Gregory P. 1962. Appearances and the self. In *Human Behavior and Social Processes*, ed. A. Rose. Houghton Mifflin.

Stone, Sandy. 1995. Split subjects, not atoms; or, how I fell in love with my prosthesis. In *The Cyborg Handbook*, ed. C. Gray. Routledge.

Stout, G. F. 1888. The Herbartian psychology, part 2. *Mind* o. s. 7: 477–505.

Strawson, Galen. 1994. *Mental Reality*. MIT Press.

Strawson, Galen. 1994/2010. *Mental Reality*, second edition. MIT Press.

Swanson, James M., and Marcel Kinsbourne. 1976. Stimulant-related state-dependent learning in hyperactive children. *Science* 192: 1354–1357.

Thelen, Esther, and Linda B. Smith. 1995. *A Dynamic Systems Approach to the Development of Cognition and Action*. MIT Press.

Thompson, Evan. 2001. *Between Ourselves: Second-Person Issues in the Study of Consciousness*. Imprint Academic.

Thompson, Laura A., Keith L. Williams, Paul R. L'Esperance, and Jeffrey Cornelius. 2001. Context-dependent memory under stressful conditions: The case of skydiving. *Human Factors* 43: 611–619.

Thomson, Gregory. 1982. An introduction to implicature for translators. *Notes on Translation* 1: 1–82.

Thorndike, Edward L. 1932. *The Fundamentals of Learning*. Teachers College.

Tolstoy, Lev Nikolaievich. 1898/1932. *What Is Art?* Oxford University Press.

Tomasello, Michael. 1991. Processes of communication in the origins of language. In *Studies in Language Origins*, ed. W. von Raffler-Engel, J. Wind, and A. Jonker. John Benjamins.

Tomasello, Michael. 1992. The social bases of language acquisition. *Social Development* 1: 67–87.

Tomasello, Michael. 1994. On the interpersonal origins of self-concept. In *Ecological and Interpersonal Sources of Self-Knowledge*, ed. U. Neisser. Cambridge University Press.

Tomasello, Michael. 1988. The role of joint attentional process in early language development. *Language Sciences* 10: 69–88.

Tomasello, Michael. 1995. Joint attention as social cognition. In *Joint Attention: Its Origins and Role in Development*, ed. C. Moore and P. Dunham. Erlbaum.

Tomasello, Michael. 1998. Social cognition and the evolution of culture. In *Piaget, Evolution, and Development*, ed. J. Langer and M. Killen. Erlbaum.

Tomasello, Michael. 1999a. The cultural ecology of young children's interactions with objects and artifacts. In *Ecological Approaches to Cognition: Essays in Honor of Ulrich Neisser*, ed. E. Winograd, R. Fivush, and W. Hirst. Erlbaum.

Tomasello, Michael. 1999b. *The Cultural Origins of Human Cognition*. Harvard University Press.

Tomasello, Michael. 2004. Learning through others. *Daedalus* 133: 51–58.

Tomasello, Michael. 2008. *Origins of Human Communication*. MIT Press.

Tomasello, Michael, with Carol Dweck, Joan Silk, Brian Skyrms, and Elizabeth Spelke. 2009. *Why We Cooperate*. MIT Press.

Tomasello, Michael, and Katharina Haberl. 2003. Understanding attention: 12- and 18-month-olds know what's new for other persons. *Developmental Psychology* 39: 906–912.

Tomasello, Michael, and Hannes Rakoczy. 2003. What makes human cognition unique? From individual to shared to collective intentionality. *Millennial Perspective Series in Mind and Language* 18: 121–147.

Tomasello, Michael, and Jeffrey Farrar. 1986. Joint attention and early language. *Child Development* 57: 1454–1463.

Tomasello, Michael, and Jody Todd. 1983. Joint attention and lexical acquisition style. *First Language* 4: 197–212.

Tomasello, Michael, Malinda Carpenter, Josep Call, Tanya Behne, and Henrike Moll. 2005. Understanding and sharing intentions: The origins of cultural cognition. *Behavioral and Brain Sciences* 28: 675–691.

Tulving, Endel. 1976. Ecphoric processes in recall and recognition. In *Recall and Recognition*, ed. J. Brown, 37–73. Wiley.

Tulving, Endel. 1979. Memory research: What kind of progress? In *Perspectives in Memory Research*, ed. L. G. Nilsson, 19–34. Erlbaum.

Tulving, Endel. 1983. *Elements of Episodic Memory*. Oxford University Press.

Tye, Michael. 1996. *Ten Problems of Consciousness*. MIT Press.

Tye, Michael. 2000. *Consciousness, Color, and Content*. MIT Press.

Varela, Francisco J., Evan Thompson, and Eleanor Rosch. 1991. *The Embodied Mind: Cognitive Science and Human Experience*. MIT Press.

Vera, Alonso H., and Herbert A. Simon. 1993. Situated action: A symbolic interpretation. *Cognitive Science* 17: 7–48.

Voloshinov, V. N. 1930/1973. *Marxism and the Philosophy of Language*. Seminar.

Walker, Jeffrey. 2000. *Rhetoric and Poetics in Antiquity*. Oxford University Press.

Ward, J. 1883. Psychological principles. *Mind* o. s. 8: 465–486.

Warren, William H. 1984. Perceiving affordances: Visual guidance of stair climbing. *Journal of Experimental Psychology: Human Perception and Performance* 10 (5): 683–703.

Whittaker, T. 1890. Volkmann's psychology, part 2. *Mind* o. s. 15: 489–513.

Wilde, Oscar. 1891/1982. The decay of lying. In *The Artist as Critic: Critical Writings of Oscar Wilde*, ed. R. Ellmann. University of Chicago Press.

Wilkes, Kathleen V. 1988. Yishi, duh, um and consciousness. In *Consciousness in Contemporary Science*, ed. A. Marcel and E. Bisiach. Oxford University Press.

Wilson, Robert A., and Andy Clark. 2009. How to situate cognition: Letting nature take its course. In *The Cambridge Handbook of Situated Cognition*, ed. P. Robbins and M. Aydede. Cambridge University Press.

Wittgenstein, Ludwig. 1953. *Philosophical Investigations*. Blackwell.

Zaki, Jamil, Niall Bolger, and Kevin Ochsner. 2008. It takes two: The interpersonal nature of empathetic accuracy. *Psychological Science* 19: 399–404.

Index

Adams, Fred, 2, 15–16, 20, 26–28, 55, 68, 75, 84, 105, 153, 165, 171–174, 190, 212–214, 220–221
  and binaries, 77–82
  critique of EMT, 70–74
Adolphs, Ralph, 151, 153
Affect, 20
  and foreign words, 52–55
  research on, 17–21
  shared evaluative, 158
Affect-becoming-conation, 6–7, 22, 166, 169, 174–175
  -becoming-cognition, 27, 120, 167
  and encouragement, 111
  reticulated through the group, 158
  and tools, 55
Affect Control Theory, 18–24, 28, 147–148, 169
Affect Infusion Model (Forgas), 62–63
Affective communication, 28, 102, 112
  as the displacement of force (Derrida), 68
Agre, Philip E., 207
Aizawa, Ken, 2, 15–16, 20, 26–28, 55, 68, 75, 84, 105, 153, 165, 171–174, 190, 212–214
Allport, Alan, 178
Altieri, Charles, 193
Aristotle, 6, 89, 122, 149, 218
  on *doxa*, 155–159
  on emotion, 221
  on *ēthos* and *pathos*, 150, 198
  on persuasion, 110–113
  on shame, 24, 164
Artificial intelligence, 207
As-if body loop (Damasio), 110
Attachment theory (Bowlby), 153
Austin, J. L., 7, 21–22, 28, 68, 85–102, 115, 188, 195. *See also* Speech acts
  read by Bourdieu, 107–109
  read by Cavell, 87–88, 91–92
  read by Derrida, 89–103
Automaton theory, 213–214
Avramides, Anita, 213

Bagozzi, Richard P., 46
Bakhtin, Mikhail, 7, 28, 68, 88–89, 102–107, 140, 169
  on metalinguistics, 215
Banissy, Michael, 152
Baron, Robert A., 62
Barsalou, Lawrence W., 69
Bartlett, James C., 60
Baudelaire, Charles, 188
Beer, Randy D., 207
Behaviorism, 17
Benveniste, Émile, 96
Blackmore, Susan, 220
Block, Ned, 2
Bodenhausen, Galen V., 63

Body-becoming-mind, 6–7, 170
  collective, 149, 164
  extended proprioception of, 59
Body English, 58–59
Boghossian, Paul A., 136
Bohart, Arthur C., 221
Bohm, David, 32–33, 57
Bourdieu, Pierre, 28, 89, 107–109, 155, 169, 215–216. *See also Habitus*
Bower, G. H., 62
Bowlby, John, 153
Brodie, Richard, 220
Brooks, Rodney A., 207
Buridan, John, 221–222
Burke, Kenneth, 192–193
Burton, Robert, 203
Butler, Judith, 188

Carpenter, G. R., 223
Carpenter, William, 150
Carpenter Effect, 150–153
Categories (Aristotle), 122
Cavell, Stanley, 87–88, 91–92, 107, 109
Chalmers, David, 1–3, 29, 178–179
Chapman, David, 207
Chemero, Anthony, 2, 3
Chlopan, Bruce E., 221
Chomsky, Noam, 53, 65, 75, 104, 218
Churchland, Paul A., 69, 220
Cialdini, Robert B., 221
Clancey, William J., 207
Clark, Andy, 1–5, 42–43, 70, 82, 120, 171–174, 207, 220
  on Chalmers' Hard Problem of Consciousness, 12
  and embodied mind, 24–27
  on Fodor, 44, 74–76, 84
  on language as verbal labels, 28, 68–70, 101, 212
  on literal extension, 40, 65, 170, 182
  on qualia, 7–15, 29, 31, 143–145, 207
Clark, Andy, and David Chalmers, 1–2, 8, 16–17, 27, 38, 43, 45, 53, 57, 115, 150, 172–174, 190
  and the Parity Principle, 9–13, 31
Clark, Arthur J., 221
Clark, Margaret S., 62, 63
Clore, Gerald L., 62, 63
Clynes, Manfred, 1
Cognition, 17, 20
  and the Computational Theory of Mind, 166–167
  distributed, 56–57
  embodied, 32, 56–57, 207
  enactive (Noë), 8, 65–67, 207
  existential, 207
  extended, 22, 26, 32, 147
Collins, Randall, 18, 169
Commodity fetishism (Marx), 39
Computational Theory of Mind (CTM), 28, 65, 75, 166–167
Conation, 20, 22, 46–49, 145. *See also* Affect-becoming-conation
  as force, 28, 68, 112
  in qualia/interpretants, 142
  in speech acts, 99–103
Connerton, Paul, 28, 57–58, 149, 165–168
Constative linguistics (Felman/Robinson), 85–86, 207, 216
Cooper, W. E., 177
Cooperative Principle and its maxims (Grice), 193
Crane, Tim, 121–122, 177
Cretan liar paradox, 190–196
Crisafi, Anthony, 7, 35–38, 208
Cyborg Handbook, The (Gray), 1–2
Cyborg theory, 1–2

Damasio, Antonio, 79, 110, 151, 189–190
  and body-becoming-mind, 26–27
  on the homeostasis machine, 214
  on somatic markers, 153, 162, 205–206

Index

Davis, Mark H., 221
Decadence, 187
"Decay of Lying, The" (Wilde), 7, 29, 142–143, 180–202
Decety, Jean, 151, 152, 221
Deigh, John, 221
Deleuze, Gilles, 6
Dennett, Daniel, 69, 80, 108, 118–120, 136, 178, 217
Denzin, Norman K., 18
Deonna, Julian A., 221
Derrida, Jacques, 7, 28, 68, 89, 102–104, 140
 on Austin, 89–103
 read by Cavell, 91–92
 on the displacement of force, 100–103
 on iterability, 92–100, 168–169, 170
Descartes, René, 37, 56, 125, 145, 208
Dewey, John, 17, 135
"Discourse in the Novel" (Bakhtin), 215
Dissipative structure/system (Prigogine), 141
Distributed mind/cognition, 56–57
Doxa (Aristotle), 155–161, 221
Dretske, Fred, 75, 137, 178, 214
Dualism, 177–179
 mind-body, 37, 56, 125, 145, 208
Durkheim, Émile, 17–18

Eich, Eric, 60, 63
Eidelberg, Ludwig, 150
Embodied mind/cognition, 32, 56–57, 207
Empathy, 67
 social neuroscience of, 148, 149, 150–154, 162, 166, 171
Enactive mind/cognition (Noë), 8, 65–67, 207
Encouragement, 111, 210
Encyclopedia of the Philosophical Sciences (Hegel), 27, 36–37, 50
Endorsement (Clark and Chalmers), 9–13, 115, 172

Enthymeme (Aristotle), 110–111, 113, 155
EPA (evaluation, potency, activity: Osgood), 20–21
Epimenides of Knossos, 191
Epistemic artifacts (Sterelny), 9, 13, 31, 147
Esterhammer, Angela, 68
Eubulides of Miletus, 191, 194, 222
Existential cognition, 207
Explanatory gap between materialism and qualia (Levine), 119, 177, 203
Expressive implicature (Altieri), 193
Extended body-becoming-mind, 22, 26, 32, 147
 and Bakhtin, 104
 and force, 101

Face (Aristotle/Goffman), 67, 156–162
Felman, Shoshana, 21, 207, 216
Fernandez, A., 60
Flanagan, Owen, 119–120, 124, 142
Fodor, Jerry, 16, 20, 28, 43–44, 65, 69, 70, 81–82, 84, 104, 138, 174, 214
 critiqued, 74–77
Force, conative, 112
 communication as, 68
 displacement of in speech acts (Derrida), 89, 100–103
Forgas, Joseph, 62–63
Freud, Sigmund, 35
Friedman, Howard, 150
Functionalism, 9–13
Fuzzy logic, 78–80

Gabora, Liane, 220
Gallagher, Shaun, 7, 16–17, 35–38, 208
Gardner, Helen, 184
Gilbert, Margaret, 142
Glenberg, A. M., 60
Goffman, Erving, 19, 28, 163, 169
 on face, 24, 149, 157–164
 on frames, 93, 98

Gopnik, Alison, 220–221
Graphematics (Derrida), 215
Gray, Chris Hables, 1–2
Greenberg, Leslie S., 221
Grice, H. Paul, 93, 140, 192–193, 197
Griffiths, Paul, 17, 80–81, 112
Grush, Rick, 24–26, 33
Gulliver's Travels (Swift), 182

Habitualization
  as extended body-becoming-mind, 49–51
  Hegel on, as internalization, 45–46
  and ritual, 169
  as Third, 195
Habitus (Bourdieu), 28, 89, 107–109, 169, 155
  and laughter, 109–110
  and persuasion, 110–113
Haraway, Donna, 2
Hard Problem of Consciousness (Chalmers), 3, 12, 29, 119–120, 179, 191, 199, 203
Harman, Gilbert, 137
Hatfield, Elaine, 150
Havelock, Eric A., 155
Hegel, G. W. F., 6, 7, 27, 35, 44, 49–50, 218, 208
  on mind, 35–42
  on the phenomenology of tool-use, 55, 59
  on speech, 52
Heidegger, Martin, 6, 42
Heider, Fritz, 19
Heise, David R., 18
Hess, David, 2, 64
Heteroglossia (Bakhtin), 104, 215
Hochschild, Arlie R., 18
Hodges, Sara D., 221
Hofstadter, Douglas, 203–204
Holquist, Michael, 215
Homeostasis, 81, 189–190, 214
How to Do Things with Words (Austin), 91

Hut, Piet, 179
Hutchins, Edwin, 207
Hutton, Christopher, 194–195, 218–219, 222–223

Ickes, William, 150–151, 221
Idealism, 14, 15, 65, 177–178, 200
  fractured, 32, 29, 65–66, 180
Ikäheimo, Heikki, 37, 208–210
Illocutionary act, 86, 88, 92, 113–114
Implicature
  conversational (Grice), 93, 140, 197
  expressive (Altieri), 193
  invocative (Robinson), 92
Inclusion-of-Other-in-Self (IOS) scale, 210
Indirect speech acts (Searle), 22, 154, 188
Individualism, 171–172
Interpretants (Peirce), 102, 116–117, 139–140, 218–220
  emotional as affect, energetic as conation, logical as cognition, 20
  logical as habit, 131
  and music, 127–131
  as qualia, 28, 67, 135–140, 149, 171
Intimidation, 215–216
Intracraniality, 70, 167, 171, 220
Invocature (Robinson), 92
Isen, Alice M., 62
Iterability (Derrida), 89, 92–100, 102–103, 168–169, 170, 174–175

Jackendoff, Ray S., 129–131, 218
James, William, 17, 18, 81, 122, 177, 189
  on feeling, 217–218
  and neo-Jamesian neuroscience, 26–27
Judgments, distinguished from qualia (Clark), 11–13

Kant, Immanuel, 14, 142, 184, 187, 188–190, 197
Keeley, B., 121–122, 126, 135

Kelso, J. A. Scott, 207
Kemper, Theodore D., 17
Kinsbourne, Marcel, 60
Kirsh, David, 56–57
Kline, Nathan, 1
Kluge, 1
Kögler, Hans Herbert, 221
Kohut, Heinz, 153
Konstan, David, 157
Krashen, Stephen D., 210
Kremer, Michael, 58
Kugler, Peter Noble, 205
Kuhn, Thomas, 15, 200–201

Lamm, Claus, 221
Lang, Berel, 195
Language
  as conative force/speech acts, 67, 172, 174–175
  as labels, 28, 67, 172–174, 212
Language of thought (LOT: Fodor), 20, 28, 65, 68, 75–76, 81, 82, 104–105. *See also* Mentalese
Language-of-thought hypothesis (LOTH: Fodor), 16, 28, 43–44, 69, 70, 74–77, 80, 84, 187
Laughter, as perlocutionary effect, 109–110
Lerdahl, Fred, 218
Leslie, Kenneth, 152
Lewis, C. I., 121, 122, 217
Liar paradox, 183–184, 187–199, 201–204
  Cretan, 190–196
Liar-paradox monism (Robinson), 29, 65–66, 180, 205
Literality
  of cognitive extension, 2–5, 40, 170, 182
  of Wilde's claims, 182, 186
Loggia, Marco, 152, 221
"Logic of Science, The" (Peirce), 121
Low-tech cyborgs (Hess), 2, 64
Ludwig, Arnold M., 60

Lycan, William G., 137
Lynch, Aaron, 220

Macaulay, Dawn, 61
MacKinnon, Neil J., 18–21, 23–24, 147–148
Malle, Bertrand F., 221
Manstead, Anthony S. R., 63
Marcus, Gary, 1
Martin, Leonard L., 63
Marx, Karl, 39
Materialism, 2–5, 14, 15, 32–34, 64–65, 119–120, 143, 177–178, 189–190, 200, 205
Mathematical modeling, 207
McCall, George J., 19
McClamrock, Ron, 207
McDougall, William, 17
Mead, George Herbert, 16–17, 19, 23–24, 169
Memes (Dawkins), 220
Menary, Richard, 2
Mencius, 195
Mental and physical monism (Strawson), 177–178, 205
Mentalese (Fodor), 43–44, 74–77. *See also* Language of Thought
Merleau-Ponty, Maurice, 18
Metaphysical conceit, 184
Metzger, Richard L., 60
Miller, Geoffrey F., 220
Miller, Susan, 112
Mind
  body-becoming-, 6–7, 59, 149, 164, 170
  as embodied/enactive, 5
  extended proprioception of, 59
  as internalized tool (Hegel), 49–50, 52, 55, 59, 64
  as phenomenology, 4–6
  as qualia, 5, 7–15
Mind-body dualism, 37, 56, 125, 145, 208
Mind-reading (Ickes, Tomasello), 151

Mirror neurons, 102, 151–152, 155, 166, 171
Misfires (Austin, Derrida, Searle), 99–100
Monism, 177–179, 191, 199, 202
    fractured, 14
    liar-paradox, 29, 65–66, 180, 205
    mental and physical, 177–178, 205
    neutral, 205
Mood-dependent cognition, 34, 60–63
Moylan, Stephanie J., 62

Nagel, Thomas, 177
Naturalized semantics (Dretske), 75–76, 78–79, 214
Nichols, Shaun, 221
Nietzsche, Friedrich, 90
Noë, Alva, 8, 56–57, 207
Normal science (Kuhn), 200–201
"Notes for Eight Lectures" (Peirce), 217

Oakeshott, Michael, 165
Otto's notebook (Clark and Chalmers), 8, 38, 45, 57, 115, 150, 172–174, 212

Pain, as quale/interpretant, 137–140
Pandemonium model of consciousness (Dennett), 217
Parity Principle (Clark and Chalmers), 9–13
Parkinson, Brian, 17
Pater, Walter, 187–188
Pathetic fallacy (Ruskin), 33
Paul of Tarsus, 191
Peirce, Charles Sanders, 6, 7, 21, 62, 102, 105, 116, 170–171, 195, 208, 217–219
    on interpretants, 126–131
    on literality, 182
    on qualia and interpretants, 28, 120
    and Strawson, 124–127, 135
    on the symbol/icon/index triad, 138
    on the tone-token-type triad, 28, 132–133, 194
Perception studies, 207
Performative linguistics (Felman/Robinson), 216
Performatives, 90
    as iterability, 92–100, 102
Periperformative (Sedgwick), 88
Perlocutionary act/effect, 86, 88, 113–114
Perrot, David A., 63
Persuasion, 110–113, 134
Phantom limb, 58
Phenomenalism, 14, 31–32, 34, 137
Philosophy of Right (Hegel), 38
Piccinini, Gualtiero, 75
Pistis (persuading-becoming-believing: Aristotle), 110–113
Plato, 68, 76, 173, 195
Port, Robert Frederick, 207
Postman, Neil, 43
Preston, Stephanie, 151, 153, 221
Prigogine, Ilya, 141
Principles of Psychology (James), 122
Prinz, Jesse J., 2
Prior, A. N., 221–222
"Prolegomena to an apology for pragmaticism" (Peirce), 132, 134
Proprioception, 170
    extended (Bohm), 32–33

"Quale-consciousness" (Peirce), 217
Qualia, 179, 191
    influenced by art (Wilde), 184, 200
    empathetic simulation of, 149
    and the explanatory gap, 119, 177–179, 203
    as First (Peirce), 126–127
    and homeostasis, 190
    as interpretants, 28, 67, 135–140, 149, 171
    and lying, 201

coined/theorized by Peirce, 121–124, 170, 218
and prequalia, 80–81
as primary in mind, 7–15, 202–203
quined (Dennett), 118–120, 217
as shared, 13, 120, 147–148
as transcranial, 14–15
as transparent (Tye), 136–137, 204
as trap (Clark), 5, 8, 14, 29, 143–145, 207
Qualisign (Peirce), 132–133
Queer theory, 188

Rationalist philosophy of language (ROPL), 67–68, 69, 83, 92, 96, 98, 104, 118, 174
as constative, 85–86
Ravenscroft, Ian, 220, 221
Realism, direct, 204
Recognition (*Anerkennung*: Hegel), 37, 208–210
Reductive representationalism, 16, 136–137, 204
Reus, Victor I., 60
Revolutionary science (Kuhn), 200–201
Rhetoric (Aristotle), 89, 110–113, 149, 155–156, 221
Ritual (Connerton), 67, 164–167
Rizzolatti, Giacomo, 151–152
Robinson, Douglas, 21, 68, 88, 108, 136, 216
Rosch, Eleanor, 207
Rosenberg, Gregg H., 179
Rossetti, Dante Gabriel, 187
Royce, Josiah, 122
Ruby, Perrine, 221
Rupert, Robert D., 2, 26
Ruskin, John, 33
Russell, Bertrand, 191

Sacks, Oliver, 58
Santrock, John W., 60

Saufley, William H., 60
Saussure, Ferdinand de, 75, 104, 216
Sawyer, Keith, 88
Scarantino, Andrea, 17, 80–81, 112
Scheff, Thomas J., 17
Schore, Allan, 152–154
Schwarz, Norbert, 62
Seager, William W., 179
Searle, John, 14, 96, 142
on group minds, 14, 220
on illocutionary acts, 88
on indirect speech acts, 93, 115–116
Searle–Derrida debate, 90, 93–95, 99
Sedgwick, Eve Kosovsky, 88
Self-incorporation (*Sicheinbilden*: Hegel), 49, 210
Self psychology (Kohut), 153
Shakespeare, William, 197
Shame (Aristotle, Goffman), 158–164
Shared intentionality (Searle), 14
Shepard, Roger N., 179
Short, T. L., 218
Shott, Sue, 17
Simmons, Jerry L., 19
Simon, Herbert A., 207
Sinfield, Alan, 188
Singer, Tania, 152
Situated
  activities, 148
  identities, 18, 19, 22, 148, 163
  mind, 56–57
Smith, Linda B., 207
Social act(or)s, 18, 22
Sociality, 16, 67, 212, 214
Social memory through ritual (Connerton), 28, 165–168
Solomon, H. Yosef, 207
Somatic-marker hypothesis (Damasio), 153, 161–162, 205–206
Sonnby-Borgström, Marianne, 152
Sorites series, 6, 70, 78, 80–84, 114–118, 154

Speech acts (Austin), 21, 28, 85–89
  constative theory of, 116
  group, 89, 107–109, 112
  group indirect, 154
  indirect, 22, 93, 114–118, 147, 188
  and laughter, 109–110
  as transcranial conations, 22, 175
Stampe, Dennis, 75, 214
Sterelny, Kim, 9, 11, 13, 31, 67, 212, 214
Stich, Stephen, 220
Stone, Gregory P., 19
Stone, Sandy, 216–217
Strawson, Galen, 124–125, 189, 190
  and experience/qualia, 177–179
  and the explanatory gap, 207–208
  on pain, 137–140
  and Peirce, 127, 135
Studies in the History of the Renaissance (Pater), 187
Stueber, Karsten, 221
Swanson, James M., 60
Swift, Jonathan, 182
Swinburne, Algernon, 187–188
Symbolic interactionism (Mead), 16–17, 19
Symbol/icon/index (Peirce), 138
Symons, Arthur, 187
System of Ethical Life (Hegel), 27, 35, 38

Tamir, Maya, 63
Terrell, Tracy D., 54
Thelen, Esther, 207
Thompson, Evan, 207, 221
Thompson, Laura A., 61
Tolstoy, Leo, 129
Tomasello, Michael, 14, 53, 142, 151, 220
Tomkins, Silvan, 17
Tone (Peirce), 222
  as interpretant, 133–135
  as quale/qualisign, 132–134
Tone-token-type (Peirce), 105, 132–133, 194–195, 208, 218–219

Tools, as externalized mind (Hegel), 49–50, 52, 55, 59
Transcraniality, 70, 118, 120, 167, 171
  and natural language, 23
  of qualia, 14–15
Transparency of qualia, 136–137, 204
Tulving, Endel, 60
Turing, Alan, 65, 75, 173
Turner, J. M. W., 182, 186
Turvey, Michael T., 205, 207
Tye, Michael, 137, 178

Unification of language as project (Bakhtin), 103–107, 140, 169

van der Pligt, Joop, 63
van Gelder, Timothy, 207
Varela, Francisco J., 207
Vera, Alonso H., 207
Verizon Wireless Test Man, 72–74
Voloshinov, V. N., 88

Walker, Jeffrey, 111
Ward, Jamie, 152
Warren, William H., 207
Wellman, H. M., 220–221
Wilde, Oscar, 7, 29, 142, 180–202, 223
Wilkes, Kathleen V., 178
Wilson, Robert A., 2
Wittgenstein, Ludwig, 62, 68, 76, 131, 142, 195

Zaki, Jamil, 221